Dancing betwee and Despair

Trauma, Attachment and the Therapeutic Relationship

Sue Wright

 macmillan education palgrave

First published 2016 by
PALGRAVE

Palgrave in the UK is an imprint of Macmillan Publishers Limited, registered in England, company number 785998, of 4 Crinan Street, London, N1 9XW.

Palgrave Macmillan in the US is a division of St Martin's Press LLC, 175 Fifth Avenue, New York, NY 10010.

Palgrave is a global imprint of the above companies and is represented throughout the world.

Palgrave® and Macmillan® are registered trademarks in the United States, the United Kingdom, Europe and other countries.

ISBN 978–1–137–44123–2 paperback

This book is printed on paper suitable for recycling and made from fully managed and sustained forest sources. Logging, pulping and manufacturing processes are expected to conform to the environmental regulations of the country of origin.

A catalogue record for this book is available from the British Library.

A catalog record for this book is available from the Library of Congress.

Printed and bound by CPI Group (UK) Ltd, Croydon, CR0 4YY

To the spirit of 'Little Tyke' that lives in all of us – that spirit of courage, tenacity, integrity and hopefulness that enables us to keep going when life seems impossible – and to all the people I have been privileged to work with who have taught me about this and so much more.

Contents

List of Figures and Tables

Figures

Tables

Preface

Writing on this subject has, perhaps not surprisingly, taken me on my own journey of shifting hope and despair. However, I would not have believed when I conceived the project of writing a book how much it would come to mean to me and how devastating were the periods when, for various reasons, I had to face the fact that there might be no birth after such hopes and dreams. I think it was only in the periods when I had to consider letting the book go – or at least my vision of it – that my reasons for this subject became clear.

For me this has been much more than an academic project. I wanted to inspire other professionals who get stuck in despair along with their clients. I also wanted to honour the stories of the many people I have worked with – to act as a witness to their suffering, not only in the past but often for years after the original wounding experiences. Trauma does not stop when the guns are laid down. My clients have inspired me and repeatedly remind me how incredible the human mind and body can be. Despite the immensity of all they have suffered, people find amazing ways to survive – creatively adapting in order to avoid harm, ensure attachment or protect themselves from overwhelming thoughts and feelings. For the survivor of extreme trauma just getting through an 'ordinary' day is an act of heroism.

I wanted to be a voice for what Donna Orange calls the 'suffering stranger' (2011). But I came to realise that to do so I had to stay true to my own voice, however informed I might be by other writers or by the comments of people who have kindly read sections of the book. And, interestingly, I discovered that some of my despair moments came when I had to mute my voice. I began to understand why the trauma of disconfirmation – something I mention often in the book – has been a subject of such interest to me and why it feels so important to honour my subjectivity and that of others. I have needed to reflect on my own experiences of being disconfirmed and to face with shame and regret when I disconfirm the truth of others.

When I began to study hope and despair I could not have known how pervasive the subject is – in my work, my life, in things I read. My work has informed the book. But perhaps more important, my research has informed and altered how I work – and perhaps subtly who I am. I feel the richer for it at many levels. And so I dedicate the book with gratitude to my clients past and present for all they have taught me and with admiration for their courage. As stated, I wanted to be a voice for them. But I also honour the privacy of all that they have shared with me and so I have done all I can to disguise the identity of individuals by changing details and sometimes using composite examples for illustrative purposes. I have also decided that my preferred way to honour gender neutrality is to alternate between using the words he and she rather than what for me is the rather clumsy and unrelational term he/she.

I am indebted to the many people who have helped the book along in various ways. In particular I would like to thank Jim Pye who has been a sounding board for ideas throughout the project and for all his wise comments as he read each emerging chapter. My thanks are also due to Jenifer Elton Wilson, whose sound advice guided me at the beginning, and to my other readers – Caroline Vacara, Sarah Tate, Helen Hastings-Spital, Christine O'Neil, Paula Biles, Julie Gurnell and Adrian Roberts. I have greatly appreciated all your thoughts and encouragement. I am very grateful to the people I have worked with who gave permission for me to refer to our work and to those who read sections and offered their valuable thoughts. From Palgrave Macmillan I should like to thank Louise Summerling and Peter Hooper as well as Alex Antidius Arpoudam, the production project manager. You all gave me the answers I needed when asking 'anxious author' questions and respected my request for flexibility around some of the things you suggested.

Chris Wright also deserves a mention for advice and encouragement from the publishing side. Lastly, huge thanks to Paul who has solidly backed me in this crazy project as he has always done – compassionately tolerating the hours I have devoted to it, listening to my worries and excitements, humorously putting me in my place if I got too excited, reading and offering comments from a scientist's mind and helping straighten tables and text with the computer wizardry that I lack.

Acknowledgements

The author and publishers wish to thank W.W. Norton for kind permission to reproduce Figure 1.1, page 6, and Figure 9.1, page 160.

1

Introducing the Dance

If one does not hope, one will not find the un-hoped for, since there is no trail leading to it and no path.

(Heraclitus, cited in Shabad, 2001, p. 35)

The endless rain story

'If we don't hope, we won't find the un-hoped for'. There is something elusive, but obvious, in Heraclitus's words, written many centuries ago, that speaks of what can unexpectedly emerge when we risk something – something that exceeds our plans and our dreams. It is something I observe time and again for myself and my clients within the deeply relational process of psychotherapy. We risk when we enter wholeheartedly into the unknown territory of a therapeutic relationship. We risk when we allow ourselves to hope. Yet we need to take such risks. That said, why is hoping so fundamental to our existence? And if it is, why might it sometimes be adaptive not to hope? These are questions that I invite us all to hold in mind as we encounter things in our work or in our own lives which challenge both our capacity to stay hopeful and our beliefs in what we do. There are other questions that I am also curious about. What inspired my interest in the dance between hope and despair? What drew you to reading this book? And most important, what leads our clients to seek counselling or psychotherapy? There will probably be something for us all about our personal relationship to hope, and for our clients it may be a mix of hope and despair that brings them to our doors. They may come because they feel stuck and desperate but have little hope that anything will change. At the same time they may harbour the hope that we will 'fix' them or make them feel better or help them to get rid of an unwanted aspect of themselves or their lives.

I will come to the subject of beginning hopes later. But to return to my own interest – I cannot point to a specific moment or event which made me realise that I had to write about hope. However, once the seed had been planted I became increasingly fascinated by the subject. It mattered to me and I began to appreciate how central the theme of hope is in our work as psychotherapists and counsellors. I was encouraged by the enthusiastic interest of those I spoke to about the project, and my interest was further fuelled the more

I encountered the theme in my work, my reading and my life. I began to notice subtle shifts in my clients as they move between hope and despair – shifts in how they use language about themselves and the future, how they perceive things, in their energy or posture or interpersonally. I also realised the importance of studying what we do as therapists that engenders hope and of becoming sensitive to what we do, say or fail to do that squashes a fledgling hope or pulls someone back into despair. I also became curious about the things I myself do when I start to feel hopeless and the things that give me hope and inspiration.

As an example, let me describe a personal story of hopelessness. I suspect that we all encounter brief moments of hopelessness which punctuate our day and colour it in a way that affects what we do and how we view ourselves and others, and sometimes we may go through prolonged periods of despair and stuckness, when we question the very purpose of life. We could term these 'small d' and 'big D' lows in the same way that Shapiro referred to 'small t' and 'big T' traumas (2001)[1] – and for people who have experienced the latter or who struggle with an enduring health problem 'big D' lows are very common. This example was certainly not one of the 'big D' moments in my life, yet it is interesting because of what it told me about my own relationship to hope. I call it the 'endless rain story', my response to the weeks of uncharacteristic, relentless and sometimes destructive rain that the UK endured in 2012. Over that summer I moved through a range of different responses as week after week there seemed no let-up in the weather, no shift into the sun and warmth I longed for. The messages that my hope-seeking self came up with progressed from 'it will be better tomorrow' to 'by the weekend' to 'surely next month will be different!' Like a client who told me she could cope if she knew that there would be an end to her suffering, this was the reassurance I was seeking – that the weather would improve – and like my client when hoped-for ends failed to materialise, I slipped into a reactive state of mind. Because being outside and in touch with nature is such a resource for me, the repeated experience of getting soaked, the lack of sun plus damp penetrating the fabric of my house began to impact my mood. I remember my response when I learned that things were unlikely to improve for weeks because the jet stream was stuck. In a moment of frustrated disappointment I protested vehemently 'well move it!' I wanted someone to take responsibility, to do something and was ready to blame anything I could.

However, in calmer, more reflective moments I reminded myself that getting upset and protesting would not help. I needed to find a place of acceptance. For me this included capitalising on good moments and reminding myself that the inconveniences the rain caused me were trivial compared to how others suffered – both in this country and in countries subject to far worse climatic disasters. As Victor Frankl said, 'when we are no longer able to change a situation, we are challenged to change ourselves', and what I needed to do on the gloomiest days was change my perspective (2004, p. 116). Whilst this sounds obvious, changing our attitude, which Frankl described as 'the last of the human freedoms', is not easy (2004, p. 75). We can all slip into hopeless-ness or blame when faced with something we find hard to endure and which feels endless, and it is certainly not easy for people who have been fighting to survive for years. However, as I shall discuss later, I believe that some of the most important and moving change moments that occur in therapy are when something enables a shift in perspective. Whatever form this takes, it opens the door to hope.

In this book I intend to explore the lived experience of people whose cir-cumstances have left them without hope or who oscillate between hope and despair – for instance, people who have endured overwhelming trauma and loss or who struggle with debilitating mental and physical health problems. Alongside this I shall explore the experiences of those who work with them and who face the challenge of balancing the tension of supporting clients when they are in the depths of despair, whilst at the same time keeping a candle of hope alight. Here, one of my hopes is that the book will encourage clinicians to keep questioning how they can avoid becoming caught up in the hopelessness and despair of their clients and getting pulled into non-mental-ising responses to a client's urgent seeking for, or vehement dismissal of hope. I shall draw upon a range of theoretical perspectives and refer to the work of therapists from different traditions as well as to research on attachment, child development, trauma and neuroscience and will turn to client examples to illustrate the application of theory to practice.

To outline the material to be covered in the book, in Chapter 2 I begin to explore the differences between realistic and illusory hope by considering how the therapeutic world has conceptualised hope. I also set the scene for my own evolving relational approach. Chapters 3 and 4 explore how states of hope and despair can be viewed from an evolutionary and a developmental perspective. The next two chapters look at the dance of hope and despair through a trauma lens. For instance, in Chapter 5 I return to developmental issues and consider how trauma and attachment failures at different life stages can contribute to the loss of a sense of hope and optimism about the future. Chapter 6 examines in more detail how trauma and attachment failures can impact the individual's relationship to hope and expands upon earlier points about the differences between flexible, realistic hoping and hope which entails a dependency on magical solutions. My focus in Chapter 7 is on the internal dance between hope and despair. Here, the examples presented will enable me to study in more depth the shifting states of mind and body that accompany hopelessness and how we can all have multiple relationships to hope. In Chapter 8 my interest is in how the dance gets played out intersubjec-tively, for example, in the therapeutic relationship or within teams and wider systems. Then, in the last three chapters I describe how I work with people caught in chronic despair and hopelessness and discuss how I position myself in terms of working in a more active, directive way or through what emerges in the relationship itself. My trainings in Integrative Psychotherapy, psycho-dynamic work, Dance Movement Therapy and Sensorimotor Psychotherapy all inform how I work, and what I offer here is an approach that is highly relational with an emphasis on integrating mind, body and emotions.[2]

As the book moves on you will find that certain themes keep appearing in addition to the overarching theme – the dialectic between hope and despair. The first is the relationship between states of hope that involve creative imagining but are grounded in reality, and states of what could be described as 'wishful' or 'magical' thinking. For the former I will generally use the term realistic hope and for the latter illusory hope. It will become clear that I believe both are important and sometimes crucial in helping people to keep going in unendurable situations. However, a reliance on illusory hope also brings problems, and one of the changes that we can hope for is that this reliance will shift over the course of a therapeutic journey. Because I often use the language of mentalising when discussing this theme, a brief explanation of my understanding of the concept is called for.

Mentalising, or self-reflective functioning, is the process by which we make sense of the contents of our own minds and the minds of others (Allen, 2006; Bateman, 2005). Without this capacity we could neither empathise nor make predictions about how others might behave or respond to us. It also enables us to hold different perspectives rather than seeing things in black and white terms and quickly making assumptions. It is a fluid capacity and we are all more likely to react rather than to reflect when strong feelings are around or if we are tired, unwell or in pain. We can also momentarily lose our ability to mentalise when something feels endless or is blocking our progress – as my vehement protest about the jet stream illustrates. The ideal is to be able to recognise when this happens and quickly come back to a more reflective place.

The second sub-theme concerns the interplay between hope as an individual and an intersubjective phenomenon. Intrapsychically, one of my basic premises is that we all have multiple relationships to hope. In response to context and environment – and that includes the intersubjective context – we can shift from feeling more hopeful and optimistic to defeated and desperate in a matter of moments or over a longer time span. We can cling to hope at all costs or we can cynically push away anything that offers a little hope. When considering hope as an intersubjective phenomenon I will stress the importance of our earliest environment in laying the foundations for a capacity to dream and to hope, and will explore the impact of attachment failures and trauma on the individual's relationship to hope. Through the lens of individual stories I will show how the dance between hope and despair can be played out in the interactions between people with attention to the relationship between therapist and client and to interactions within wider systems.

One of my beliefs is that positive relationships support the growth of hope. I will highlight how the therapeutic relationship can be a crucial factor in the transformation from despair to hope and from non-mentalised 'wishful thinking' to a more grounded, flexible form of hoping. This rests in part on what we 'do' as therapists and counsellors. But more fundamental is the fact that if we are willing and courageous enough to look into the face of their suffering and stay with their despair we can offer the people we work with a new and deeply healing experience. When we truly listen their truth can be heard rather than repeatedly disconfirmed and denied. When we attune to their subjective experience with compassion and curiosity we help them to step out of stuck relational and internal patterns and to reflect on their experiences in a non-judgemental way.

Another *leitmotiv* that threads through the book is the interconnectedness of hopelessness, shame, blame and responsibility. I have become interested how when we feel hopeless we can often shift into shame or into the paradigm of responsibility and blame. Within organisations and teams working with people with little hope of change it is interesting to see who feels most responsible and who ends up blaming whom. In Chapter 7 I discuss how blame and shame can form part of the internal dance and in Chapter 8 turn to an exploration of the interlocking paradigms of hope–despair and blame–responsibility in wider contexts.

I have stated my intention to study the dance between hope and despair by exploring the experiences of people who have survived multiple traumas, whose unique individuality has been disconfirmed and who struggle with serious and enduring health conditions. But more specifically, I want to draw attention to the more hypoaroused clients, who can challenge us in ways that are different from people who are predominantly hyperaroused and tend to attract more focus in clinical consultations and theoretical literature. As Elizabeth Howell points out, 'until fairly recently PTSD has mostly been understood in terms of over-arousal and anxiety – involving hyperactivation of the noradrenergic system, with symptoms of increased heart rate and blood pressure' (2011, p. 113). But it is now understood that there are two types of Post-Traumatic Stress Disorder (PTSD), one involving hyperarousal and one involving hypoarousal. Fight and flight reactions characterise the former. It is a state where there is too much emotion – for instance, states of overwhelming anxiety, fear or anger. Hypoarousal, meanwhile, is a state of low emotional tone associated with depression, hopelessness, passivity, numbing, depersonalisation and dissociation. After trauma some people tend towards one more than the other. However, oscillating between states of high and low arousal is also common and this itself can contribute to the erosion of hope, as it feels so out of control.

When talking to clients about which state most applies to them I often refer to the window of tolerance model (Siegel, 1999, pp. 253–8; Ogden et al., 2006, pp. 26–40). It helps to develop a shared, non-stigmatising language about their fluctuating moods and how they learned to cope with them. The model is best explained visually. When we are in our window of tolerance – the middle band in Figure 1.1 – we can feel but still think. In the top band there is too much emotion or sensation. We are hyperaroused and likely to be less able to mentalise. States of numbness, depression and dissociation fit in the lowest band, and in these shut down states thinking is again compromised and it is harder to be with others. Sometimes I add the idea of warning zones

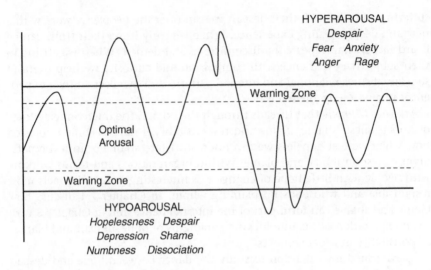

Figure 1.1 The Window of Tolerance
(Adapted from Ogden et al., 2006)

to encourage people to be curious about the first signs of slipping out of their window. I say more about how I use the model in Chapter 9 when discussing ways of working with hopelessness. But now I want to explore what we mean by hope and despair, to consider what contributes to states of hope and of hopelessness and then to return to the question 'what leads our clients to seek counselling or psychotherapy?' by examining what we can discover about their language of hope in our very first encounters.

The characteristics of hope and of despair

How do we define hope? Is it an emotion? A state of mind? A blend of emotions? An existential position? In everyday conversation we tend to be sloppy about how we use words like hope, hopelessness and despair. For instance, sometimes we say 'hope' when we mean 'wish', which could be a wish that rationally we know will not be fulfilled. On another occasion we might be conveying a faith or trust in the possibility, even if only tiny, that something will occur. The imprecision of our use of the word hope is partly because it is both a noun and a verb and because it can relate to the desire for something specific or more generalised. When used as a noun we talk about losing or finding hope or we quantify it (O'Hara, 2013, pp. 5–9). When speaking of it as an object we can take a passive position – as one refugee said, 'my hope was stolen from me'. Alternatively, O'Hara suggests to think of hope as something growing or diminishing that 'can have a self-empowering aspect' because 'if hope can grow in quantity then human effort can make a difference' (2013, p. 6). Meanwhile, as a verb there is someone doing the hoping and a sense of being active, of having a belief in something desirable and positive worth striving or hanging on for. It holds the richness and open-endedness of future possibilities. We can hope for something specific and oriented to a precise time frame, such as an object or of doing something: 'He hopes to get that job' or 'I hope I can finish this book by the end of the year.' Or what we hope for can be generalised and open-ended: 'I hope that something good will come from writing it.'

One way of looking at hope is to think in terms of linked emotional states such as optimism, excitement and interest or, alternatively, as a quieter, more serene state of acceptance and trusting that 'all will be well'. The former all involve a level of high physiological arousal – a 'buzz'; the latter state, a resting of one's trust in something outside the self, leads to calm states of both body and mind. When these emotional states are around we generally feel good about ourselves and are more likely to reach out to others. Because hope about one aspect of our lives can feed others, we are also more likely to try new things. We have a greater sense of mastery and control over our destiny. The way we think and interpret things is also affected by and influences how hopeful or otherwise we feel. People who are hopeful by nature tend to have a flexible style of thinking and relating. They are able to entertain alternative perspectives and to imagine and play with future possibilities. They also tend to be realistically optimistic that their actions will result in positive outcomes and that they will be able to find a way through difficulties (O'Hara, 2013, pp. 13, 58, 132).

Despair meanwhile is linked with the emotional states of hopelessness, disappointment, defeat, numbness, shame and sometimes cynicism and anger. When despair strikes our thinking is more likely to be black and white and we tend to interpret things negatively. Physiologically, it is often associated with hypoarousal, in other words low energy and physical exhaustion. However, people who are familiar with despair can also be hyperaroused – acutely anxious, fearful, vigilant and on edge. On the whole I use the words despair and hopelessness interchangeably throughout the book, as I think we do in everyday usage. But are there distinctions between the two? Grammatically, yes. For example, we can *be* hopeless and so can a situation, but we *feel* despair, and sometimes the word hopeless is used pejoratively instead of useless. We could also argue for making a distinction in terms of degree as Meltzer did when he wrote that whereas 'hopelessness is still grasping after hope and is very painful ... despair has given up hope and is no longer in pain' (1985, p. 40). I am not so sure. I believe that in a state of utter despair the individual can indeed become numb and detached. But equally he or she can feel intense, abject pain. There is an acuteness to it, whereas I see hopelessness as a flatter, greyer state. This is why I place hopelessness in the lowest band on the window of tolerance chart, whereas I associate despair with both the upper and the lower bands. There are also people who argue that behind despair there always lingers a hint of hope. It is not always a total giving up of hope, and as I work with desperate and hopeless people and write about the dance between hope and despair, I endeavour to always keep that small lingering hint in mind.

Another characteristic of hopelessness is that it involves a disruption to our sense of efficacy, time and meaning. People without hope often tell us how everything they have tried so far has failed and how whenever they seek help they only meet with blocks. Their despair is made worse because of a tendency to make comparisons – between self and others, how things are and how they used to be or how they would like them to be, and the let-downs and attempts that get nowhere; when compounded with such 'discrepancy mode' thinking (Segal et al., 2002) this leads to people feeling useless and powerless. The chronically hopeless often speak of feeling trapped, especially if all their perceived options have potentially negative consequences; for instance, the dilemma of not feeling safe with a current partner, but being terrified of living alone. Their sense of time is disrupted because there seems to be nothing to reach towards that offers a better future. They are facing something that feels endless and unendurable. Over time their sense of meaning and purpose erodes. There is little to live for.

In writing about depression, which is often the clinical manifestation of chronic hopelessness, Morgan emphasised how it 'involves turning away from experience in order to avoid emotional pain' (2005, p. 130). It is a 'turning away from life'. The people we see who are trapped in despair appear to have lost any sense of life or joy or vitality. They live in what Hobson described as 'a persistently detached-from-life-and-people way' and 'teeter on the abyss of unthinkable no-being' (1985, p. 127). Such people could be described as 'psychically numb', a term developed by Lifton to describe the numbed, automatic state of functioning he observed in the survivors of Hiroshima.[3] Albie Sachs captures this in the account of his imprisonment in solitary confinement in apartheid South Africa. He wrote, 'the worse symptom of all ... I am losing the will to resist. Nothing seems to matter anymore. I feel flat and lonely, and I do not seem to care about anything. "So what" sums up my attitude. Life is purposeless. To continue to live like this is purposeless. I feel powerless to achieve anything. Time and isolation have dissipated my emotional energy' (1966, p. 254).

One of the problems of being caught in such a state of hopelessness and purposelessness is that it can become self-perpetuating. To understand why I am going to use Daniel Siegel's definition of a state of mind; namely, 'a pattern of activation of recruited systems within the brain responsible for perceptual bias, emotional tone and regulation, memory processes, mental models and behavioural response patterns'. Put more simply it includes feelings, thoughts, memories, attitudes, beliefs and desires. Our state of mind influences our behaviour and interactions with others and it can rapidly change in response to environmental cues (1999, p. 211). We are responsive to places, times of day, the weather, noise, temperature, the task we are doing and whether this is pleasurable or stressful, the people we are with and the nuances of social interactions. Our state of mind can also be coloured by internal cues such as physical changes, pain, worries or things remembered or imagined (1999, pp. 213–4). Particularly important to remember is that our state of mind is especially sensitive to perceived levels of safety. Our emotional tone, bodily state and attentional bias will be very different if we are somewhere that evokes a sense of danger compared with being somewhere or with someone where we feel safe. In Figure 1.2 I have tried to capture the key elements of a state of mind as defined by Siegel with some adaptations, including adding body sensations, because of my understanding of the close interaction between mind, body and emotions.

States of mind can become engrained. Siegel gives the example of a state of despair because of repeated neglect as a child. 'In this excessively low energy state, perceptions of the world are marked with a sense of rejection; emotions are filled with shame and hopelessness; memories may evoke previous experiences of being rejected; a model of self as unlovable and of others as unavailable may be activated; and there may be a behavioural tendency to withdraw.' Because our state of mind or mood shapes how we interpret things and because feedback loops can develop between mind and body, over time this state of despair can be activated in response to even minor hints of rejection (1999, p. 212).

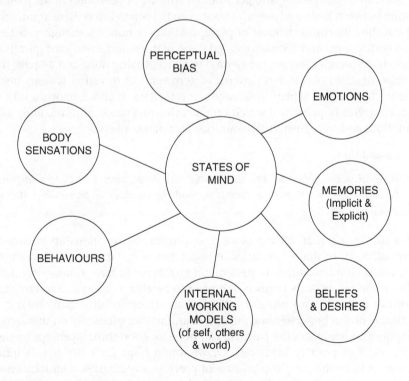

Figure 1.2 The Constituents of a State of Mind

Williams et al. said something similar when explaining why depression relapse is so common. Over time, they argue, a lower mood[4] can become easier and easier to trigger because each time it returns, the thoughts, feelings, body sensations and behaviours that accompany it form increasingly strong interconnections. Eventually, any one element can trigger depression itself. Hence, 'a fleeting thought of failure can trigger a huge sense of fatigue. A small comment by a family member can trigger an avalanche of emotions such as guilt and regret, feeding a sense of inadequacy. Because these downward spirals are so easily triggered by small events or mood shifts, they feel as if they come from out of nowhere. And once depression takes hold, we can feel powerless to prevent it from getting worse or to make it better' (2007, p. 29). Our thoughts about how we feel are influential. If to feeling sad, hopeless or depressed we add beliefs about being useless and inadequate the downward spiral gets worse. According to these researchers 'this is why we can react so negatively to unhappiness: our experience is not simply one of sadness, but is coloured powerfully by reawakened feelings of deficiency or inadequacy'. 'We feel not good **now** without being aware that this is a thinking pattern which belongs to the past' (2007, pp. 38–9). This, I argue, is one of the reasons why some of our clients get stuck in chronic hopelessness and why this state is so often linked with shame.

As I talk about people who get stuck in chronic hopelessness or keep oscillating between hope and despair I invite you to keep in mind these arguments about the interconnectedness of perceptual bias, emotions, thoughts, beliefs and bodily states and about engrained states of mind and downward spiralling moods. Although there are many ways to conceptualise hope and despair, the notion of states of mind as patterns of activation of recruited systems helps me to capture and explain this interconnectedness. It also supports a way of working with hopelessness which honours the integration of mind, body and emotions and our sensitivity to our interpersonal context.

Hope and time

Hope likes the yet-to-be, the changeable, the ambiguous ... [it] goes forward, beyond even a lifetime or outwards beyond the confines of probability. (Boris, 1976, p. 150)

It is interesting that, from a place of optimism, our relationship to time is very different to that when stuck in hopelessness and despair. Indeed a fundamental characteristic of hope is that it enables us to have a future in mind: the 'yet to be' as Boris terms it. We need to be able to hope and to envisage positive futures – and yet, as I will illustrate, there are situations when it is adaptive not to hope. Because our hopes and wishes often rely on memories, hoping also references the past. We can hope for good things, perhaps fuelled by a bank of positive memories. Or we might hope for a life that is quite different from the past, and because of previous experiences, simultaneously anticipate that nothing will come of our hopes, or worse, that something bad will emerge. In the act of hoping we are therefore bridging past, present and future, but in the process also having to grapple with uncertainty rather than absolutes. As the quotation from Boris highlights, we are entertaining a vision of a state beyond now – sometimes even beyond this existence; of something potentially different, but also conditional, uncertain and holding the risk of disappointment.

We could argue that to hope is an essentially human characteristic – a cortical activity. Our brains can run simulations of the future and being able to predict, weigh up possibilities and consider courses of action is one of the things that has enabled our species to survive (Hanson, 2009, p. 49). For the individual too the process of envisaging a future can be life sustaining, as Frankl discovered. 'It is a peculiarity of man' he wrote, 'that he can only live by looking to the future ... and this is his salvation in the most difficult moments of his existence' (2004, p. 81). Without this 'salvation' we risk becoming detached from life, as Frankl knew very well. He described the distorted sense of time of those trapped in a 'provisional existence of unknown limit' and observed how the lack of a future in mind, coupled with the limitlessness of their suffering, meant that many in the concentration camps gave up (2004, pp. 78–81).

In terms of our cognitive development it is interesting that the advent of language plays a significant part in our capacity to hope. This is partly because it gives children a way of conceptualising time and partly, as Daniel Stern points out, because once we can use symbolic language we can 'entertain and maintain a formed wish of how reality ought to be, contrary to the fact' (1985, p. 167). We can imagine a different now and dream dreams about the future. Children begin to use future-oriented words from about 18 to 24 months and then a little later words relating to the past. Before that they appear to live only in the present – at times perhaps a state of wonderful timelessness, but if gripped by fear or pain then an unendurable and inexplicable endlessness. These two polarised states frame the dialectic of hope and despair. What we dread is being caught in something endless, whilst in a more magical thinking way our hopes can focus on something limitless, blissful, an ideal. Molnos speaks about the 'magical lure of timelessness' – a state which takes us away from our terror of finite time, endings and death. She reminds us that 'the human mind, once the here and now becomes intolerably frightening or painful, escapes into another time, another place and idealises it' (1995, pp. 1, 60). This begs the question – how can we tell when are we in a more healthy, future-thinking mode and when caught in something illusory involving denial and splitting? Interestingly, wishing is part of the magical realm of childhood – the good fairy appears and grants three wishes. We seem to need this kind of illusion, and like children we can't always bear the wait before our longings are fulfilled. As I write I am remembering a moment when my client Jan said after a moving, transformative moment in a session, 'I'm always hoping that things will get better just like that.' But the problem, O'Hara points out, is that 'hope exists in the *in between* world of waiting' and we have to find a way to manage the fact that 'all hopes have a time delay ... if hope is to be sustained' (2013, pp. 12, 15). The laugh that accompanied Jan's words seemed to acknowledge that she knew this and had heard my caution that it might take some time before what she had suddenly learnt about herself would really take root. However, when people are desperate there is often an urgency to their hopes and we can get caught up in this, perhaps by doing too much or distancing in some way. I talk about some typical countertransference responses in Chapter 8.

What fosters hope?

In my endeavour to determine the prerequisites for a hopeful, optimistic personality I have identified certain factors which I call the 'dimensions of hope'. I shall describe them briefly, but will add further detail in the final chapter when I consider how they can be fostered in therapy. The dimensions include:

- *A sense of mastery and strategies to feel in control of ourselves, our emotions and our world*
- *Something that gives meaning to our experiences*
- *Discovering a purpose to our lives*
- *A sense of a future with good things to look forward to*
- *Trust in others and the capacity for meaningful relationships*
- *Faith in something larger than the self*

The foundations for the six dimensions are laid down within the matrix of our earliest attachment relationships. They need to be embedded in a climate of safety – which is represented in Figure 1.3 by the surrounding circle – and trauma and attachment failures can have a deleterious effect on all these fundamental self-experiences. This is especially true of the fifth dimension – trust in others and the capacity for meaningful relationships. In Chapter 5, when I discuss how trauma at different life stages affects our relationship to hope, I mention how a lack of safety in the earliest months of life can have long-lasting consequences. If others have contributed to the unsafeness this may include expectations about being abandoned, let down or hurt if we get close to people.

A sense of mastery is also born within the context of a secure base. From birth onwards we have a need to make things happen and to be seen and responded to as intentional beings. It has been shown how very young babies become passive, unresponsive and physiologically shut down when their efforts to elicit a response from a caregiver or manipulate something keep failing. Slightly older infants, meanwhile, might become more actively avoidant of anything to do with the problem (Alvarez, 2012, p. 30; Hudson Allez, 2011, pp. 26, 48–9). Both reactions to a feeling of inefficacy – avoidance and passive unresponsiveness – remind me of clients who have endured traumatic events

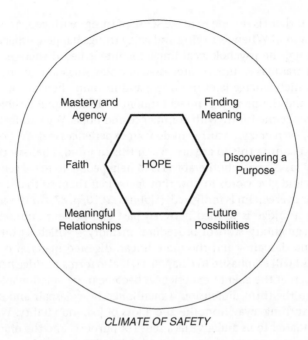

Mastery and
Agency

Finding
Meaning

Faith   HOPE

Discovering a
Purpose

Meaningful
Relationships

Future
Possibilities

CLIMATE OF SAFETY

Figure 1.3   The Dimensions of Hope

which overwhelmed and robbed them of their capacity to act and whose lives continue to be controlled by the psychological and somatic after-effects of trauma. For them shutting down and avoidance are familiar strategies when faced by potentially overwhelming situations. It also reminds me of people who, for different reasons, feel defeated after repeated unsuccessful attempts to change things and who sink into a state of hopeless and helpless collapse in which nothing and no one seems to matter anymore. As I will discuss in Chapter 3, shutting down is one of the hard-wired, defensive systems which we share with other animals. It is important as a temporary solution, but can have serious consequences if it becomes habitual.

The second dimension concerns our innate need to find meaning in our experiences in order to form a coherent story of our lives. Again we could argue that the foundations of meaning-making lie in infancy and the earliest 'conversations' between primary caregiver and baby. The mother's capacity to mentalise and reflect back in modified form what he or she is experiencing helps to transform raw sensory experiencing into something that can be modulated, understood and shared. Then, as Daniel Stern discussed, the advent of language in the second year of life 'brings about the ability to construct a narrative of one's life story with all the potential that holds for changing how one views oneself' (1985, p. 174). It is part of the emergence of what he called the 'verbal self', the self that can become an object of reflection and can negotiate shared meanings with others (1985, pp. 165, 170).

But what if there is no one to make sense of things with you, as is often the case after trauma? When terrifying and crazy things happen, especially when you are young, the psychological impact is intensified if there is no one to turn to. The traumas cannot be processed and stay stuck as body memories or fragments which emerge later in bizarre and incomprehensible ways. Events in the past and the present can feel random and incomprehensible and it is hard to envisage the future with confidence and hope. You can feel alienated from others, even crazy, so different do your experiences feel. Yet you have no means of explaining this to anyone. With this in mind, I believe that one of our primary tasks as psychotherapists is to help people to make sense of their experiences and give words to how they feel about them so that 'their power to distress or overwhelm is mitigated' (Holmes, 2010, p. 87). In the co-creation of meaning a bridge is formed between past and present and between the formless, fragmentary stuff of procedural memory – which so often evokes both fear and despair – and the more linear, digested material of narrative memory.[5] As I will emphasise in Chapter 11, it also forms a bridge between self and other so that the client's experiences become more 'relationable'.

Turning to the third dimension, I mentioned how despair and depression can lead to turning away from life and a loss of joy and vitality. We all need things that matter to us and give us a sense of purpose, and the objects of our hopes and desires can act as reference points to illuminate what is important and encourage us to keep turning towards life (O'Hara, 2013, pp. 10–11). For many of us our parent's own relationship to hope will play a part in this. For instance, we may identify with things that matter to them and 'adopt' their vision of what our life purpose should be. Adolescence should be a time to challenge their visions as we struggle to form our own identities. But it depends on how securely attached the young person feels. Some people have a clear sense of purpose from early in life. For others what matters and drives them keeps changing. We can also go through periods when we lose all sense of purpose and this is especially true if life events shatter our world and turn everything upside down. But out of this, I firmly believe, can come not just healing, but the reappraisal of what matters most and the discovery of a new direction and a more vital sense of meaning to our lives.

The fourth dimension, a sense of future possibilities, would not be possible without having developed a solid sense of our ongoingness and that of the world. If a child is brought up in a world of relative safety, where other people are reliable, attuned and responsive, this serves as a platform for developing this sense of ongoingness and an expectancy for obtaining what he/she needs. Robert Hobson conveyed this when he wrote that from the beginning a child 'anticipates the future in terms of possible satisfaction and dissatisfaction, of hope and fear'. If the young child's forays away from his secure base are too frightening and if, when he runs back to the security of his mother's arms, his fear is reinforced by her anxious and overprotective prohibitions, then 'his exploratory drive is inhibited' and 'the development of an attitude of hope with the expectation of rewarding achievement is arrested' (1985,

p. 215). A child needs to be able to 'play' with future possibilities, and the capacity to imagine and dream dreams flourishes when other people see his potential and support his initiative and aspirations. The same could also be said for us as adults. If we see hope in the eyes of others and hear encouragement in their voices we are more likely to feel confident about ourselves and the future.

The final dimension concerns the transpersonal. For many people faith in something greater than the self helps them to keep going through seemingly endless, unimaginable ordeals. Others have an intuitive or 'sixth' sense that even though the odds are against them all will be well. They may not be able to say what it is that gives them this quiet hope, and perhaps we don't need to know any more than we need absolute proof of a deity or higher power. The important thing is that it holds and inspires us and offers a vision of a different future.

What destroys hope?

Having considered what fosters hope, my next question is what type of life experiences might leave people without hope or endlessly oscillating between hope and despair? There seem to be a number of factors that take people into the place of despair, but in my experience they often fall within the following categories:

- *Enduring overwhelming trauma and loss*
- *Repeatedly being disconfirmed by others*
- *Struggling with debilitating mental and physical health problems*
- *Feeling trapped with no choices and no way out*
- *Repeatedly trying to make things better but finding that nothing works or seeking but never finding help*

Some people learn very early in life not to hope for too much – children living in chaotic homes, facing neglect and abuse or witnessing terrible things. But trauma experienced at any age can be a hope killer. The event or events shatter the sense of ongoingness and of basic trust in others and the world. Indeed one of the criteria for complex PTSD as defined by Judith Herman is that it entails an alteration in systems of meaning and more specifically, a 'loss of sustaining faith' and a 'sense of hopelessness and despair' (1994, p. 121). Often it is not just the awfulness of the events themselves but the after-effects, what I call 'trauma's tsunamis', which contribute to a sense of being out of control, a loss of sustaining beliefs and states of despair. Van der Hart et al. write: 'survivors often speak of the helplessness and hopelessness they feel as they perceive a random and chaotic world, where nothing is predictable or safe' (1993, p. 23). These after-effects include the very debilitating symptoms of a nervous system that is 'out of kilter' because of repeated shifts between being on red alert and varying degrees of numbness and shutting down, intrusive memories, the need to avoid any reminders of the trauma, the loss of trust in others and a sense of self as bad and worthless. Over time this can build up into a profound state of aloneness, helplessness and despair.

From a trauma perspective hopelessness is also one of the consequences of being objectified in some way – a body to be used; a child implicitly or explicitly expected to perform certain roles in the family system such as the 'good girl', the 'peace keeper', the 'gifted pianist' or 'the joker'; and later in life, a number in a bureaucratic system, a problem or diagnostic label to be fixed. It follows experiences when one's subjectivity is shattered, when personal reality is distorted and denied, when healthy strivings are squashed or ridiculed. I still recall feeling a chill of horror when one man who had been brought up in an abusive cult said, 'they teach you to be a nothing'. A no-thing allowed no thoughts and actions of his own, no opportunities to choose or experiment with ways of being, and sadly still controlled – as is the case with many survivors of abuse – by emotional and body memories and by acute fears of engaging in everyday life. Moreover, when someone's life has been rigidly controlled and when his truth has repeatedly been disconfirmed, it can become hard to know what he wants, let alone strive for it.

One situation I have often encountered is when people have worked, been effective parents, managed daily life and then, because of a traumatic event or situation which brought to the foreground repressed memories about previous traumas, they suddenly crashed into illness. They found themselves subject to intrusive thoughts and flashbacks which kept them in a state of fear and alertness and made it hard to be with people and to go out. They had to stop work and began to avoid social events. Such dramatic changes left them confused, frightened about what was going on and even fearing that they were going mad. They compared life now and before falling ill and struggled with guilt about no longer being the person they used to be. Typically, these people present with a combination of depression and anxiety, and sometimes with additional somatic problems. What they don't realise is that their 'symptoms' are not shameful or mad, but may owe their presence, as I will discuss in Chapter 3, to the way evolution has shaped our physiological responses to danger.

The language of hope

For people who have crashed into illness and despair the question 'what are you wanting in coming to therapy?' often leads to the reply that they don't know. This is especially true if they have been referred. Moreover, even when someone can articulate an explicit goal or reason for seeking help, underneath there can be hidden hopes and fears. The individual's 'language' of hope emerges in subtle ways and I believe we need to be particularly attentive to how hopes are revealed in the early stages of therapy. I agree with Erskine that to enquire specifically about someone's hopes can 'open a whole storehouse of information'. It can help to identify goals to work towards and to understand 'the deep wants and needs that thread through that client's life' (1999, pp. 42–3). Sometimes, if it feels right, I will ask specific questions. However, I have come to appreciate that if we listen carefully to the stories our clients tell us, especially about their relationships or past experiences of seeking help, it can reveal a lot about their hopes, fantasies and fears.

Let me give an example of what can be learned about a client's relationship to hope in the first meeting. My first impression of Mae, a woman whose story I shall turn to at later points in the book, was how burdened she seemed. She arrived for that meeting weighed down with a heavy bag, which she put down with a weary sigh, then, wincing with pain, carefully straightened her back. She told me she couldn't wait for her next cortisone injection as it always gave immediate relief. She added, 'I wish they'd find a permanent cure – something that would get rid of this back problem once and for all.' I speculated whether she might have a wish for a similar emotional cure? Mae agreed. She said she keeps expecting instant results. She wants a miracle cure. I acknowledged the wish and how understandable it was. Even after seeing so many professionals over the years, she still struggled with debilitating pain, anxiety and depression. However, I suggested, maybe what was really needed was to be able to face and tolerate the pain first. And so began a long journey together in which we worked on many intensely moving, tragic stories from Mae's childhood and made sense of how traumatic experiences coloured her relationships, self-beliefs and expectations about the future.

This beginning illustrates what we might call a dependent relationship to hope – the ongoing quest for the miracle – an investment in illusory hopes when there is a reification of the capacities of others or the potential effects of objects and substances. Other clients tell us about a lack of hope, perhaps by listing people they have contacted and everything they have tried which has not worked. Alternatively, they might express ambivalence by appearing eager to attend, talking about their hopes, then quickly dismissing them, discounting themselves or saying they don't believe anything will help. Magda, another woman I shall mention later, communicated her ambivalence on our first encounter when she said, 'I'd really like things to change, but I'm scared it will end and nothing will have happened.' Later she asked sadly, 'am I too broken or just a pain in the arse and need to pull myself together?' When I enquired what Magda meant by 'too broken' she explained, 'things haven't changed even with lots of input. I've never been able to use help and everyone loses patience with me'. Another woman said she thought she'd be wasting my time and that therapy wouldn't help. But in the next breath said 'this is my last hope'.

One thing I listen for are hints about attachment patterns in the hopes and fears people arrive with and how they are presented. Sometimes they speak of attachment gone wrong. They communicate a longing for a different sort of relationship – perhaps for the love or care they never had; for someone who understands them, who encourages and lets them be themselves. They hint at being let down, tricked, laughed at or rejected. They can also tell us about the strategies people have evolved in order to be with others or get their needs met, such as clinging, being resolutely self-reliant, trying hard to avoid being criticised or never risking asking for anything. Even with the minimal details in the examples above it might be interesting to speculate what these women's early relationships were like and what might drive someone to the point when therapy becomes the 'last hope'. We might also find clues about the client's attachment story and about the contexts in which their expectations were developed if we ask who or what are the hopes invested in – the client herself? us? some other professional? God? fate? a potential acquisition or life change? And who or what might block or disapprove of the hoped-for or become a useless object in the client's mind for their 'failure to *deliver*'.

Another thing to listen for is the 'elasticity' of the client's hopes. How far into the future do they stretch? Is it a hope for something immediate, to be achieved by the end of therapy or beyond this lifetime? Does it stretch beyond 'the confines of probability' and perhaps fall into the category of illusory hope, or is it realistic and achievable? Are our clients' hopes driven by perfectionism – an addictive pursuit of the ideal and terrible anxiety about failure? Or like Mae by wanting to be fixed quickly and not have a problem anymore? I am also curious about whose hopes they are. Do they belong authentically to the person in front of me or to someone who persuaded her to come? Or maybe they were 'adopted' from parents long ago.

One more lens should be considered – our responses to our clients' hopes. For instance, do they challenge or enmesh with our personal hopes and aspirations and how might the latter get in the way? If the individual is fixated on a particular outcome, do we feel a failure for not making this happen or argue the case for alternative possibilities? Or can we stay curious about why this is so important? And when people are sceptical or pin their hopes on another professional, such as the man who said 'I don't think anything will improve until my medication is changed. I want to see another psychiatrist,' do we catch their hopelessness and fall into doubt about what we can offer or try hard to convince them of our worth?

There are many ways in which hope could be categorised and O'Hara gives a range of examples from different research studies in his book *Hope in Counselling and Psychotherapy* (2013). In my own attempt to define some of the typical ways in which we can position ourselves in relation to hope I have developed what I call the Hope Scale. The model is informed by my observations of how the survivors of overwhelming trauma and loss conceptualise the future and speak about hope, and tries to capture the difference between mentalised and non-mentalised hope, to draw in the intersubjective dimension and to provide a means of tracing our multiple relationships to hope. I use the word

Table 1.1 The Hope Scale

Realistic, creative and flexible hoping	Aspirations and belief in future possibilities, but a capacity to accept and adjust in the face of thwarted hopes
	"Live as well as I can in the circumstances"
Faith and trust That all will be well	
When hoping keeps The self alive	Mentalised or non-mentalised hope?
	Realistic or illusory?
	Active or passive?
	Self-reliant or relational?
Adaptive not to hope	Don't trust or risk being hopeful
Chronic hopelessness	Shut down Give up
Hope destroyed	Despair
A-hope	No capacity to imagine, dream or hope

scale, but not in the sense of something measurable, although we could certainly think of a hierarchy from states of utter despair to progressively more hopeful states of mind in which the individual feels able to turn to things that provide hope and has a greater sense of being in control of his or her destiny. Instead I have a musical scale in mind because I think this captures far better that these are not either/or categories. The individual can move between the different positions or experience two or more simultaneously in the same way that notes in a scale can be played together or separately in different combinations. Bearing in mind my point that hope is both an intrapsychic and an intersubjective phenomenon, and expanding upon the musical analogy, these changing positions are often coloured by the responses of others or the 'notes' they play. In Chapter 6 I give a detailed account of each position when discussing the impact of trauma on the individual's relationship to hope. But for reference I set them out in Table 1.1.

Being with despair

In this beginning I have signposted what follows and raised questions that I hope will encourage you to be curious in new ways about what you notice as you work. Any research raises more questions than it answers and writing this book has been a journey of exploration. It has introduced me to new authors and taken me back to familiar works, but now read from a very different place. Amongst the latter is a well-thumbed copy of Robert Hobson's *Forms of Feeling*. Hobson writes from the heart with a poetic honesty. He says much that resonates and makes me think, and in the context of the dance of hope and despair the following had a particularly strong impact. He pointed out that we don't know how to speak *to* the core of loneliness, although we might talk *about* it (1985, p. 271). Reading this made me realise that I don't just want to talk *about* despair – although you will certainly find a lot *'about'* the subject as you read. What I am trying to grasp and to convey is how to *be* with despair. How can we join our desperate clients in their suffering yet, as said earlier, not get caught up in it for too long and lose our capacity to think? In an article about mindfulness and depression Morgan described this as 'finding the heart of depression' and as 'a form of open-heart surgery' (2005, pp. 139, 142). For me this metaphor speaks of two challenges. The first is of helping those we work with to turn towards rather than avoid the experience of emotional pain. The second is of developing the capacity to open our own hearts to the rawness and overwhelmingness of their pain and despair. This, ultimately, is what can make a difference.

Notes

1. I would define 'big T' traumas as events at the extremes of human experience that often occur over a long period.
2. Because Sensorimotor Psychotherapy strongly informs how I work with the survivors of trauma, the book includes specific examples of how I integrate this approach. Other Sensorimotor psychotherapists may not always agree with my opinions or emphasis and I recommend Pat Ogden's books for anyone interested in learning more (2006, 2015).
3. Lifton described psychic numbing as 'a form of desensitisation [which] refers to an incapacity to feel or to confront certain types of experience due to the blocking or absence of inner forms or imagery that can connect with such experiences' (1967, cited in Wilson, 2004, p. 123).
4. These researchers use the term mood, rather than state of mind. For our purposes the important point is that both influence how we perceive things and both are susceptible to recursive feedback loops.
5. Implicit or procedural memory is memory for the nonverbal aspects of experience. It includes skills knowledge, for instance, all the muscular processes that are involved in riding a bike, and emotional, body and sensory memories. Explicit or declarative memory is verbal and factual such as what we remember and narrate to others, or facts that we learnt at school. Explicit memory is partial – we don't remember every detail of an event, and it is not fixed for memories are constantly being modified as we access them and associate them with other experiences. This includes experiences in the therapeutic relationship.

2

Desperately Seeking the 'Happy Ever After': Some Theoretical Perspectives on Hope

To love is to risk not being loved in return
To hope is to risk pain
To try is to risk failure
But risk must be taken,
Because the greatest hazard in life
Is to risk nothing

(Buscaglia, 2006)

Seeking 'happy ever afters'

In the first drafts of this book I was aware of a pull to present examples with a 'happy ending', just as in fairy tales we need and indeed expect to hear that 'they all lived happily ever after'. Did I choose, and of course we are selective, to end my narratives at positive moments? And if so why? Why is man drawn to or needs to believe in 'happy ever afters' and to seek certainty and absolutes? There is a neatness about this – a sense of closure. And it is about certainty – the novel with a definite ending; the piece of music that returns to the home key, rather than something suspended in mid-air or with an ambiguous conclusion. But real life is not like that. It is conditional, uncertain, changeable, and as Buscaglia's words emphasise, entails risk if we are to move forwards. Of course, as therapists, we hope for a 'happy ending' and with our longer-term, more complex clients we feel optimistic and perhaps relieved when we encounter a moment of transformation and things appear to change. But then suddenly they are thrown back into crisis, leaving us anxious, disappointed or feeling hopeless to be here again. Another reality is that we are only privileged to read a chapter of each client's life. We cannot know whether there is a happy ending; whether they are able to build on the changes we witnessed or whether life continues to deal a cruel hand.

I began to think that whilst I genuinely believe that hope keeps people going, it can also be an 'obstacle'. It needs to be viewed from a dialectic position. The central theme of my book is the dance between hope and despair. But there is another dialectic that holds my attention. We can think about hope as something progressive which keeps us striving for things that enhance and expand life. This is the sort of hope that can be linked with creative play, imagination and inspiration, but is grounded in reality. However, as mentioned in the Introduction, there is another version of hope – hope that is vested in illusion. Victor Frankl talked about the 'delusion of reprieve' and our human tendency to cling to shreds of hope (2004, p. 23). I believe that as therapists we can be pulled into this delusion and into trying to provide shreds of hope in non-mentalising ways. Instead of responding to a desperate client from a well thought out position, we can slip into 'doing mode'. 'Only action will do' is one of three states which, in developmental terms, precede the more mature and flexible ability to mentalise. In 'teleological mode', as this state is known, positions become polarised – for instance, between good and bad or between absolute certainty and absolute doubt (Bateman et al., 2004).[1]

'If only' thinking can be a clue to when we might be in teleological mode. For instance, we might find ourselves thinking 'if only I knew how to ... or was trained in ... ; other people did their bit; she attended regularly; he was more motivated' or 'I was allowed to work with him for two years'. From our clients' perspective a list of wishful thoughts might include: 'If only you did this for me; they stopped that; people listened; someone cared; I could go back home; I could do this ... it would all be OK'. The 'if only' list might also include a change of treatment or personnel: 'If only I could see someone else; be sent to that expert or change my medication'. For people in the client's world, meanwhile, the script might be: 'If only someone else took over; he or she grew up; he got off his backside; she stopped moaning' and so on. Interestingly, in all these examples there is some form of discount (Shiff, 1975). Each member of the system will either discount his or her capacity to do anything, or the ability or willingness of others to make a difference or, at worse, the solvability of the problem – and unchecked discounting rapidly contributes to futility.

The tensions of the dialectic between creative and illusory hope are evident in some of the conflicting positions that have been taken by writers in the psychoanalytic tradition. Interestingly, it is also a dialectic discussed by Buddhist philosophers. Buddhists advocate letting go our attachment or 'addiction' to the hope for change. As Pema Chodron argues, hopelessness is 'the beginning of the beginning. Without giving up hope – that there's somewhere better to be, that there's someone better to be, we will never relax with where we are or who we are' (1997, p. 38). This stance offers a deeper connection to the present moment and to ourselves. 'Giving up hope is encouragement to stick with yourself, to make friends with yourself, to not run away from yourself ... if we totally experience hopelessness, giving up all hope of alternatives to the present moment, we can have a joyful relationship with our lives' (1997, p. 45). Thich Nhat Hanh also wrote about this (1991, p. 41):

Hope is important because it can make the present moment less difficult to bear. If we believe that tomorrow will be better, we can bear a hardship today. But that is the most hope can do for us – to make some hardship lighter. When I think deeply about the nature of hope I see something tragic. Since we cling to our hope in the future, we do not focus our energies and capabilities on the present moment. We use hope to think something better will happen in the future, that we will arrive at peace, the Kingdom of God. Hope becomes a kind of obstacle. If you can refrain from hoping, you bring yourself into the present moment and discover the joy that is already there.

There can certainly be an addictive quality to hope, or rather to false hopes. But whilst agreeing that in some circumstances hope can be an obstacle, I cannot agree that joy is always there to be noticed. How can it be if the present is haunted by a traumatic past? Perhaps anticipating objections, Thich Nhat Hanh added, 'I do not mean you should not hope, but that hope is not enough.' What he seems to be saying is that a permanent future focus, which fits with the idea of non-mentalised hoping, stops us noticing the present. Even if hope, and likewise seeking change, could be an obstacle or an illusion if that helps someone to get through the day does it matter? One could argue that the very experience of mastering a day may provide a potentially new experience which in itself is the *real* hope upon which the individual can build. It is about constructing a new narrative and updating procedural memories.

When someone appears to be stuck in a repetitive cycle of misfortune, self-destructive behaviours and self-limiting beliefs, I hold on to the notion of a spiral of growth. What may appear like endless looping can become an upward spiral in which, whilst people may certainly encounter the same external difficulties and relational struggles and periodic troughs of despair, each time they go round a loop they bring to it new insights, skills and resources. I would also add that hoping on behalf of our clients is hugely important. We need to safeguard the 'patient's hope denied' and retain a sense of the possible, the yet-to-be and as yet un-hoped for (Holmes, 2010, p. 150). It is about allowing ourselves to risk hoping because, as Buscaglia said, the greatest hazard in life is to risk nothing.

The people who come to see us are indeed risking hope and as a motivating factor this is important. As research has shown, it is one of the four 'common factors' in promoting change.[2] Hope or, I would add, despair motivates the individual to seek help in the first place and hope encourages him or her to keep coming. Hope also motivates those of us who work in the helping professions to persevere in the work we do. But alongside our respective hopes there will also be a range of conflicting fears and expectations.

When trauma is in the field the swings between hope and fear are likely to be particularly strong and this is another dialectic that I hold in mind. From a Buddhist perspective hope and fear are two sides of a coin. As long as there is one, there's always the other argues Pema Chodron (1997). The Tibetans represent this linguistically with the term *re-dok*, which combines their words for hope – *rewa* – and fear – *dokpa*. The two are interconnected in many ways. When we are very scared, holding on to the hope of something different offers us a lifeline. We can swing between optimism and fearing that our hopes will never be met. Or we might fear some form of punishment or scorn for entertaining certain hopes, especially if they are for things that are 'forbidden' in our family or culture. It is important to bear in mind that our clients' quest for the 'happy ever after' may be driven by archaic fears. To quote Stephen Mitchell: 'old hopes are born from dread. They are solutions to situations that no longer exist', and he argued that 'what is most therapeutic is our ability to find opportunities for new growth embedded in old hopes' (1993, p. 221). So another question to consider when we first meet someone is what the hopes she arrives with might reveal about things she fears and what this might tell us about her past.

A small example of the hope/fear duality – which I would guess is illustrative of a bigger template – occurred when one woman showed me a poem she had written. She admitted to hoping that I would approve. When I read the poem tears came to my eyes. It moved me and I said how beautiful it was. The woman was surprised, but only later told me that she always expects anger or disapproval and that seeing my emotion changed something inside. I am glad she risked allowing the hope. But for some people their dreads prevent them from daring to hope and trying something new.

The duality of hope and fear does not only apply to our clients. What fears lurk behind our hopes as therapists? For instance, what do we fear if our work with someone does not end well? I wonder if the therapeutic community, and indeed our culture as a whole, is desperately seeking the 'happy ever after' in its focus on outcome measures, evidence-based treatments and accountability? Might we be looking for the security of knowing that something works, and works for all, rather than facing the uncomfortable truth that perhaps some of our clients won't get better, or not in a way that can be quantified nor as speedily as our 'quick fix' world would like? Do our clinical hopes sometimes serve to avoid knowing that the here-and-now problems someone encounters are truly awful and something that no one person or system can fix? Or that some people's journey is one of snakes and ladders and they may come back months, even years after we first met facing yet again something hopeless and unbearable? And what might our professional quest for certainty, for the thing that will solve or fix the problem, tell us about our personal anxieties and dreads?

This is a question to keep attending to – and for me it is especially important when, as one response to feeling stuck or hopeless during a session, I drift into pulling for change in some way. For example, it might be in suggesting something a client could try at home, such as experimenting doing something different or mindfully noticing thoughts and sensations rather than reacting to them. Or I might catch myself challenging stuck beliefs too forcefully. I can fall into the trap of behavioural change and going into teleological mode.

This is not to say that sometimes adopting a more directive, problem-oriented approach is not important. It **can** be in supporting people to regain a sense of hope and possibility. However, it becomes a trap if my client goes along with my suggestions and then feels even more hopeless after trying hard, but finding the task impossible. It is also a trap because whenever we become too focussed on solutions and outcomes we risk 'wasting the moment of hope' (Winnicott, 1958, p. 309). We need to keep asking is this really supporting growth? Are we both avoiding facing something painful? Or am I wanting a 'happy ever after' – for the session to end well; for the person not to have to keep suffering (or telling me) this problem? The more we can hold our hopes lightly and catch moments when anxieties are driving us, the likelier it is that we can help our clients access what is hopeful and meaningful for them.

Theoretical perspectives on hope

For the remainder of this chapter I want to examine some of the different and at times polarised ways that psychotherapists have viewed hope. I have selected themes which have helped me to clarify my own thinking and which provide pointers to how we might conceptualise our work with desperate individuals. I am not going to cover how different schools of psychotherapy think about what engenders hope. That is a big subject in its own right and is connected with the beliefs about what it means to be human and about what leads to change that are emphasised in different traditions.[3] However, in the final section I will consider how the theories discussed influence my ever-evolving practice.

Hope in the analytic tradition

If we were working in the early days of psychoanalysis we would be aware of two very different and conflicting perspectives on hope. One – the classic Freudian position – was that hope is regressive and linked with fantasy and illusion; the other that hopes can be progressive and concerned with enriching our experience. This view holds in mind early deprivation and seeking something reparative. We would also have encountered a slightly different duality in the writing of Melanie Klein. Taking the regressive view first, a Freudian would argue that illusory hoping is 'embedded in primary process thinking and wish fulfilment', such as the wish for infantile sexual or aggressive impulses to be gratified (Mitchell, 1993, pp. 204–7). It is divorced from reality and our focus should therefore be on the need to let go of infantile hopes and transform them into 'rational understanding' (Mitchell, 1993, pp. 15, 205). A key aspect of this approach would be to interpret the dreads that go with the patient's illusory hopes – for example, of fantasised punishment for forbidden wishes – and the defences used to deal with fears and disillusionments when the object of desire is not forthcoming. As Boris pointed out, 'when life becomes unbearable and we cannot change the people, events or conditions we depend on for the fulfilment of our hopes and desires' one defence might be to try to alter our perception of experience. For example, we might try to convince ourselves that we didn't want the hoped-for after all; that it is not worth having or that something is wrong with us, so of course we can't have it (1976, p. 147).

In subsequent chapters I shall give examples of hope which is divorced from reality. But I cannot agree with the position that hope is essentially regressive or that our role should be to establish a 'rational normality'. In my experience, for a child or adult who faces a bleak, unwelcoming and hostile world wishful thinking may well keep him going. Moreover, if you cannot change or escape your environment, altering your perception of experience or your physiological state can be crucial for emotional and physical survival. To assume that this survival strategy is negative is to engage in what Orange calls the 'hermeneutics of suspicion', a therapeutic stance of believing that in the client's narrative things are not what they seem and every perspective conceals another (2011, pp. 30–1).

Klein's views on hope

Klein's idea of the paranoid-schizoid and depressive positions offers another way to conceptualise illusory hope. In the former hope is seen as a longing for something easily controlled and easily exchanged. It seeks absolutes, splits experience and preserves idealisation and omnipotence. In the depressive position, with the growing capacity to integrate good and bad and to feel concern for others, we start to realise that the 'bad' is not as terrible as feared and, according to Klein, 'feelings of hope emerge' (Mitchell, 1993, pp. 212, 261; Klein, 1975, pp. 75, 196). But in this version of hope there is risk because it entails facing uncertainty and finitude. Mitchell argues that 'hope in the depressive position requires great courage, a longing for an all-too human, irreplaceable object, outside of one's control'. He also says, 'to love in a committed fashion over time is to hope; and to hope is to impart value in an inevitably uncertain future. Both love and hope are extremely risky' (1993, p. 212). His words remind me that we cannot ignore the vicissitudes of time. The people we love may disappoint, betray, leave us or one day die. Likewise, the people the abused child hopes will one day say they love her will, in all likelihood, fail her again and again. The let downs, losses and inevitable changes have to be faced and grieved. If we can do this it opens up the possibility for what Mitchell describes as 'a more mature version of hope – generated through the capacity to sustain an integrated, textured experience of self and others despite loss and vulnerability' (1993, p. 261). This is one of the things that I hope for my clients. To develop an integrated, textured experience of self and others is an achievement that is built on the capacity to hold multiple perspectives – one of the themes in Chapter 10 – and, crucially, upon the foundations of secure relationships. The writer I turn to next understood this.

Winnicott's progressive view of hope

Winnicott took a more progressive view of hope. One of his main, and in his day radical, arguments was that infantile hopes are not defensive or pathological demands for illusory satisfaction. They represent a self-healing return to the point at which psychological growth was suspended or 'frozen' because of some form of relational failure (Mitchell, 1993, p. 207). Winnicott believed that for anyone deeply wounded by relational trauma a regression to dependency represents a developmental search for psychological recovery. It is a hoping for a new start or 'developmental second chance' (Orange, 2011, p. 153). What makes regression useful, Winnicott argued, is 'that it carries with it the hope of a new opportunity for an unfreezing of the frozen situation and a chance for ... the present-day environment, to make adequate though belated adaptation' (1955 cited in Orange, 2011, p. 153). Winnicott's belief that therapy can offer a 'renewed experience in which the failure situation will be unfrozen and re-experienced' but in a different way presages contemporary views on enactments. It is not that infantile hopes and longings need be renounced. But if 'reanimated and brought to life' they can 'grow into more mature hopes through a natural, organic growth process' (Mitchell, 1993, p. 207).

Winnicott did not shy from offering more than many of his contemporaries would have done to support his patients and he was adept at looking for hope in their difficulties.[4] For example, when writing about troubled youths, Winnicott argued that the 'anti-social tendency' implies hope. It emerges when 'the child becomes hopeful of a positive response from the world once more. His hope leads him to protest against his deprivation and try to put matters right.'[5] To me this speaks about the healthiness of protest, and I have often observed that when people stuck in hopelessness and hypoarousal begin to feel and express anger they become more alive, energised and ready to take action. Winnicott also saw glimmers of hope in his work with psychotic individuals, again arguing that 'the regression represents the psychotic individual's hope that certain aspects of the environment which failed originally may be relived, with the environment this time succeeding instead of failing' (1965, p. 128).

What I particularly like is Winnicott's stress on 'going to meet and match the moment of hope'. He wrote: 'over and over again one sees the moment of hope wasted, or withered, because of mismanagement or intolerance ... the treatment of the anti-social tendency is not psycho-analysis but management, a going to meet and match the moment of hope' (1958, cited in Mitchell, 1993, p. 206). Whatever shape it takes – whether an anti-social gesture, protest, fantasy or seeming delusion – instead of trying to interpret and too quickly transform it into 'rational understanding', can we be open to listening and learning from our clients? And can we be curious and look for seeds of something hopeful and growthful emerging?

The other theme in Winnicott's writing which offers a different way to conceptualise hope, although he did not actually use the word, is his stress on the importance of illusion and the transitional space. Unlike Freud, Winnicott did not see illusion as an alienation of the mind from reality, but as a bridge between inner and outer worlds. He believed that 'illusion lay at the heart of all creative living, both in childhood and later in life' (Turner, 2002, pp. 1063, 1077). As Orange points out, for Winnicott, illusion referred to that 'omnipotent sense of possibility that fuels creative life', and he set it firmly in a developmental context with his argument that illusion is 'supported from the beginning by the maternal environment' (2011, p. 159.) To hope also demands a sense of the possible and, as I will argue in Chapter 4, a secure attachment provides a solid foundation from which hoping and imagining can evolve. Even if we know that what we hope for might not necessarily be realistic, sometimes our hopes need to be bold. They need to come from a place of Winnicottian 'omnipotence'. In her discussion about the importance of play and the imagination, Anna Alvarez asked the important question: 'When should we tell our friends or children to "stop dreaming", "stop play-ing about" and when should we respect someone's wildest dreams?' Although she observed that sometimes our wildest dreams obstruct or pervert develop-ment, which fits the analytic view of hope as regressive, she also acknowl-edged that our dreams can be deeply creative, even visionary or at the very least healing (2012, p. 149).

Linking theory and practice: contemporary relational theories

In recent decades with what has been termed the 'relational turn' (Mitchell, 2000), there has been increasing emphasis on how a real, genuine engagement between therapists and clients is the key to healing and change. Research backs this up – for instance, showing that the therapeutic relationship 'makes substantial and consistent contributions to psychotherapy outcome irrespec-tive of the specific type of treatment' (Mearns and Cooper, 2010, pp. 2, 9, 12–15). This trend cuts across schools of psychotherapy from humanistic therapies, such as Gestalt, Transactional Analysis and person-centred, to the contemporary analytic field as well as 'third wave' cognitive therapies.

I imagine that many therapists who espouse a relational way of work-ing would resonate with Winnicott's idea of 'going to meet and match the moment of hope' and his faith that our troubled clients are looking for a 'developmental second chance'. These ideas certainly fit with the empha-sis in person-centred and other humanistic approaches on the individual's potential given the right climate in which to develop (Mearns and Thorne, 2011, pp. 33–4).[6] They are also echoed in the way Mitchell, a relational ana-lyst, views hope as 'seeking a psychological space in which a genuine desire may become possible, in which the self can find a new beginning'. As Mitch-ell argues, the goal of contemporary analysis is 'not the establishment of a rational normality but the capacity to generate a sense of self and relation-ships felt as important, meaningful and deeply one's own'. (1993, pp. 37, 39). It honours how subjectivity can emerge in the interactions between therapist and client and how we are always working with multiple meanings rather than single, objective truths. Again echoing Winnicott, it also appreciates the need for a 'safe domain' in which the client 'can pursue an authentic personal experience' (1993, pp. 205–6).

The 'new beginning' is born in the context of a relationship that is different from those in the past. It is a particular type of relationship offering not just a holding presence, nor the core conditions, but a willingness to make use of ourselves in the service of a client and to honour his or her subjectivity. It is not about being an 'expert', but 'a fellow human being who will understand his longings, losses, hopes and fears; someone who will engage with him as he struggles to work out a happier, healthier way of being with others in the world' (DeYoung, 2003, p. 15). I believe that such a relationship should also be grounded in compassion. So often shame gets in the way of finding a new beginning. When we communicate our compassion for how our client's story and difficulties have contributed to how he organises and perceives his experiences, the grip of shame diminishes.[7]

Our respect and compassion for what Rogers called the 'otherness' of the other is even more important when working with survivors of trauma who have repeatedly been treated like objects. This is an ethical stance shared across traditions that is epitomised in Buber's 'I-thou' attitude (1958). The relational stance also includes what Orange calls 'an attitude of receptivity'. She argues that we are called, not merely to actively involve ourselves with our clients, but to truly listen and learn from them.[8] It is about the 'hermeneutics of trust' rather than of suspicion – to trust that the people we work with are 'trying to communicate their truth to us, by whatever they are saying or doing, and that is up to us to try to understand' (2011, pp. 30, 67–8). We have to suspend our theories and assumptions, something that Buber describes as 'perilous' because 'the well-tried context' is loosened and 'one's security shattered' (Mearns and Cooper, 2010, p. 42). Yet in this loosening of our security lies an enormous potential for growth.

One day, whilst working on this chapter, a woman said to me 'I was too scared to be my own self.' I recall a stab of sadness in my chest. Then I had a sense of this self, her potential self, hiding somewhere deep inside her core – longing to emerge and express herself through her art, yet dreading that people might respond to her as her parents had done in the past. The words of the existentialist Kierkegaard came to my mind. 'The deepest form of despair', he said, 'is to choose to be another than himself', and if this is so, then 'to will to be that self which one truly is, is indeed the opposite of despair' (cited in Rogers, 2004, p. 110). My client's ongoing despair when over and over again something blocked her attempts to translate her creative ideas into action was tragic to observe – and even more tragic was how she interpreted this as being useless and a failure. If only she could have known that all too often it is our fears which get in the way of our hopes.

There is a poem by Anne Sexton which connects the idea of being the self one truly is and the growth of hope, and I would like to end this chapter with her words. The poem was written as a riposte to her mentor's advice to use less of herself in her work (Middlebrook and George, 1991, p. 26).

> *And if I tried to give you something else,*
> *something outside of myself*
> *you would not know*
> *that the worst of anyone*
> *can be, finally, an accident of hope.*

If we are to help our clients to be their authentic selves we have to not only provide a 'safe domain', but risk being truer to ourselves and willing to share our subjectivity. This is what lies at the heart of the relational attitude and this is where our hope lies.

I believe that we must never forget the centrality of our presence in this work and the importance of a real and genuine engagement. But it takes courage to go into the unscripted territory of intersubjectivity. It also calls for a scrupulous honesty with ourselves, and sometimes this means getting to know our own 'worst'. In my experience, although I may not always like what I find, if I can reflect on this and if and when it feels right talk with a client about what I have discovered and how we might have impacted each other, something new and important emerges. We both change in the process. Maybe it could even be argued that we – or rather *we-together* – are the 'accidents of hope'.

Notes

1. The other two proto-mentalising states are 'pretend mode' and 'psychic equivalence mode'.
2. Lambert et al. identified that about 15% of change comes from hope and expectancy. The other three factors are client variables or extra-therapeutic factors [40%]; the therapeutic alliance [30%] and theory/technique [15%] (O'Hara, 2013, p. 63).
3. I suspect that individual therapists will probably have been drawn to their particular training model because of their own relationship to hope (see Adams, 2014, Chapter 6). I am also mindful that all theories are embedded in time and culture.
4. See Orange, 2011, chapter 5.
5. This is reminiscent of the phase of protest Bowlby (1989) observed in young children when separated from their mothers.
6. This premise is supported by attachment theory.
7. This view is informed by the philosophies and research underpinning Compassion Focused Therapy (Gilbert, 2005).
8. In a sense this is about being mindful as well as mentalising therapists (Wallin, 2007, pp. 312–13).

3

Hoping, Imagining and Dreaming: An Evolutionary Perspective

The survival logic of chronic hopelessness: immobilisation as a defensive system

Within the fortress of your depression –
Shutting you down, shutting me out, shutting you up –
In the safe cocoon of lethargy
Somewhere dormant lies a pearl of hope waiting to be found.

In this chapter I look at the dance of hope and despair from an evolutionary, neurobiological perspective. In the Introduction I said that as well as wanting to explore how the dance plays out in the lives of people who have survived complex trauma, I intend to draw attention to clients who get stuck in states of depression and hopelessness. My rationale for taking an evolutionary perspective is that I believe it provides insights that can help us to respond more effectively to the chronically hopeless. In the first part of the chapter I will explore the survival logic of states of hypoarousal. In part two I look at the other side of the coin by asking why mankind developed a capacity to hope and how might that have promoted our survival as individuals and a species?

Evolution has primed the brain to mobilise the body in readiness for fight or flight in response to danger or, if these strategies are not possible, to go into freeze or down-regulate into a state of shut down or feigned death. 'Shut down', or what is sometimes referred to as tonic immobility, is evoked by situations when fear is coupled with feeling trapped and being unable to escape. It is characterised by a loss of energy and muscle tone, whilst heart rate, blood pressure and breathing rate all go down (Howell, 2011, pp. 124–5). This is accompanied by emotional numbing and a slowing or shutting down of cognitive processing, in other words, a more dissociative state.

Before going further a brief explanation of the terms sympathetic (SNS) and parasympathetic nervous system (PNS) is called for (see Figure 3.1). These two branches of the autonomic nervous system (ANS) regulate involuntary body processes. The former could be described as our 'get up and go system'. It is mainly involved in arousal and preparation for action and is activated during states of pleasurable high arousal, such as excitement, and states of distress,

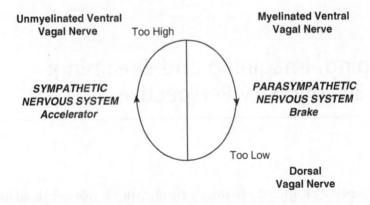

Figure 3.1 The Autonomic Nervous System

fear and anger. It provokes the production of chemicals necessary for fight and flight. The parasympathetic branch is involved in lowering arousal and could be called our 'calm down and rest system'. When activated it decreases heart rate, breathing and blood pressure. It is also involved in digestion, repair and immune functions and supports rest and sleep. The PNS is associated with states of relaxation and peacefulness and the emotional states of sadness, disappointment and shame. The ANS works in cycles to maintain homeostasis. Ideally, we have moments of high arousal, then of rest. Ongoing trauma can make the ANS very unstable – a bit like having a foot on the accelerator and the brake at the same time – with consequences for both physical and emotional health (Rothschild, 2000, pp. 46–50).

The functioning of the ANS depends on messages being communicated between the brain and the body. This is via two major nerves. The dorsal vagus is an unmyelinated nerve. It mediates the PNS and helps to ensure survival by conserving energy and reducing metabolic demands. In other words, it acts like a brake or dimmer switch which slows down our body's and brain's responses (Shapiro, 2009, p. 18). By contrast, the ventral vagal nerve aids survival by mobilisation. When it is 'on' we go into red alert and the body is primed for fight or flight. This is SNS functioning. In mammals there is also a myelinated ventral vagus which connects to the brain areas that control the facial muscles – in other words, the organs of social engagement. When we are safe it dampens down the sympathetic fight/flight circuits and creates a calm and alert state (associated with PNS functioning) so that we can engage socially and optimise metabolic resources (Porges, 2012; Shapiro, 2009). The three elements of the vagal system map neatly onto the window of tolerance.

To sum up, whereas the hyperaroused states of fight, flight and freeze[1] are all associated with the SNS, shut down or feigned death is mediated by the PNS (Porges, 2012; Corrigan et al., 2011). The way the dorsal vagus puts a brake on functioning and down-regulates the mind and body is highly adaptive in situations where it would not be safe or possible to fight or to flee. Porges (2012) describes how this process helps people survive horrendous things by raising pain thresholds and thus reducing the pain actually experienced. It also facilitates survival by cutting down on demands for oxygen and food until resuming activity is safe. In the face of a violent aggressor it can be a crucial way to minimise harm and thus, in some situations, to stay alive. Yet many people see shutting down as a shameful 'giving in' rather than an important strategy to preserve both the mind and the body. A similar state of physiological shutdown has been observed in animals and young children in response to the death of, prolonged absence of or lack of response from their mother.[2] For instance, there can be a significant reduction in body temperature and oxygen consumption in such infants and behaviourally there is evidence of a decrease in social interaction, play and appetite along with hypo or hyper-responsiveness. There can also be long-term effects on the body's immune system (Hofer, 1984 and Coe et al., 1984 cited in de Zulueta, 2000, pp. 54–6).

As a normal part of the cycle, dorsal vagal braking is also linked with recuperation, the resting and healing which our bodies need after enduring illness or some form of danger. Then, after a period of recuperation, there should be a return of energy, interest, motivation and pleasure in being with people. However, trauma survivors often get stuck in this hypoaroused state which includes a significant lowering of mood. Sometimes there is a collapse into persistent exhaustion and depression if the individual has been on red alert for a long time in response to actual or perceived danger and unable to make use of instinctive fight or flight responses.[3] Sometimes shutting down mentally and emotionally in response to threat or emotional overwhelm can become a habit that is adopted increasingly under stress. Thus 'a mental state that is biologically determined for a brief and immediate response to attack can become chronic' (Corrigan et al., 2011, p. 22).

The subjective experience of what has been called 'hunkering down', especially if prolonged, includes feelings of hopelessness and helplessness and beliefs about being worthless, useless and about the impossibility of change (Gilbert, 2005, p. 21; Shapiro, 2009, p. 13). Such beliefs can unfortunately be reinforced over time by hurtful comments from others. The other common subjective experience is a withdrawal from people. Siegel reflects how helplessness can pervade our whole system and limit our responsiveness and thinking. 'It shuts down our sense of possibility' – something so important as far as hope is concerned – 'as we isolate ourselves from involvement with others and even ourselves' (2010, p. 23).

Again, what people don't appreciate is that in terms of interpersonal safety there can be a survival logic to giving up hope and hanging onto beliefs about personal defectiveness. Janina Fisher (2012) described hopelessness as an ingenious way to avoid disappointment and argues that all the hypoaroused states that our clients present with – despair, depression, shame, numbness, lethargy – have a protective element and it is our job to be curious what this might be. Such states, she explains, keep people 'below the radar', and in dangerous homes and violent relationships this is highly adaptive. It keeps you a little safer. Beliefs organised around hopelessness prevent us from venturing out of our comfort zone. If you don't expect much and your nervous system is predominantly hypoaroused you don't risk. As a child you don't risk moments of excitement being cruelly squashed; of playfulness earning a slap; of being ridiculed for natural childish showing off or inquisitiveness. Meanwhile, as an adult, depressed states combined with the shame-based beliefs which frequently go hand in hand with a pessimistic outlook reinforce submissive responses and keep the individual in what may be a safer position of avoiding and hiding rather than risking being hurt even more because of complaining or fighting (Corrigan et al., 2011).

In his work on motivational systems, or what he calls social mentalities, Gilbert also emphasises interpersonal safety as the driver behind states of submission and hunkering down.[4] According to Gilbert social mentalities are 'different co-assemblies between motives, emotions, information processing routines and behaviours [which] give rise to different internal patterns of neurophysiological activity' (2005, p. 15). Functionally, these evolutionary patterns aid us in navigating the social world and in solving particular forms of interpersonal challenge. A particularly important social mentality is social ranking. Human beings are sensitive to levels of social control and threat and to our status in the eyes of others. In the face of threat from someone dominant or when seeking his or her protection and help, we may resort to appeasement and submissive behaviours as one way to cope (2005, p. 33). In this way, as an animal that needs to live in groups and has to compete for resources, we maximise our chances of being included rather than rejected and thus of surviving as individuals and a species.

At this point I should point out that whilst submissive behaviours and shut down/feigned death are both crucial ways to minimise harm and maximise survival there are also differences between them in terms of arousal levels and emotional and mental state (Ogden et al., 2006, p. 96). The latter includes emotional detachment, numbness and depersonalisation. Submission includes actions, postures and gestures that are designed to be as unnoticeable as possible as well as automatic obedience, mechanical behaviour, crouching, bowing the head and avoiding eye contact. 'I had to sit very still and say "yes please" and "I'm fine"', said one survivor of ritual abuse, and in the present she continued claiming to be fine however she felt and trying to fathom out what others might expect from her. Another client – also incredibly quiet – became intensely anxious if he imagined anyone might be cross with him and apologised repeatedly if he thought he had done something wrong. We often worked with this as his anxiety extended to the fear that I might either become angry like his rageful father or rejecting like his mother and suddenly terminate the work. To preserve his attachment to both parents he had to resort to submissive behaviours and this got played out in our relationship.

Whereas shut down is typified by a deadening of subjective states, the submissive child or adult is often in a state of hyperarousal or frozen watchfulness. Despite seeming not to look at others, such a child is highly attentive to tones of voice and sudden movements as well as being mentally hyperactive in a 'figure-it-out' way. I believe that this 'figure-it-out' or 'worrier' part of the personality is engaged in the constant task of trying to fathom out the next move of someone threatening or work out what she might have done to enrage him or should do to please him. In each case the aim is to avoid being hurt or abandoned. Again, what is an understandable survival strategy in childhood can become a more obsessive type of hyper-mentalising in later life.

Both clients mentioned above were highly vigilant and had a 'figure-it-out' self. Both also went into states of shut down when being so mentally 'wound up' became overwhelming or if anything else took them too far out of their window of tolerance. This highlights that we should not assume that compliant states are necessarily states of hypoarousal. Sometimes they are sympathetically driven and involve heightened arousal: in situations, for instance, where subjectively the individual fears being attacked or abandoned. Sometimes, and perhaps this is the more chronic state, when someone goes into submit the PNS is dominant. It is a more collapsed, giving up, 'below the radar' state and is often accompanied by clinical depression. And lastly, there is the state of dorsal vagal mediated complete shut down – a last ditch solution to being overwhelmed.

Linking theory and practice

To illustrate different manifestations of shut down and submission let me turn to material from sessions with three clients. The examples capture how rapid and automatic our body responses can be and also how responses that were highly adaptive in the past often lie behind current symptoms and relational patterns.

The first example is of a woman who complained about always feeling sluggish, mildly depressed and lacking in vitality. On one occasion she mentioned how important her grandfather had been when she was little. Greta knew that her birth father had been violent to her mother when she was pregnant and had left shortly after her birth. Her mother had manic depression. She remembered feeling safe when Grandad was around because she didn't have to be so alert to her mother's changing moods. She trusted that he would take charge. However, because he often worked abroad, there were long periods when she would long for him to come home. She missed his smile, his kindness and his reliability. She said rather sadly, 'but there wasn't anything I could do to make him come. I just learned to wait patiently'. As Greta said this she noticed how sleepy she felt and I observed her head lolling to one side as if she might drift off. I asked if she could track what was happening. She said it felt as if all she could do was to shut down and wait and that this was very familiar. I had a sense of a scared, lonely child unable to reach out to anyone for comfort and was struck how the experience of passive waiting and detaching as a little girl was still held in her body. It reminded me of Bowlby's stage of detachment and how one cause of passivity in a child, and later adult, is the experience of waiting endlessly for something that does not come and being too little to do anything more active.[5] Greta also had a tendency to accommodate to others, a more submissive state. As a child she believed that if she was naughty it made Mum worse – a belief fostered by things her mother said and by Grandad's injunction to 'be good and look after Mummy' whenever he said goodbye. She had learned to downplay more vitalising emotions such as excitement or anger in order to keep things safe. As we slowly worked using a sensorimotor approach we discovered that her body certainly knew other emotional states, and when therapy ended Greta said with a laugh and emphasis on the last word, 'I've connected with the authentic me. I feel as if I found my aliveness'.

The second example also illustrates how shutting down can be re-enacted during a therapy session. It occurred when a woman called Maxine made a connection between a tendency for her mind to go blank in group settings and when she was assaulted at the age of 6. Maxine had used the words 'feeling exposed' and this suddenly reminded her of what had happened. She looked scared and I noticed her head dropping and her body drawing inwards. She said she was felt she was shrinking. 'What would happen if that kept going? If it was exaggerated?' I asked. 'I'd be curled up in a foetal position', she replied. 'And as you think that, what's happening now?' 'I'm going blank. It's harder to think.' To keep Maxine in the window of tolerance I gently reminded her – 'It's over. It's not happening now. I'm here with you'. She straightened up and made eye contact again. Once she was calmer we talked about how freezing is like a circuit breaker. It stops us feeling overwhelmed and can protect us when it might not be safe or possible to fight or run away. I asked what she thought might have happened if she'd tried to fight her abuser. With a scared look Maxine said, 'he was big … he'd have killed me'. I acknowledged how scary that thought was and how shutting down kept her safe. But I pointed out that in the present it was getting in the way. This enabled us to discuss what would alert Maxine to the first signs of shutting down and how she might try to stay present during stressful events. But as with many survivors of child-hood abuse, the circuit breaker operates so rapidly that it entailed repeated work on resources and a slow, often painful, re-connecting with memories and split-off feelings before Maxine was able to stay more anchored in the present moment.

Megan also had tendencies for both submissive behaviours and to freeze then shut down because of a traumatic childhood. The latter meant that she found it incredibly hard to keep abreast of household tasks and she became increasingly dismayed as things mounted up and she seemed to achieve so little. On many occasions she said she felt like giving up. Late afternoon was a particularly difficult time for Megan. It evoked body memories of the mount-ing fear she felt as a child walking home from school. Once home she was expected to work in the shop run by her grandfather and father. Both men had violent tempers – well hidden from their appreciative customers – and from about 7 Megan was sexually abused by the former. She suspected that her father knew but did nothing, and she could not turn to her mother – a cold, impatient woman for whom nothing she did was ever good enough.

In one session we identified an inner battle between a part of her that had learned to stay safe by being hardworking and dutiful and a part that was angry about always being used.[6] In the former state of mind she feared getting into trouble unless she did what others wanted. When I asked what would have happened if she had said 'no', Megan said 'they'd have shouted, hit me, told everyone how bad I was'. She tensed and shrank back as she said this. When I reflected that she had to do what she was told in order to stay safe it was as if a penny dropped. 'So I didn't have a choice!' she said with surprise. As we continued to explore this Megan began to understand why she felt so much anxiety about doing things for others. She worried obsessively about letting people down and feared that if she did they would be cross and reject her. Thinking from an evolutionary perspective we could say that shutting down protected Megan from overwhelming fear, whilst compliance protected her from anticipated attachment ruptures. The tendency to shut down and to submit had left Megan believing she was useless and deeply ashamed of herself. Starting to learn how her body was trying to protect her was a first step in dissolving the shame and developing a more compassionate relationship with herself. It also began to sow some seeds of hope.

To sum up what I have said about immobilisation as a defensive system: we have a number of elements – physical immobilisation marked by lethargy, loss of energy and motivation; emotional numbing marked by states of depression and hopelessness; a tendency for submissive, appeasing or harm-reducing behaviours and entrenched beliefs about personal defectiveness and futility. Before leaving this subject it is important to stress Ogden's point that 'as a result of chronic abuse it is not uncommon for traumatised people to respond to threat cues with mechanistic compliance or resigned submission', *but* it is important that we see this submissive tendency as 'defensive behaviour rather than as conscious agreement' (2006, p. 96). Resorting to compliance and shutting down are learned behaviours. They become automatic after many repetitions of threat and danger. However, what was designed to ensure safety can become a source of shame and hopelessness for many adult survivors like Megan.

Another damaging consequence is that all these aspects of the immobilising, minimising-harm defences contribute to a withdrawal from people. In other words, the chronically hopeless stop using their social engagement system which, like fight, flight and freeze, is one of our instinctive responses to danger. As Porges put it, 'the human nervous system is on a quest, and the quest is for safety and we use others to help us feel safe' (2012, p. 5). Our attachment system primes us to reach for a trusted other when we are in danger and in more ordinary contexts at a neurological level we use right-brain to right-brain connections in order to calm and be calmed by another person's nervous system. Hopelessness reduces our capacity to socially engage and anything that thwarts or compromises social engagement is likely to contribute to despair. Over time this also leads to a state of profound aloneness as well, frequently, of shame. In subsequent chapters I will talk more about shame. But now, having argued that down-regulating the mind and body is an adaptive survival response in situations where it would not be safe or possible to fight or to flee, let us consider why in evolutionary terms man should have developed a capacity to hope, to dream and to desire.

The seeking system and man's evolutionary need to hope and to dream

Desire was a relative latecomer to our universe. Indeed, it was the last of three great miracles in cosmic history. The first miracle was the creation of the universe itself: that there should be something rather than nothing is miraculous. The second miracle was that some of the inanimate matter formed by the first miracle came to life.

And the third great miracle was that some of those living things gained the ability to be motivated, to seek, and even to hope. (Irvine, 2006, p. 144)

When I read Irvine's book on desire, and in particular these words, I was struck by the amazing way evolution has shaped us to survive as a species. Not only have we evolved a range of highly adaptive strategies to defend ourselves, but we also have hard-wired strategies to ensure that we reproduce and provide for ourselves, and I need to describe them as part of my endeavour to answer the question why *homo sapiens* developed a capacity to hope. These 'daily life' systems lie behind the motivation and seeking Irvine refers to. In addition, as he points out, the 'miracle' for mankind is that we developed a capacity to desire and to hope, a capacity without which how could we have thrived as individuals and as a species?

The 'daily life' systems are also found in other animals, and in particular in primates. Different authorities use slightly different terms and ways of categorising them including 'action systems' (van der Hart et al., 2006; Ogden et al., 2006), 'emotional operating systems' (Panksepp, 1998), 'emotional circuits' (Hudson Allez, 2011), 'emotional regulating systems' (Gilbert, 2009) and 'behavioural systems' (Bowlby, 1991). But there is agreement that these neural circuits are fundamentally designed to promote survival and that each system is associated with specific neurochemicals which evoke physiological changes that in turn motivate certain sensorimotor, emotional and cognitive responses. Whilst some systems are specifically geared for defensive action in the face of threat others are concerned with activities needed for survival on a daily basis. Table 3.1 lists the action systems as classified by van der Hart et al.

Table 3.1   Action Systems

DEFENSIVE ACTION SYSTEMS*	ACTION SYSTEMS OF DAILY LIFE*	EMOTIONAL OPERATIONAL SYSTEMS**
Social engagement (Attachment)	Attachment	Seeking
Fight		Rage
Flight		Fear
Freeze		Panic
Submit Feigned death (Shut down)		
	Care giving	Care
	Sociability or affiliation system	
	Exploration	
	Play	Play
	Reproduction/ sexuality	Lust
	Energy regulation	

(*Van der Hart et al., 2006; **Panksepp, 1998)

and Panksepp. All are activated by external and internal stimuli. For example, both seeing and thinking about a former attacker might evoke one of the defence systems and trigger a rapid physiological response. The other important feature of action systems is that operationally they are closely linked and can inhibit or support each other. For instance, when the defensive systems are 'on line', the daily life systems will be inhibited – something important to bear in mind when trying to understand how someone in a state of depressed 'shut down' can feel unmotivated to tackle daily tasks, meet other people or engage in stimulating pursuits.

The Seeking and Exploration systems are of particular relevance to understanding states of hope and hopelessness. For some time I struggled to reconcile what has been written about each within a common framework, before coming to the conclusion that it makes most sense to view seeking and exploration as closely linked motivational systems with the important distinction that the former aims to promote attachment, whereas exploration is dependent upon or in other words *follows* a secure attachment. According to Panksepp, seeking is basic to survival and operational from birth and he views it as a super-ordinate system which provides a 'scaffolding' for all the other basic systems (2006, p. 30).[7] Seeking is evident in the way a baby instinctively searches for the mother's breast and begins to focus on her face. The infant is primed to seek safety and care and to bond with a caregiver. If the mother is absent or unavailable in some way and the young child feels unsafe he or she will try to regain proximity. Panksepp also lists several other survival seeking activities in this category such as foraging for basic resources like food, warmth and shelter.

Whilst at its most basic level the Seeking system is involved with our need for relational security and perhaps might more precisely be called the proximity seeking system, because it involves curiosity and excitement it stimulates the infant and later the child and adult to interact with and explore the world. It is at this point that I think it more accurate to think in terms of exploration, which, in the classification used by van der Hart et al. (2006) and Ogden et al. (2006), is seen as an action system of daily life, rather than a defensive system. In other words, it only comes 'on line' when we feel safe and survival systems like fight, flight and freeze are not engaged.

As we know from attachment studies, children who are securely attached feel free to explore their world, from those early days when the toddler refers to what he sees on his mother's face before crawling towards something new or picking up a strange object, to the older child who balances using the caregiver as a 'secure base' from which to venture forth and a 'secure haven' to return to if distressed (Ainsworth et al., 1978). Later, as adults, we are more likely to venture out of our comfort zone if we have a trusted companion or guide, or to explore if our environment is relatively free from danger. But we retreat to the familiar when threatened in some way and the need to focus attention on survival shuts down our capacity to experiment, investigate and play with ideas. The Circle of Security model based on the safe haven/secure base paradigm captures beautifully the interface between proximity seeking and exploration and will be considered in more detail later (Marvin et al., 2002).

Another helpful model which highlights the relationship between security and seeking or exploration is provided in a book exploring the interface between attachment, neurobiology and personality formation by Hudson Allez (2011). The author describes how unpredictable, unavailable or aversive mothering sets up a template which she calls the Loss circuit. Using Panksepp's terminology Hudson Allez contrasts this with the Care circuit which is the hallmark of a securely attached individual. Returning to what I said about proximity seeking, the Care circuit involves the following sequence: When the child for whatever reason begins to panic – maybe because of briefly losing contact with Mum or feeling uncomfortable inside – his Seeking system is activated. All being well, Mum responds to his cries and promptly offers care. This means that once soothed, seeking can shift into play and exploring his world. He can imagine in a creative way and he can hope. However, if the caregiver fails to offer a timely and attuned response the infant shifts into the Loss circuit. One consequence may be that the child goes into a fight or flight response, in other words, some form of separation protest when the body is pumped with adrenaline and cortisol. Alternatively, he may go into a state of freeze or shut down (2011, pp. 47–8). Physically, the child can become floppy and lethargic. He averts his gaze; he becomes small. Emotionally, there may be a combination of fear, grief, shame and despair. For a child for whom there has been minimal experience of basic trust the Loss circuit is likely to be repeatedly activated as he encounters subsequent experiences of loss, rejection or humiliation and he or she is likely to develop some of the trauma-related relationships to hope that I will discuss in Chapter 6.

Trauma and the loss of attachment figures at any age constrict seeking. When overwhelmed by fear our brain protectively tries to reduce the amount of information being attended to. We can think of this as 'selective inattention' (Sullivan cited in Howell, 2005, p. 97) or a 'retraction of the field of consciousness' (van der Hart et al., 2006, p. 102). Whilst there is often heightened alertness to any possible signs of danger, other more ordinary and potentially interesting and hopeful things go unnoticed. For instance, Anna, the victim of a sadistic sexual assault, often complained of always being on edge and unable to stop worrying about minute details – both indicative of the 'figure-it-out' self mentioned earlier. Since the assault she had found it very hard to relax or to fully concentrate on anything because of chronic hypervigilance. This formed a backdrop to her days. Anna caught herself listening intently to distant sounds. She was jumpy if the phone or doorbell rang and aware that she was always looking over her shoulder when she went out. Physically, this manifested as chronic tension and restlessness and, because of difficulties sleeping, a permanent state of exhaustion and low mood. Anna used a lot of energy to keep memories of the assault out of her mind. But she felt that they were always there waiting to leap out, especially when least expecting it. She was desperate for respite but could not allow herself to relax for fear of what might happen if she was not on guard. Her attention was so outward focussed that Anna missed noticing things about herself such as if she was hungry or had hurt herself.

Like many other trauma survivors Anna had progressively reduced the sphere of what she did on a daily basis in an attempt to avoid being triggered by reminders of the trauma and she became increasingly depressed and hope-less.[8] Effectively, her seeking had become restricted to the basics of seeking safety and proximity to the one or two people with whom she still felt safe. Old interests and pursuits fell by the wayside. This retreat from living life to the full highlights a point made by Caroll that all the emotional operating systems operate on a spectrum from the fulfilment of basic needs to 'elaborate abstract expressions of the human spirit' (2002). This is clearly demonstrated in the relationship between seeking and exploration. Seeking is the more basic and primitive of the two. Exploration, meanwhile, is an increasingly complex and sophisticated system which evolves over the individual life span and phylogenetically over the course of civilisation. In terms of the life span, for instance, there is a progression from exploring the environment via play to exploring other minds and the world of ideas in increasingly sophisticated ways. At the most abstract level, at certain points in our lives, exploration often entails searching for meaning in life.[9] Phylogenetically, there has also been a progression over the course of civilisation as man has explored increasingly challenging contexts (the Americas, the Antarctic, Everest, the Moon) and ever more complex, sophisticated concepts and ideas in the realms of philosophy, science and the arts.

One thing seeking and exploration have in common, whatever the object of search, is that both are motivational systems. Seeking mobilises action. It energises us and keeps us going. It is not only the pleasure or relief of finding whatever we seek, but the pursuit itself is stimulating. This is because when we are searching and exploring dopamine and endogenous opioids, the body's natural pleasure hormones, are released and this in turn produces further interest, excitement and a sense of reward (Caroll, 2006, p. 54). I can resonate with this when I think of the experience of researching this book. When I come across a stimulating new idea my energy goes up; my mind begins to make connections with other ideas, which in turn adds to the intellectual excitement. There is an impulse to pull out other books from my shelves or track down articles on the Internet and I forget that it is late and I had planned an early night. This contrasts with moments – frequent – when my writing gets stuck. My mood drops and I can get frustrated and now and then slip into 'give up mode'. Panksepp captures the motivational aspects of the Seeking system when he describes it as the 'foraging/exploration/investigation/curiosity/interest/expectant/seeking system' that 'fills the mind with interest and motivates organisms to move their bodies effortlessly in search of the things they need, crave, and desire' (1988, cited in Ogden et al., 2006, p. 114).

In this way the Seeking-Exploration system connects with the state of hoping which, as mentioned in Chapter 1, is bound up with curiosity, expectancy and desire. Indeed, as Caroll observes, 'from an evolutionary perspective it is crucial for survival that we experience seeking as affectively positive [as intrinsic desire] and that it is focussed and goal-directed. Hope, excitement, anticipation, determination and curiosity provide the motivation and force to keep going, to move forward, to follow the scent' and, I would add, the process of exploring and finding often generates more hope (2006, p. 55). On the other side of the coin, anyone personally affected by depression knows how depression and despair entail a loss of motivation, and clinically we know that regaining a sense of purpose and curiosity can play a significant part in helping people out of joyless, hypoaroused states. Also important to bear in mind is that both seeking and hope are future oriented, whereas depression and despair entail being stuck in what often feels like an endless present. As Caroll says, without the activation of the seeking system 'there is a lack of hope – we feel flat, or stuck in a process of mourning that knows no end' (2002).

Some clinical applications of seeking and exploration

I believe that seeking and exploration are of great relevance to therapeutic work. First, something is needed to motivate clients to keep coming and that something is often a quest for something better or a curiosity about why they have the problems they do or a wish to discover more about themselves. For things to work we need an element of expectancy, anticipation and curiosity (Frank, 1974; O'Hara, 2013) and if we inspire curiosity in our clients this can help them to return to an optimal state of emotional arousal rather than being stuck in hyper or hypoarousal. It can also help them to step back from entrenched beliefs and behavioural patterns and experiment with something new. I will expand on this in Chapter 10. At a neurological level, curiosity helps to interrupt old patterns and promote the growth of new neural pathways, in other words, it fosters neuroplasticity. Moreover, as the following example illustrates, curiosity can also regenerate a sense of hope.

Bill knew all too well that experience of feeling stuck in 'a process of mourning that knows no end' and had lost touch with a livelier part of himself that was curious about the world. Bill was referred to me after a long period of depression which had left him feeling hopeless and unable to see any way out of his current problems. These included being out of work, in debt and in a failing marriage. He oscillated between days of intense anxiety and a collapsed, depressed state, both of which inhibited his engagement with the outside world and daily life tasks. Nothing gave him joy anymore and it took tremendous effort to do the simplest tasks. During our first meeting Bill said he felt ashamed that he was not coping and letting the family down and shared his belief that in being made redundant he had failed. Hearing this I asked Bill if feeling he had failed was familiar. He said yes and suddenly looked tearful. I asked what was happening in his body as he thought about this. Bill said he was aware of a lump in his throat and his chest was very tight. My guess was that he was chronically tense and that his rigid torso probably held back a lot of emotion.

In the belief that it could be helpful right then to awaken Bill's curiosity, because the more he listed his problems the more collapsed he appeared, I asked if he would be willing to experiment and to think for a moment about one of the books he was reading. Bill had explained that when he had more energy he immersed himself in scientific books and that he had always dreamt that one day he might be able to work part time and study for a degree. After talking for a few minutes about a topic that interested him I checked what was happening now in his body. Bill said with surprise that the lump in his throat had gone and he noticed that he was no longer frowning. He was also looking directly at me for the first time and his face seemed softer. I asked if he would like me to explain why I had asked these questions and began to explain about the influence of thoughts and emotions on the body and vice versa and about mindfulness and the 'noticing brain'.[10] As he listened Bill seemed excited. He said it gave him some hope to think that there could be something he could do rather than relying on medication to pull him out of depression.

By turning to an experiment and to psychoeducation, my aim had been to evoke Bill's exploration system and along with that more social engagement. This seemed more important than getting a detailed history, which I guessed would probably raise his anxiety and reinforce his depressed mood because it would rekindle those debilitating feelings of despair and shame which had troubled him for so long. And this interface between experimenting, being curious about present moment responses and sharing theoretical ideas which might interest Bill, became the backdrop of our work. Slowly, Bill began to resume contacts and activities that he had been avoiding for months. It was exciting to see his smiles at the end of sessions which often began with hopelessness and ended with curiosity and enthusiasm.

When considering the relevance of seeking and exploration to therapeutic work it is also important to hold in mind the 'attachment-exploration balance' (Ogden et al., 2006, p. 114). Being aware of the tension between needing security and the urge to explore, in the same way that we need to be aware how attachment and fear systems work in tandem, is crucial for effective work with complex clients. It can help us to understand why some people are so fearful of trying anything new and get stuck in the mire of hopelessness and helplessness – for instance, as time went on I came to appreciate how fear of his father had inhibited Bill's natural inclination to be creative and curious. It can also guide how we pace the work – knowing when it might be important to ignite the exploratory system and when attachment needs or the need to pay attention to the therapeutic alliance demand prioritising.

Sometimes, however, the Seeking system can be a trap. For instance, internally there may be an excess of meaning making, that 'figure-it-out' part of the personality mentioned earlier, and interpersonally both therapist and client (and/or supervisor and supervisee) are sometimes pulled into the process of exploring and making links without, as Caroll (2002) says, 'attending enough to the shadow side of seeking – frustration, disappointment and lack' or to other painful emotional states. In other words, seeking meaning can serve as a flight strategy. For some people it also clearly served, and still serves, as a way to try to avoid harm or to maximise the chances of attachment. The anxious need to figure everything or everyone out is an example of hyper-mentalising. It is a tendency I have observed in many clients who experienced relational trauma from an early age, and research evidence confirms that exposure to chronic and episodic life stress and to backgrounds in which, even if there was no abuse, there was an absence of secure attachment figures whose protective presence could buffer the child against the effects of stress contributes to the development of hyper-mentalising.[11] Whilst adaptive in contexts where rapidly working out how someone threatening might respond could enhance your chances of minimising harm, hyper-mentalising inhibits noticing the world in a more flexible way and makes it hard to see alternative perspectives and to concentrate on a task.

It could also be argued that the Seeking system has gone awry when people come to rely on addictive substances and behaviours. I mentioned that seeking and exploration are associated with the release of dopamine and endogenous opioids, the body's natural pleasure hormones. In states of loss, panic, fear and rage the production of these hormones and of oxytocin, the neuro-chemical associated with care and attachment, is inhibited. At the same time the body is flooded with stress hormones: adrenaline, cortisol, acetycholine and glutamate. To compensate for the lack of pleasure hormones produced naturally through stimulating relationships and activities people often seek external opiates (MacClean, 1990, cited in Hudson Allez, 2011, p. 91). This can lead to a range of addictive behaviours which over-regulate and lend urgency to the Seeking system. In other words, instead of being motivated by curiosity and excitement, the individual becomes driven by obsession and need (Hudson Allez, 2011, p. 191). In time the addictive substance itself can become a source of hope in a more magical thinking way. However, I would argue that the compensation for missing attachment figures is not simply a chemical process but can be thought of from an object relations perspective. The drug or compulsive behaviour becomes the longed-for caring other to salve the pain of loss and loneliness. It serves as a reliable 'best friend' when people cannot be trusted. For example, Gina, a woman who had been abandoned at birth and adopted when she was nine months old, said that when she first got hooked on alcohol it was not to escape, but because when she first had a drink as a young teenager it gave her a warm, comforting feeling which felt like the experience of being mothered she had always longed for. So of course she wanted more.

Gina also helped me to understand how the compulsive drive to seek out new experiences without ever quite landing anywhere or completing or truly enjoying anything is another manifestation of seeking gone awry. She kept booking onto courses, even though she could ill afford them, in her quest for hope. First, she decided to train as a yoga teacher and threw herself into a hectic schedule of classes and workshops. Then she became fascinated by aromatherapy and changed course. She didn't like the trainer and gave that up. A few months later she started two A-levels in order to get the grades needed to enrol for a degree course. Nothing came of that because she read about another alternative therapy which sounded wonderful and booked onto a series of workshops. On one occasion I challenged Gina because she never seemed to have a free weekend and was always struggling to pay for her trainings. I asked curiously, 'what would happen if you simply decided not to do that particular course, even though it sounds tempting?' She said 'I'd be missing an experience'. Then, after a pause, she continued with deep emotion, 'I'm terrified of getting stuck in despair again – it's so awful. I've got to keep going – do something that might be a breakthrough'. I asked what she envisaged life would be like if she found the breakthrough. Gina replied 'I'd be normal'. I felt sad hearing this and suddenly unsure how to respond. I think I offered a rather lame remark about 'what is normal?' Only later did I realise that in that moment I failed her in not empathising with how terrifying it was to contemplate slipping back into loneliness and despair and how important it was for her to do things that gave some hope. So, in the same way that Gina avoided the pain by resorting to drink or endlessly doing new things, I too had avoided the need to face head on her sense of isolation and to grieve the experiences she really lacked.

Another client also comes to mind when I think of the 'if only' quality of this particular form of compulsive seeking. Andrew kept changing jobs. Each time he began full of hopes and expectations but before long became dissatisfied with something about his boss and would spend a lot of the therapy hour denigrating and complaining. I suspect that he was really seeking something far more elusive than money or promotions – for instance, that part of him was seeking the father he never had in his encounters with managers and other authority figures. Andrew longed for somebody who would recognise him as someone with potential, as not merely competent but special, and his sarcastic complaints masked an envy of those who seemed to have but withhold that specialness he craved. He lacked those early mirroring experiences which lead to feeling grand and believed in, and so of course he was endlessly dissatisfied because, as with Gina, the real loss and deficits needed to be faced and mourned.

If we go back to the idea of that 'third great miracle' which Irvine spoke of, and add a fourth: – It is not simply that living creatures gained the ability to be motivated, to seek, and even to hope – it is that we, as *homo sapiens,* also acquired the ability to think about the desires, wishes, hopes and motives of ourselves and others. Although their backgrounds were very different, my impression is that neither Gina nor Andrew had parents who offered this on a consistent basis. Gina's adoptive mother seems to have been practical but not emotionally available and caught up looking after her own three children, Gina and a disabled mother. The picture of Gina left alone in a pram at the bottom of the garden for hours, something she was told when older, seems to epitomise the kind of attention she received when very young. Andrew's mother was very different, but equally unavailable and unable to see her son except as either a nuisance or a cute child to be shown off in front of her many friends. Everything in the house revolved around the mother's needs, and his father, a highly successful man, only seemed interested in his son as someone to eventually take over the family business.

Deep down both clients were aware of an emptiness, something missing relationally, which however restlessly they sought out new experiences and chased illusory hopes was never filled. My speculation is that they were seeking a type of attachment relationship that neither of their caregivers could provide – and at the same time I believe they were trying to find themselves. Interestingly, from an attachment perspective we can think about the baby's need to be found as well as to find the mother. As Fonagy argues, 'the child needs to find her mind in the mind of the parent or caregiver' (2001, pp. 167–8).[12] From this she internalises the latter's image of her as an intentional being, someone who responds and acts with intentions in mind and, something which is so important for the development of a capacity to hope, as someone who has potential, who can be dreamt about and who can have dreams.

Notes

1. In Type 1 freeze the body is on red alert and ready to explode into action if necessary. In Type 2 freeze the individual is still hypervigilant but feels trapped, para-
   lysed and terrified. The SNS and the PNS are simultaneously aroused, which is like
   having the accelerator and brakes on at the same time, until eventually the heart
   rate slows down, blood pressure drops and tense muscles collapse and become still
   (Scaer, 2007, p. 18). The mind becomes numb and dissociated, and memory access
   and storage are impaired. This is a state of dorsal vagal dominance. See Ogden for a
   fuller description of the differences between Types 1 and 2 freezing, feigned death
   and submissive behaviours (2006, pp. 93–8).
2. Experiments by the Papouseks illustrate passive shut down in infants when they
   cannot make something happen (1975, cited in Alvarez, 2012, p. 30). This is particularly serious if it becomes a repeated strategy when a baby tries to elicit lively
   responses from a depressed, shut down mother.
3. One of the major problems for survivors of severe trauma is that natural defensive and restorative processes often remain incomplete or truncated (Levine, 1997;
   Scaer, 2007). For instance, once the danger has passed an animal will normally
   move out of a state of freeze or shut down into a phase of shaking, trembling,
   perspiring and deep breathing. Scaer calls this the freeze discharge and argues that
   it effectively completes the truncated somatic and autonomic activation initially
   mobilised for the possibility of fight or flight. Humans rarely go through this discharge, which means that the survival brain may stay in threat mode. This could
   account for many persistent and unexplained medical symptoms (Scaer, 2007,
   pp. 19–22).
4. Although I use the words submit and submission at various points in the book, the
   reaction of a number of clients to the idea of submission as something shameful
   means that I prefer if possible to use the words shut down or minimising harm
   instead.
5. Although this was not an infantile experience, I wondered whether Greta might
   have experienced similar moments of detachment as a baby, given what she told
   me of a mother who was often distraught or frenetically active.
6. With Megan, as with many other highly traumatised clients, I used a sensorimotor
   approach with an emphasis on 'bite-sizing' talking about the trauma and on noticing here-and-now responses to the memories, rather than narrating. By helping
   people to stay in the present and develop dual awareness they slowly become more
   able to think and talk about traumatic events without going out of their window
   of tolerance. See Ogden (2006, 2015) for detailed discussions about this way of
   working.
7. In Panksepp's categorisation, Fear and Rage are also basic to survival in all animals
   and operational from birth. The other four emotional operating systems, Panic,
   Care, Lust and Play, are dependent on the maintenance of social bonds for survival
   and are particular to mammals (Caroll, 2006, p. 51).
8. For some people inhibiting seeking and exploration develops as a response to developmental injury rather than overt trauma. For instance, some children assume the
   role of the constant carer and companion of a chronically ill and needy mother.
   Others learn that love and approval are conditional on working hard and sup-
   pressing spontaneity and curiosity. A more subtle relational configuration occurs
   when a parent envies the child's freedom or success and finds ways to denigrate or
   constrain his or her exploratory steps (Shabad, 2001, pp. 6, 169).
9. This progression in the Seeking and Exploration systems can be mapped onto
   Maslow's hierarchy of needs.

10. Asking mindful questions about present experience, as I did with Bill, and inviting an experimental attitude is one of the hallmarks of Sensorimotor Psychotherapy. Neuro-imaging has shown that when we respond to mindful or self-referencing questions the medial pre-frontal cortex, or what we could call the 'noticing brain', lights up. This is also true when meditating or engaging in structured forms of mindfulness. The medial pre-frontal cortex has a connection to the amygdala, and it is thought that to mindfully notice one's subjective experience or external phenomena, such as sounds, colours, shapes and textures, can calm the amygdala when triggered (Ogden et al., 2006, pp. 193–5, 169).

11. In their research on mentalising problems in young people, Sharp and Venta discovered that adolescents diagnosed with schizophrenia or borderline personality, and the children of someone with a psychotic mental illness are likely to hyper-mentalise (2012, pp. 38–40). I agree with their speculation that the tendency for borderline adolescents to hyper-mentalise may be attributable to trauma histories.

12. This is a key premise of mentalisation theory.

4
Our Need for Hope and its Roots in Childhood

Intimately bound up with hope, fear and trust is a basic need for attachment, a secure bond with another person.

(Hobson, 1985, p. 215)

The examples of Gina, Andrew and Bill illustrate the tight interface between seeking, exploration and attachment and provide a good entry point into a fuller discussion of the attachment system and its relevance to the theme of hope and despair. In thinking about attachment, my overriding questions are: in the context of our earliest attachments, what fosters an optimistic outlook and provides a buffer if we encounter periods of helplessness and despair, and what destroys the capacity for hope? When I first began to think about hope in developmental terms my initial assumption was that we cannot hope until we have acquired the cognitive and linguistic skills to contemplate future possibilities. However, if we think about hope not as a construct or set of beliefs but as an embodied state, then we can locate the roots of hope in infancy and our earliest interactions with our caregivers. This certainly accords with Hobson's point and was the view of Erikson who was writing at a similar time to the early attachment theorists, but from a different perspective.

Hope during the stage of trust versus mistrust

Erikson identified hope as the first and most basic of what he called the 'vital virtues'. When writing about the first of his Eight Ages of Man he commented that 'the oral stages form in the infant the springs of the basic sense of trust and the basic sense of mistrust which remain as the autogenic source of both primal hope and of doom throughout life' (1968, p. 233; 1965, p. 74). During this period from birth to 18 months, Erikson's view was that our task is to deal with the conflict between trust and mistrust and to form the basis of a sense of identity (1965, p. 241). With good enough care we can internalise a feeling of consistency and feel confident that whatever is most essential for our well-being will be possible to attain. This basic trust in the reliability of others and in our own ongoingness can then serve as a secure platform for the development of an optimistic outlook and a self-reliant, 'well-adapted' personality. As one commentator said, 'hope, in an Eriksonian sense is a mental outlook of what constitutes goodness, trustworthiness, comfort, regularity, predictability and consistent object-relations. Hope is a dispositional attitude of expectancy for obtaining what is needed to sustain self-vitality' (Wilson, 2006, p. 9).

Erikson had trained in Freudian analysis and his hypotheses about infancy and child development came primarily from work with adults, rather than direct observation. Yet, whilst couching his writing in the language of Freud, his work is a departure from classic Freudian theory in that he argued that the development of trust and the formation of a sense of identity are 'dependent on the quality of the maternal relationship'. What he lacked, as Karen points out, was a convincing theory to explain why this should be (1998, p. 92). Erikson had not appreciated that it is not so much about meeting physiological needs but, as Hobson says, through the early 'conversation' between a mother and baby, in which she responds to his non-verbal cues using auditory, visual and tactile means, that 'the infant learns *basic trust and hope*, the sense that his mother is reliably there and will be consistently responsive to his needs' (1985, p. 213).

This is where Attachment Theory comes in. Erikson's points have since been substantiated by what we now know about attachment and the evolving brain concerning the fundamental need for a reliable, attuned and responsive other during the first two years of life in order to establish what Erikson calls basic trust, but attachment theorists think of as a secure base.[1] For instance, we know from the observation of infants in laboratory and home settings and from longitudinal studies how securely attached children and adults are generally autonomous, have confidence to explore the world, are able to form positive relationships and are both self-reliant, but can also turn to others for help and support when needed (Bowlby 1989, p. 107; Karen, 1998, 183–90).

Let me say more about the infant's need for an attuned, responsive caregiver because it is these attributes of secure parenting that also contribute to the formation of a solid therapeutic relationship and, as I shall argue in Chapter 11, there are connections between them and the dimensions of hope that can help a client to move out of states of depression and despair. We all feel safest when there is a degree of consistency to our world, and for the dependent child the predictability and reliability of others enables him to trust in his own ongoingness. But we also need buffers when facing the unfamiliar or things that alarm us, in other words, things that trigger our survival brain, including both what lies outside and inside us such as overwhelming feelings or body sensations. This takes me to an important finding of infant research that 'the modulation of infant affect by an attuned and responsive mother is the essential precursor of secure attachment' (Holmes, 1996, p. 55). The responsive mother is able to pick up that her baby is distressed, reflect on what she notices and 'contain' or in Bion's terms digest raw, unmetabolised emotion and 'give it back' in modified form (1962). To do this she needs to be able to regulate and mentalise both her own emotional state and that of her child. Remember, by mentalising we mean that the caregiver is able – most of the time – to 'hold the child's mind in mind' and to see him or her as an intentional being. In other words, she can appreciate that his actions and shifting moods are meaningful, in the same way that she can understand that her responses are based on her personal thoughts, beliefs, desires and emotions. An aspect of attunement and 'giving the baby back to himself' (Winnicott, 1967, 1990) is that she can mirror her child in a way that is accurate, yet sufficiently different from the child's experience in order to avoid exacerbating an uncomfortable emotional state.[2] Over time such attuned mirroring enables the child to mentalise and regulate his own emotional states (Allen and Fonagy, 2006, pp. 67–8).

Attunement also involves interactional synchrony – that early 'conversation' which Hobson saw as a foundation of basic trust and hope, and through its nuances of me and you, connecting and disconnecting, rift and repair also contributes to a sense of security and trust in the world. A key element of interactional synchrony is that it offers an optimal balance between too much and too little emotion; too close and too separate. It also entails a balance between the provision of a 'secure base' and a 'safe haven'. Children need both. They need a secure base from which to be able to play and explore freely and for a parent to encourage this. But if the child falters, if he begins to panic because the novelty becomes too great or something goes wrong, he needs to be able to run back to Mum as a 'safe haven', trusting that she will welcome and help him to manage his distress. Over time this optimal balancing between encouragement and the provision of security in what Marvin and colleagues (2002) called the Circle of Security enables a child to increasingly trust in his own resilience and capacity to manage overwhelming feelings. How the dialectic between exploration and proximity seeking is managed is therefore also fundamental to the acquisition of basic trust and the capacity to hope.

Of course, just as none of us are always able to contain our emotions and to mentalise, so no parent will always be able to consistently get the balance right between encouragement and the provision of security. A basic premise of the Circle of Security model is that there will be occasions when there are interactional failures with mis-cuing by either the parent or the child. It is also argued that because of individual attachment styles a parent may feel more comfortable acting as a safe haven than a secure base or vice versa. For example, someone who is warm, loving, there for the child when distressed and good at attuning to his or her affective states may not always be so good at supporting his exploration and thus promoting resilience through mastery building experiences. Meanwhile a parent who actively encourages the child to explore the world, even to be tough, may feel less comfortable about providing a safe haven. I would argue then that an optimistic, hopeful perspective is more likely if someone's parents were able to offer both a safe haven and a secure base from which to step out into the world than for someone whose parents mis-attuned to either his attachment or his exploratory needs, and in cases of minimal provision of either, then the child would have to find alternative auto-regulatory strategies to create any sense of safety and hope.

Another attribute of secure parenting is that interactional failures, miscuing and rifts in the interactional dance can be repaired relatively quickly. Indeed, we know that the process of rift and repair or the gradual disillusionment of the infant helps to foster resilience (Winnicott, 1990, pp. 10–11). As Holmes reminds us, 'the secure base is never entirely safe. Breaks, gaps and losses are as intrinsic to the rhythm of life as are attachment and connectedness' (1996, p. 54). With this in mind, my argument could be expanded to say that it is not just the foundation of a secure base or basic trust that fosters an optimistic outlook on life, but the successful navigation of the course between rift and repair, absence and presence, excitement and disappointment, idealisation and disillusionment which enables us to retain a sense of hope when things are going badly. As Bowlby said, securely attached individuals are people who 'have a capacity to maintain trust', or let's add the word hope, 'in what might seem conditions of distrust' (1989, p. 107). But, they can also generally distinguish unrealistic hopes from realistic ones and can, to adapt a quotation from Martin Luther King, 'accept finite disappointment', but 'never lose infinite hope' (King, 1985, p. 25). In other words, the securely attached individual is not pulled into believing in a polarised world of perfect good and utter bad.

But what if the mother is repeatedly not there when the child falters or is emotionally unavailable in some way? Another writer who opened a way into thinking about a pre-verbal state of hope and who eloquently fashioned a language for experiences when some form of maternal failure threatens the formation of basic trust is Donald Winnicott.[3] For instance, he speculated about a baby's experience of being separated from his mother for a length of time. For a short while he can hang onto the illusion of the 'wished for mother' and so 'in x + y minutes the baby has not become altered. But in x + y + z minutes the baby has become traumatized ... trauma [implying] that the baby has experienced a break in life's continuity' (Winnicott, 1990, p. 97). Drawing on Winnicott, Shabad writes that 'as long as the mother remains absent, the infant exists outside the bridge of creating and finding, stuck in the limbo of emptiness in between' (2001, p. 46). That trust in his mother's ability to provide him with what he needs **when** he needs it is momentarily shattered. I say momentarily, because ideally with her return the baby's search is contained by her renewed presence and, again quoting Shabad, 'bridging the gap to the mother instils the hope that such sufferings can be redeemed, that bad can be made good again' (2001, p. 46). Using Hudson Allez's model we could say the infant is back out of the Loss circuit into the Care circuit; in practical terms this means that as time goes on periods of increasing absence or 'optimal frustration' can gradually be tolerated (Winnicott, 1990, pp. 10–11). Erikson also understood this. 'The infant's first social achievement', he wrote, 'is his willingness to let his mother out of sight without undue anxiety or rage, because *she has become an inner certainty as well as an outer predictability*' (1965, p. 239).

In Bowlby's terms the young child has been able to form an internal working model of reliable care. The problem is if there really is no external predictability, for instance in a home where one or other parent suffers from mental illness or uses substances or if the child is unexpectedly separated from his mother for prolonged periods. 'If a bridge to the mother were not discovered', says Shabad, 'and the baby's sufferings continued indefinitely, the despair of madness and bitterness would overwhelm the hope to find the good' (2001, p. 46). This is the place of Winnicott's 'unthinkable anxieties' and 'falling forever' (Davies and Wallbridge, 1981, p. 58).

Let me anchor this with an example from my work with a woman called Sandra whose recurrent experience of terror when she woke early in the morning was to my mind an example of such primal despair. From things Sandra said about her mother my speculation is that for her there was little of that early conversation between mother and baby through which Hobson argues the infant learns 'basic trust and the sense that someone is reliably there and will be consistently responsive to his needs' (1985, p. 213). She was a woman who was always busy and seemed to resent having to look after the large family house her husband had inherited. Sandra also believed that she resented her. In one session a memory emerged of being in bed as a young child feeling very scared and alone. Sandra wanted to go and find her mother, but knew she'd get told off if she disturbed her. So she lay there clutching her teddy and trying not to cry. Sandra also remembered nightmares as a child when she was falling through a vast sky with nothing to hold onto. 'It was terrifying' she said. 'It felt like I was shattering into pieces. I used to wake up shaking. I wanted someone to hold me tight.' But there was no one there. She spoke with her hands as she described this – grasping them tightly as if desperately clinging onto something and I had the image of an infant hanging onto the bars of a cot. I thought of Winnicott's 'nameless dread' and 'falling for ever' and reflected how in these scenes there was no one containing and reassuring to turn to. 'There never was', she replied. 'It was always like that – going to nursery school, to children's parties – I wanted Mum to come and stay with me. Like other mums. I didn't know what to do, how to play with them.' But she just said 'don't be silly. Off you go'. Perhaps not surprisingly, in time Sandra developed a tough self-reliant shell – relying on herself for soothing and increasingly hiding away in books and work rather than seeking the contact of others.

Whilst Winnicott focussed on how a baby might experience maternal absence, Bowlby approached the subject by studying the responses of slightly older children who were unexpectedly separated from their mothers. He identified a sequence of three phases: protest, despair and detachment. 'At first', he wrote, 'with tears and anger [the child] demands his mother back and seems hopeful he will succeed in getting her' (1989, p. 48). Now we would describe this as hyperaroused, sympathetic nervous system dominance. 'Later the infant becomes quieter. There will be much less physical movement; his crying becomes intermittent, he appears sad and withdraws from contact' – which sounds like a shift into parasympathetic function-ing or what some call 'parasympathetic flop' (Hudson Allez, 2011). However, Bowlby points out 'the child remains preoccupied with his mother and still yearns for her return, but his hopes appear to have faded and he is in the phase of despair'. Often, and I think this deserves emphasis because this research also locates the polarity of hope and despair within the context of our earliest attachments, *'these two phases alternate: hope turns to despair and despair to renewed hope'*. In the third stage of detachment the child appears to have forgotten his mother and begins to get back to 'normal' activities. Now we would probably view this as a protective, dissociative strategy in which feelings and hopes have become compartmentalised, but have not vanished. Although this discussion pertains to young children, it has relevance across the life-cycle, for, as Bowlby argued, the phases that occur after maternal separation are characteristic of all forms of mourning in which again 'alter-nating hope and despair may continue for a long time [until] at length there develops some emotional detachment from the person' (1989, p. 49).[4] We could argue too that if early experiences of maternal absence or unavailabil-ity set up a template of oscillating hope and despair (the Loss circuit), then later losses and rejections, real or perceived, are likely to trigger the cycle all over again.

The other aspect of attachment theory that is relevant to my question 'what fosters an optimistic outlook and what destroys the capacity for hope?' is the research on different types of attachment. If people with a secure attachment style are more likely to be optimistic by nature, what then about people with insecure templates? Might there be variations in the individual's relationship to hope across the different insecure categories? In order to address this ques-tion let me first give a brief outline of the three insecure categories. Fonagy points out that 'anxious attachment implies a representational system where the responsiveness of the caregiver is not assumed [no basic trust?] and the child adopts strategies that circumvent the perceived unresponsiveness of the attachment figure' (2001, p. 12). She finds strategies to maintain a level of contact with Mum at all costs even if this means that the child is forced to split off her own feelings, hopes and wishes and is left with the pain of unmodulated emotion (Holmes, 1996, p. 55; Frankel, 2002, p. 120). Research suggests that the mothers of avoidantly attached children tend to be brusque, intrusive, controlling, over-stimulating and rejecting and that their children learn to deal with this by down-regulating affect and avoiding contact. The mothers of children classified as ambivalent/resistant, on the other hand, are likely to be inconsistent – sometimes over-involved, sometimes dismissive and unresponsive. In this case the child tends to up-regulate affect in order to deal with the stress of parental unpredictability and maximise the chance of some level of attachment. Sometimes the ambivalent child anxiously clings; some-times he or she pushes away and avoids contact (Hudson Allez, 2011, p. 55). The final category, that of disorganised attachment, is observed in children who have experienced various forms of attachment trauma and been exposed to frightening, incoherent care-giving. Attachment researchers have demonstrated that the disorganised mother is likely to be hostile or helpless or both and, as a result of her own unresolved losses and traumas, lacking in capacities to modulate emotions and mentalise her child (Lyons-Ruth et al., 2006; Solomon and George, 2011). Disorganised children often find themselves in the situation of 'fear with no solution', meaning that that they are caught in the bind of needing to approach a threatening carer for support, whilst simultaneously needing to avoid him or her. The irreconcilability of their need to seek proximity and to flee, in other words, the simultaneous activation of the attachment and the fear systems, leads to the development of multiple internal working models and the use of dissociation as the only potential solution.

Because avoidantly attached children tend to be dismissive of emotion and avoidant of intimacy, later in life we might expect someone with this style to take a sceptical rather than an optimistic position, certainly not relying on others and generally resolutely self-reliant. This is the person who says, 'I'll believe it when I see it.' Adults who fit the classification of anxious-ambivalent are likely to be endlessly preoccupied about the future, full of self-doubt and unable to stay hopeful without the support and encouragement of others. Meanwhile, I speculate that people in the final attachment category of disorganised/unresolved may flip between extremes of too much hope and giving up. In each case it is important to bear in mind the specific nature of their early experiences of trauma and attachment failure as this will have a significant bearing on their relationship to hope.

Imagination, play and hope

Another characteristic of people with a disorganised/unresolved attachment style is that they often have difficulties in mentalising. They can easily, and especially under stress or if their attachment system is triggered, slip into black and white thinking. If attachment trauma inhibits the capacity to mentalise, then it may also impact in a broader way on the capacity to imagine (Allen and Fonagy, 2006, pp. 82–3). When we mentalise we are, in effect, imagining the state of another. We are playing in our mind with different perspectives, possibilities and future scenarios. This is also what we do when we hope. We play with a vision of the possible, of the conceivable self. 'Imagination creates a future and this creative aspect of seeing, fills up the space between what is and what is not' (O'Connor and Aardema, 2005, cited in O'Hara, 2013, p. 57).

Our capacity to imagine creatively also has roots in early childhood. It is fostered in two interconnected ways – through play, which could be described as 'imagination in action', and through being held imaginatively in the minds of others. Anna Alvarez, a child psychoanalyst, talks about the important parental function of acting as 'a container for the child's aspirations'. She argues that 'mothers and fathers carry for the child not only a sense of the baby that he once was and in part still is, but also a sense of the man ... that he will become, and *is* becoming' (1991, p. 183). Parents can assist in or obstruct the process by which a child evolves a sense of his future. They can transmit hope or a lack of it through their own excitement or anxiety about future events, through the language they use about life and about the child and through the images they hold in mind of their child, even before he is born. And because children learn very early on to adapt to what they know will please the grown-ups around them, sometimes an imperative in order to minimise harm, they are likely to internalise the hopes of their parents and in so doing may split off authentic wishes, desires and emotions. If a child hears messages such as 'you're never going to do that' or 'he's as bad as his father', then such beliefs become how he defines himself and limit his aspirations. By contrast, if the child is bought up to the melody of encouragement and validation: 'go on, you can do it!' 'have a go ... it'll be OK', or 'wow! that's wonderful!', then she will be more likely to trust in her abilities and to risk taking on new things.

If there is no lively container for the child's aspirations, perhaps because the mother is depleted by illness or depression[5] or has unresolved issues about her own childhood or perhaps had never wanted to get pregnant in the first place, then it can be very difficult to see the child as a unique being with a potentially hopeful future. The helpless little being might remind her too much of her own vulnerable and needy self as a child and evoke feelings of anxiety or envy. He or she might resemble in some way a feared or hated partner. The gender or birth order of the child can also evoke strong emotional responses. The stories that each parent carries, along with the hopes and fears of previous generations, can all impact on whether or not they can unconditionally love and support the child as he or she is and as a child that 'wants to happen', or whether the child becomes a receptacle for their own unfulfilled hopes or disavowed fears.

Past histories also influence the extent to which mothers and fathers are able to support the seeds of growth and imagination that emerge in a young child's play. Play has many functions and can hold multiple meanings, but here I am interested in its role in fostering our capacity to dream dreams. Play can communicate something about the child's present reality or his past and it can represent or stand for 'a hopeful reality which does not yet exist, but which could come to pass in the future' (Alvarez, 1991, p. 179). Many examples of this in ordinary child's play come to mind: children dressing up as policemen, nurses, supermen and princesses; imagining being a racing driver whilst rolling a toy car around the floor; making pretend cakes or pushing a doll in a push chair in order to 'be like' Mum. As Alvarez emphasises, this 'prospective element ... is an important dimension in normal play and in the development of symbol formation' (1991, p. 178). Indeed, she argues that 'however negative the content of play and the imagination, the capacity to play at all and to use imagination to create forms implies some degree of hope' (2012, p. 150).

However, as noted earlier, to be able to play freely requires a secure environment in which the child feels safe to explore, knowing that there is a safe haven to return to and, initially at least, an attuned, responsive adult – someone in the language of the Circle of Security who is 'bigger, stronger, wiser and kind' – to play with or alongside him or her. When such an environment is lacking, if no one is available to assume that crucial function of containing the child's aspirations, and especially if from the beginning, indeed even before birth, things are so unsafe that, in the language of action systems, the child's nervous system is dominated by the panic and fear circuits, then in some cases – and this takes us back to the stage of trust versus mistrust – a child never develops the capacity to hope. We could call this a state of 'a-hope' in the same way that Winnicott argued for a state of privation as well as deprivation (Davis and Wallbridge, 1981, p. 89). To be deprived implies that first there was something to be deprived of. Likewise, maybe we should distinguish between a state of hopelessness in which hope has been lost and 'a-hope' when the conditions for establishing primal hope were non-existent. Such I believe, was true of Sandra. I recall once asking if something she had read inspired hope and she replied matter-of-factly, 'hope isn't a word I use', and on another occasion she remarked, 'if you let yourself hope it hurts worse'. This helped me to understand how little joy or pleasure Sandra seemed to experience from life. Sometimes I ask clients, 'did you daydream as a child or escape into books?', knowing that for some young people this can serve as a crucial form of mental escape in homes where things are unsafe but the child cannot literally escape. Two examples come to mind of women with a similar history of abuse at the hands of a sadistic father and invalidating, shaming responses from their mothers when they tried to tell them what was happening. One seemed to have gained a little comfort and a glimmer of hope from being able to fantasise that she belonged to a good family. She called this her adopted family in which as the oldest child she played a kind, motherly role towards her siblings. The other woman seems to have been so frozen in terror and needing to be perpetually vigilant that there was no space for dreaming. When I asked if she read fiction, thinking about what might resource her in the present, she cynically replied 'I don't believe in fairy tales' and she had no recollections of playing or reading as a little girl. She just sat as quietly as possible trying not to be noticed. Nothing in her young life had enabled her to develop a capacity to hope.

Anna Alvarez observed something similar to what I am calling 'a-hope' in her work with deprived, chronically abused and severely depressed children. She talks about children who are 'too despairing to imagine that [they] could ever be like an admired or idealised figure' and who have never really developed much hope. Such children, she argues, 'may have very little sense of a future; they may see closed doors and grey skies everywhere. Eight stretching to twelve may seem an impossible dream. They often see themselves as very stupid or very ugly.' They cannot yet tolerate hope. (1991, p. 186; 1992, p. 180). On re-reading Alvarez's books I have been drawn by the way, from an analytic perspective and from long experience working with children and adolescents, she grapples with one of the themes of this book – the tensions between true and illusory hope. One of the questions she poses is what can help children with little hope and low expectations, whose symbols 'may be bleak and desolate ... a vision of empty desolation and nothingness', progress to a state where they can begin to imagine the possibility of something more hopeful and of a successful 'grown up' future? (2012, p. 181). Her thesis is that such children may need someone who can 'carry hope for them, or believe in them', and this is not because they are projecting something which once belonged to them, but because of never having it in the first place. I believe that Alvarez's question can also be applied to severely depressed adults who were chronically abused as children; people for whom life continues to close doors and who cannot tolerate hope – perhaps because they never did encounter anyone to carry hope for them. With such clients our challenge is to consider how might a containing and responsive therapeutic relationship offer an experience which allows the possibility of something more hopeful to emerge? This is a theme I shall explore in more depth in the final chapters of the book.

But to return to Alvarez: one thing she observed is that there is a distinction between a child who is playing or acting in a manically defensive way in order to avoid the pain of loss or humiliation, and when such play might actually be a small sign of growth – a tentative anticipation of future 'grown-upness' and of something more hopeful emerging in his or her life (2012, p. 179; 1991, p. 182). Alvarez believes that it is an important step when severely depressed children begin to tentatively test out a fantasy with the therapist, and when more boastful, grandiose dreams do emerge she argues 'they may have to emerge first not in the mind of the child but via a particular kind of projective identification' – which she terms 'anticipatory identification' – 'in the mind of the therapist, teacher or caretaker'. For a while the latter have to hold the dreams on the child's behalf (1991, pp. 181, 177–8).

The distinction between a manic defence and a small sign of growth is helpful when I consider a woman whom I will call Margie. When she emerged from long periods of a dissociative, psychotic-like depression she often became excited and enthused by new projects. They generally involved some form of identification with people she admired. Margie decided to study for a degree. She became involved in a local voluntary project run by a group of women whom I suspect had qualities that she longed to feel in herself. After one long hospitalisation, a chance remark led to the rapid flowering of an ambition to write a book. I was often aware of misgivings, knowing of the series of projects which she had committed to then had to abandon because of relapses. There was also something naively childlike in Margie's confidence that these things were so easily achievable. I registered in myself a less optimistic series of 'buts' – 'but that takes time, but what if ...' and so on. I wanted to ask 'how realistic is that?' Yet I did not want to burst the bubble of her excitement and energy. I often wondered whether I was colluding in a narcissistic denial of limitations. But, reading Alvarez made me realise that Margie had never had an experience of the kind of parenting in which Mum and Dad share and guide the child's excited first steps – who would encourage 'you can do it, go on … you can!' as the little one haltingly stumbles. It is the adult's belief in the possibility that keeps the child going. No mother or father is going to say wisely, 'well if you work hard at walking you'll get there in time. But watch out – there are going to be lots of falls first and you'll hurt yourself and get upset.' The adult holds the hope and keeps that alive. It is other people believing in us that so often helps us to believe in ourselves.

In Margie's childhood there was either nothing and as she herself said, 'no input, no feedback' from her depressed mother, no playing with or showing how to do things by example – or there were pressures to tackle jobs which were beyond her compass and which caused the little girl considerable anxiety. Later, as a teenager there was once again an absence of interest in or celebration about what she achieved at school, and if her ruthlessly ambitious and frequently absent father did spend time with her, he never praised success but would demand to know why her grades were not even higher. Somehow Margie found a way to learn, but having so little opportunity to play and hence to imagine and dream, her learning was rote-like and repetitive. My sense then, when she arrived eager to tell me about a new endeavour or a meeting with an admired professional or a recent achievement, was that she had begun to dream, to envisage future possibilities, and she needed me to see her as a woman who **could** do these things. To have offered any cautions would have squashed and shamed these new shoots of something more alive and hopeful – in the same way that Alvarez appreciated those moments when her young patients needed her to see them as strong, tough, heroic and admirable, rather than interpreting their grandiose fantasies as a defence. As she says, 'the imagination is the great healing ground and the great area of potential development for that which can be and that which ought to be' and the therapist's mind may be 'the proving-ground where such ideas are very tentatively tried out' (1991, pp. 186–7).

When parents stifle hoping and dreaming

I want to end this chapter by returning to Bill because I believe his story draws out the link between seeking/exploration, attachment security and hope. As time went on Bill began to talk with increasing energy about his future plans and projects that he wanted to tackle. He definitely used me as a 'proving-ground'. However, Bill's fledgling confidence and hope were often eroded and we needed to keep accessing and exploring the 'narrative point of origin' of his self-doubts and tendency to shift into a state of shut down (Stern, 1985, p. 260). In particular, Bill longed to study, to be creative and to paint, or as he described it, 'make a mess' (the Exploration and Play systems). But he kept encountering a block between planning something and taking action, and this block would spiral him down into a familiar depressed, unmotivated state. Sometimes he left a session energised with thoughts about what he might do in the week to further his goals, but returned next time demoralised because something held him back. One week Bill began sketching an outline for a painting. However, he said that all the time he had a nagging feeling that this wasn't OK. He couldn't take the next step to open his paints. So yet again his mood slumped. When I invited Bill to imagine being back at his worktable with paper, pens and paint he suddenly felt sick and a wave of fear overtook him. As we explored this, the safety of our relationship enabling Bill to stay with his fear, the image of his father 'blowing his top' because he was 'mucking around' – or in our terms exploring – rather than doing his homework, came to mind. Repeated experiences like this, reinforced by his father's scornful ridiculing of things that Bill made or discovered, had led to the development of a compliant, play-it-safe self who as a teenager became sulky and unmotivated and as an adult became more and more depressed as he got stuck in a series of dead-end, monotonous jobs.

In a number of sessions Bill explored the tension between a part of him who wanted to rebel and be unconventional and a cautious, fearful, procrastinating self who felt trapped. He seemed like a caged animal that first protests, then gives up and shuts down, and I frequently observed shifts between bursts of fury as he touched on childhood memories followed by a slump into despondency. Then, as Bill began to make sense of himself and the origins of the beliefs that trapped him, there was a return to a more optimistic self. For instance, in the session when Bill recalled how Dad poured scorn on his artwork with remarks such as 'what do you want to keep that for?' his present moment responses shifted from disbelief and frustration to hopelessness and the feeling of being weighed down. When I asked, 'when your body feels like that what do you believe about yourself?' Bill replied 'I'm worthless'. We continued to explore the tension in his body between rebelling and what Bill said felt like a brake holding him back and saying 'are you sure that's safe?' 'It's like someone has stuffed the cork back in the bottle', he said, 'I don't feel like rebelling anymore. If I can't have the crazy me, I won't do anything at all.' Guessing that this was a child decision, I said 'that sounds like another part of you. How old does that feel?' Bill associated this with a stroppy teenager who didn't like doing what he was told and ended up not wanting to do anything. 'That's it', Bill said, now with more energy. 'I was always being told what to do. If only I'd had parents who were more encouraging. I had loads of plans – things I wanted to do, places I wanted to visit. But Dad always said 'what do you want to do **that** for?'

When I asked if Bill had a specific memory of this he recalled wanting to explore a disused railway line on a family holiday. He remembered those words and Dad's scornful face. I invited Bill to stay with that image and notice what was happening inside his body. 'Curiosity!' he exclaimed with a burst of energy. 'I'm curious.' This felt new, an area of 'proximal development' (Vygotsky, 1962). It did not immediately lead to collapse. So I asked Bill, 'with that curiosity what would you say to the part of you that's cautious and ends up not wanting to do anything?' His response was instant. 'Come on! Let's do something new! Let's explore!' We ended the session talking about it being OK to take risks and make mistakes. We shared playful images of being outrageous; then talked about how Bill might support the part of him that holds the fear memories of Dad blowing his top. The next time we met Bill arrived, calm and pleased that he was beginning to organise his life. 'I feel like a battery that's been plugged back in and is being recharged' he said.

I chose to cite this session in detail as it is a good example of how both fear and shame had such a pervasive effect on Bill during his childhood and adolescence. This meant he had needed to repeatedly override his Exploration system in order to prioritise safety. Here remember that both trauma and developmental injury can constrict initiative and exploration. Shutting down his excitement and trying to be good and work hard would have been the best option for Bill as a child, and when the repeated erosion of his dreams led to the emergence of a morose teenager who consistently under-achieved, I am struck how no one was curious enough to ask why this bright boy was no longer doing well. The challenge for Bill as an adult was to reconcile the tensions between the Dad he loved and respected, the Dad he feared and the Dad he was furious with so that he could reclaim his life and find his authentic self. Bill's father failed his son, first in not accepting and loving him 'on his own terms', and second because he did not celebrate his achievements or encourage him to pursue his dreams. My speculation is that he failed, not because he was a bad man, but because of projecting his own need to succeed and be respected in order to escape a violent and impoverished background. The 'rebel' part of Bill railed against this and needed to be heard. He needed to be able to acknowledge both his anger in a way that felt safe and his sadness that his Dad never spent time with him nor shared his interests before he could find compassion for himself.

According to Friedman, 'one sort of childhood need which is not only sought in analysis, but also fulfilled in analysis, is the need to identify with one's own potential *as seen in the eyes of a parent*. Being reacted to like that not only provides hope in general but structures reality in a relevant and promising fashion' (1988, quoted by Bromberg, 2011, p. 93). What Bill repeatedly saw was criticism and disappointment. However, I believe that I was able to offer a different pair of eyes. I did see potential and felt genuinely interested and excited when Bill talked about his interests. But I was also aware of a trap in investing in change and often had to contain the urge to say 'why don't you try ... ?' Friedman's argument that the therapist must 'accept the patient on his own terms and at the same time not settle for them' is relevant here. 'If he does not accept the patient on his own terms, it is as though he is asking him to be someone else, *the patient will not have cause for hope*, and he will not recognise the analyst's vision. If the analyst settles for the patient's terms, he is ignoring the concealed part of the personality and betraying the patient's wish for greater fulfilment.' Expanding on this, Bromberg talked about how accepting someone's 'capacity to change while remaining the same' is what 'most nourishes the soil of therapeutic as well as early developmental growth. It is the foundation of development because it is the foundation of hope' (2011, p. 93, my italics). Balancing the tension between accepting the people we work with on their terms, the unconditional positive regard which is so central to humanistic psychologies, whilst simultaneously believing in their capacity to change and not settling for a limited, constricted view of the self lies at the heart of what we do. We are repeatedly called to balance hope and despair, acceptance of how people are and a belief in future possibilities.

Notes

1. See Fonagy on the commonalities between Erikson's epigenetic theories and attachment theory (2001, pp. 59–61).
2. This is known as 'partially contingent mirroring' or 'markedness' (Bateman and Fonagy, 2005, pp. 66–7).
3. Winnicott's writing spans the divide between those who based their ideas on work with adults and those who directly observed babies and young children. Here I am mindful of Daniel Stern's distinction between the 'observed infant' whose behaviour is observed at the very time of its occurrence, and the 'clinical infant' or 'recreated infant' made up of 'memories, present re-enactments in the transference and theoretically guided interpretations' (1985, p. 14).
4. Bowlby later refined his model for mourning and renamed the phases as numbness, yearning and searching, disorganisation and despair, and lastly reorganisation (1989, pp. 82–9).
5. Research demonstrates the potentially devastating effect on the personality and intelligence of babies of depressed mothers who may meet the ordinary physical needs of the baby, but cannot engage in the reciprocity so necessary for developing hope and mental growth (Murray, 1991, cited in Alvarez, 1992, p. 9).

5

The Impact of Trauma as a Hope Destroyer Across the Life-Cycle

---

It's a funny thing, Markos, but people mostly have it backward. They think they live by what they want. But really what guides them is what they're afraid of. What they don't want.

(Hosseini, 2013, p. 390)

The legacy of trauma

In this chapter I shall explore how traumatic events can impact our relationship to hope by returning to developmental issues and considering how trauma and neglect at different life stages might contribute to maintaining or losing a sense of hope and optimism about the future. Traumatic events and losses can shatter our sense of ongoingness and turn our world upside down so that nothing feels the same. They set up what have variously been called trauma-related expectations, expectancy circuits or anticipatory models which colour how we see things and can have a profound effect on current and future behaviour (Pynoos et al., 1996, p. 332; Hudson Allez, 2011; Siegel, 1999, p. 13). Not surprisingly, the earlier and more severe the trauma, and especially when it is a relationship trauma, the more directly it shapes our anticipatory models. It can also have potentially serious consequences for identity formation and the development of the capacities needed for intellectual growth, emotional regulation and mentalisation. These capacities, as discussed earlier, are more likely to evolve in the context of a secure attachment with caregivers who are able to provide an optimal balance between a safe haven and a secure base and to help us negotiate frustrations and disappointments. Attachment bonds co-regulate us. They act as a form of psychological immune system.[1] If we have been buffered by a supportive social network our anticipatory models are more likely to be optimistic in tone. When encouragement and celebration of our potential is added to support, then our inner models will include trust in our capacities and future success. On the other hand, our expectations are likely to be biased towards anticipating danger, rejection and failure if our early environments were patterned by chaos, threat, neglect, disconfirmation and if our caregivers were frightened, frightening or both. As the mother in Hosseini's novel understood, we are guided by what we are afraid of.

This skewing of our expectations is due to the experience-dependent nature of our brains. As well as having certain hard-wired, pre-programmed circuits or action systems, our experiences, particularly during the first decade of life, activate certain pathways in the brain, strengthen existing connections and create new ones. Other potential pathways are 'pruned' according to the 'use it or lose it' principle (Siegel, 1999, p. 3). The experience of severe and ongoing trauma, especially when unmediated by protective others, leads to a nervous system that is organised around threat and survival. As one traumatologist points out, 'when psychological trauma interferes with or derails normal psychobiological development, particularly in infancy and early childhood, there is a shift from a brain [and body] focused on learning to a brain [and body] focused on survival' (Ford, 2009, p. 31).

The 'survival brain' is oriented towards harm avoidance.[2] It operates automatically in order to anticipate and protect against danger and constricts our attention to what is absolutely necessary for survival. When the survival brain is on line it interferes with the integration of our experiences.[3] In states of emotional overwhelm and intense physiological arousal we are at the mercy of amygdala-driven survival behaviours, and the areas of the brain which normally help us to give words to and reflect on our experiences temporarily shut down. Distressing memories may not be processed and properly encoded in the brain and instead get stored as fragments of sensory, contextless data which can later emerge in the form of flashbacks. As a temporary measure in the face of actual danger we do of course need a brain and body that can react incredibly fast. However, ongoing dominance by the reactive survival brain can impede the development of the 'learning brain', which, by contrast, is flexible and open to experience and acquiring new information. Ford summed this up when he wrote, 'if traumatic events push the brain's trajectory of development away from creative exploration and learning towards defensive states geared to promote survival, the child's biological and psychological flexibility and ability to change may be diminished or largely lost' (2009, pp. 34–5).

Although experience can shape the brain or alter neural networks at any time in life, the consequences are likely to be particularly serious and complex if trauma and neglect occur during certain one-time-only developmental windows (Ford 2009, p. 34). The first of these, the foetal stage and first two to three years of life, is a phase of rapid brain growth. If traumatic experiences in this period set up a bias towards survival responses, the development of the neural structures responsible for emotional regulation is compromised and in consequence the child's ability to deal with future stress is impaired (Siegel, 1999, pp. 13, 85, 86; Ford, 2009, p. 37).[4] The period from 7 to 24 months is thought to be particularly important for the development of self. Because attachment templates are being laid down during this period, neglect, abandonment and loss or separation from a caregiver are as potentially dam-aging as actual injury to or violation of the self. Thus, even if the child has good experiences later in life, the legacy of a lack of basic safety in the earliest months can continue to emerge in the form of physical patterns and symp-toms, autonomic dysregulation, expectations about being let down or hurt in some way and self-attacking beliefs. It can also lead to a pervasive caution about hoping too much.

Towards the end of the latency period and during adolescence (c 10–19) the second critical period of neurological development occurs. This is a phase of consolidation with another spurt of cell growth, neural pruning and rapid myelination of neural connections in areas of the brain involved in higher order symbolic thoughts and memory such as the prefrontal cortex. Trauma during adolescence has an impact on healthy brain development and hence on the ability to self-regulate. This can lead to mood swings, impulsivity and a range of internalising and externalising behavioural problems (Wilkinson, 2006, p. 117; Ford, 2009, p. 41; Hudson Allez, 2011, p. 83).[5] If the trauma is interpreted by the young person as a sign that he or she is bad and there are few messages to contradict this, then in this period it is common to test it out and to collect experiences that confirm the belief.

I believe that the bias towards the survival brain has a profound influence on whether we develop a generally negative or positive and optimistic attitude to life and is important to be aware of when trying to understand why trau-matised and troubled clients often get stuck in repeated cycles of helplessness and despair. With a brain that is on the lookout for danger and a body that reacts rapidly to anything that triggers reminders of the trauma it can become an endless struggle to get through the day. The survivors of complex trauma may be bombarded by intrusive thoughts, nightmares and somato-sensory flashbacks, and often it is this ongoing process of being haunted by intrusive memories which creates such despair in the people we work with. As Allen says, 'exposure to traumatic events can result in an illness that is continu-ally retraumatising' and people with PTSD 'cannot live in the present because they are continually haunted by the past' (Allen, 2001, p. 104).

Because repeated experiences of going out of the window of tolerance lead to an out-of-kilter autonomic nervous system, many survivors are also trou-bled by unexplained medical symptoms, recurrent pain and a range of auto-immune conditions (Scaer, 2007).[6] They can become 'phobic' of anything connected with the trauma. This can include people, places, memories, emo-tions, attachment and dependency, change and normal life and, because it is a context within which memories and feelings emerge and are talked about, the therapeutic relationship (Steele et al., 2001; Nijenhuis et al., 2004). They learn to cope by avoiding situations that might trigger them. All this inevitably wears down their resilience, especially if they also have to deal with present-day crises. Not surprisingly, we often hear people saying 'I can't go on living like this', and the ongoing sense of being haunted and trapped lies behind much suicidal ideation. This is something I shall say more about later.

The impact of trauma on how we see ourselves, others and the world

Not only does survival brain dominance make it hard to stay in the window of tolerance, it also affects how we define ourselves; how we see and relate to others and our views about the world and our future. Because each of these variables influences how we position ourselves in the dance between hope and despair let me briefly consider each in turn. Trauma can fragment the personality. The more helpless and terrified the victim feels during a traumatic event, the more enduring the impact on his or her sense of self – and this is especially true if there is a need to resort to some form of dissociation in response to feeling overwhelmed. Dissociation leads to a disruption to the continuity of one's existence in space and time. There is a lack of integration between mind and body and between parts of self. If the body itself is badly hurt or violated in some way then 'it', the hated or despised 'object', often becomes disowned. When such vandalisation occurs to a young child, he or she may never acquire what Winnicott called 'indwelling', the felt sense of having and living in a body (1965). Indeed as Bentovim argued, 'children growing up in a climate of violence develop a profound absence of self' (2002, p. 31).

It is hard to have a clear sense of an integrated, ongoing self if there is no explicit narrative memory for certain events and all one has are large blanks or disconnected, often disturbing, fragments of memory. It is also hard if we don't feel embodied. Many survivors of complex trauma talk about not knowing who they are. They are familiar with rapidly shifting states of mind and struggle with conflicting parts of self. For those exposed to the trauma of non-recognition which entails becoming the self that their parents needed them to be, this accommodation to others also makes it hard to know their true self and hence what they want. In one state of mind they might decide to try something. In another there is a strong resistance to that choice. This lack of inner coherence has a marked impact upon the capacity to hope. As O'Hara argues, 'one of the central foundations of hope is a healthy and well-formed self. When the self is confused, hope is harder to find and maintain' (2013, p. 132).

Hope is also hard to find after trauma involving humiliation and deliberate injury to the self. In the wake of any form of relational trauma people are generally left with negative shame-based beliefs, and if you believe yourself to be fundamentally bad, it follows that you don't believe you deserve good things. The block caused by this 'not deserving' is something one often encounters when people begin to recover and when we begin to feel a little more hopeful about their future. The experience of being terrified and helpless then being repeatedly hijacked by the survival brain also interferes with the development of a sense of agency. If we think of hope as about what could be or can be, then it is essential that we have experiences of mastery and have been able to internalise a sense of 'I can'. I shall say more about this in Chapter 11. We need ongoing experiences of what Pierre Janet called 'acts of triumph' – of defending ourselves, making something happen and having an impact on others (Ogden et al., 2006, pp. 247–60). Remember too that trust in our own capacities owes much to having been with others who see and celebrate our potential and act as 'containers for our aspirations' (Alvarez, 1991, p. 183). This has to be genuine and the child, or for that matter adult, has to be able to take it in. John, a young man from an incredibly deprived, abusive background who wrote about the life of his brother Jeffrey, an inmate on death row, knew how important it can be to be genuinely believed in. He wrote: 'If somebody says, "Hey, I see you going somewhere, I see a spark of something in you, I know you're going to do something great when you grow up and, you know, just keep on" – encouraging instead of discouraging. I think that's where it's going to make the difference. My grandma, she was there always from the beginning for me. She was steady. But she didn't see that in Jeffrey. She wanted to see that in Jeffrey. She always told him that, but you can tell. You can tell by the way people talk, you know, it wasn't as a firm belief. I don't know. It's hard to explain. See, kids are sensitive. They can sense every single thing about a person ... You can be telling a kid one thing, you could be saying, "you're going to be the president of the United States. You're going to be doing this and this." But ... if that adult doesn't really believe it down in their heart that they can really do that, the kid knows. It doesn't matter. Jeffrey didn't get that' (Karr-Morse and Wiley, 1997, p. 245). I found John's words moving and it made me think again about the responsibility we have as therapists for holding the balance between fostering hope in our clients, of being that encouraging other, and being able to bear the periods when there really seems to be no hope.

Trauma and neglect also interfere with the development of basic trust - that others will be supportive, loving, helpful and encouraging and will meet our relational needs. It is understandable that if people have hurt you and repeatedly let you down you will find it hard to trust people in the future. You may anticipate abandonment, being hurt if you get too close, or that to disagree or get something wrong will lead to harsh treatment. You may lack the experience of difficulties being openly talked about and disagreements negotiated. You may have learned to be constantly on the alert in order to gauge people's moods. Significantly, many people who have been hurt as children have experienced the double trauma of someone who should have cared for them assaulting and frightening them in some way and someone else who should have protected them failing to do so. Whilst both constitute a betrayal, for many survivors of childhood abuse it is the latter that hurts most. The failure to protect may have been because one parent, often the mother, was herself frightened, unable to manage her emotions and sometimes turning to the child for support. Another scenario is when the non-abusing parent failed to believe the child, perhaps accusing him so that the 'badness' and responsibility get lodged in the child.

When the brain shifts away from learning to defence, other people can evoke suspicion rather than interest and the world ceases to be a place to explore and be curious about. As discussed in Chapter 3, exploration goes off line and people's lives and their thinking can become increasingly constricted.

Sonia's story typifies a life limited by the legacy of trauma. In order to manage acute PTSD she had constructed her life around a rigidly predictable routine. She suffered from panic attacks in busy places, would spend weeks worrying in advance if she had to do anything outside her comfort zone and would collapse with exhaustion after the event because of getting so wound up. A significant aspect of our initial work was to help Sonia develop resources for managing her anxiety. But her life remained a struggle exacerbated by shame, self-loathing and loneliness. As much as she wished for friends she dare not risk getting close to others. Sonia also had very little hope of things changing.

Trauma and epigenetic stages

Having outlined how traumatic and adverse early life experiences interfere with the neurological and emotional building blocks for the kind of flexible, open-minded thinking required in order to imagine and entertain different and hopeful futures, I now want to widen the lens to the life-cycle as a whole. I shall return to Erikson's model as a framework and draw on John Wilson's research on posttraumatic growth in which he considered the potential impact of trauma on personality and identity formation at each life stage (2006, pp. 84–6). There are, of course, risks in adhering too closely to stage models. For instance, trauma does not confine itself to certain periods and its legacy ripples across the years. This is certainly true for the complex clients with whom this book is most concerned and many of the disruptions Wilson identified for each stage would be familiar to anyone who has experienced severe trauma or traumatic losses, whether this was as a young child, teenager or an adult. However, what drew me to Wilson's line of enquiry was the fact that it offered a route into thinking about the subjective, affective experience of people who have survived trauma and traumatic loss and the ways in which this might colour their sense of self and their expectations and hopes for the future.

Another caveat about using staged models is that in a rapidly changing world the tasks and challenges of each life stage are also changing. Take, for instance, the sixth stage, Intimacy versus Isolation. In the latter part of the twentieth century, and certainly when Erikson was writing, this was a stage marked by leaving home, entering the world of work and beginning to set up a home and family of one's own. Today, for complex social and economic reasons, these steps toward complete independence are becoming increasingly delayed for many young people and this sets up its own challenges. But there is also a pull for children and teenagers to negotiate far more 'grown up' issues than their parents and they are being exposed to a wider range of traumatic events. For instance, modern communication brings trauma into our homes through the images of disasters we see on television and in insidious ways through images that can be viewed online or in the form of cyber-bullying. Modern communication also makes it possible at one level to never feel alone. Yet it is leaving many people, both young and old, feeling increasingly isolated and different. Feeling very alone, especially if you imagine that other people are having a good time, is one of the pervasive causes of hopelessness and sometimes of suicide in our current age. Whilst it is not within the scope of this book to discuss how socio-cultural factors contribute to individual and societal hopes and despairs, I think it is important to bear them in mind.

Trust versus mistrust

Table 5.1 outlines Erikson's life stages alongside the corresponding 'critical periods' of neurological and personality development. I am going to discuss each stage in turn and will illustrate my points with short vignettes. The first of the critical periods of accelerated brain development, and also the period when our attachment templates are being laid down, coincides with Erikson's first and second stages (1965). Wilson argues that the impact of trauma or traumatic bereavement during stage one results in disruptions to the individual's sense of continuity and to states of hopelessness and helplessness (2006, p. 84). In Chapter 4 I discussed how the roots of hope lie in our

Table 5.1   Erikson's Ages of Man

	AGE	NEUROLOGICAL AND PERSONALITY DEVELOPMENT
Trust versus Mistrust	Pre-birth, birth, 0–18 months	Conception–2 years: Critical period of rapid brain growth
		Right hemisphere brain 'on line' from birth and begins to develop first
		Attachment templates being laid down
Autonomy versus Shame and Doubt	18 months to 3 years	Rapid neuronal growth in the prefrontal cortices and in the left hemisphere during the second year of life
		7–24 months: The 'psychological birth' of the infant
Initiative versus Guilt	3–5 years	
Industry versus Inferiority	Latency	Growth spurt in the right brain (Girls: 6–7 Boys: 8–9)
Identity versus Role Confusion	Adolescence	10–19: The second critical period of neurological development
Intimacy versus Isolation	Early adulthood	
Generativity versus Stagnation	Middle age	
Integrity versus Despair	Old age	Losses – of people, functions, purpose

earliest attachment experiences. Even if later in life the individual has good experiences, a lack of basic safety in the earliest months, and remember, this includes birth and pre-birth trauma, can continue to emerge years later in the form of defensive survival patterns, body memory, dreams and, for some people, a very tenuous relationship to hope (Hudson Allez, 2011; Karr-Morse and Wiley, 1997).

Regarding such early traumas, Hudson Allez discusses how the bonding of mother and infant occurs throughout the pregnancy as they share senses and how the woman's attitude towards her baby can be transmitted in utero.[7] If she is highly stressed, perhaps because she is in a violent relationship or dealing with a family illness or death, her heightened adrenaline and cortisol levels will create a stressful environment for the foetus (2011, pp. 7, 13). The child can become predisposed to hypervigilance and extreme reactions to stressful events. The same is true if things go wrong during the birth. Medical emergencies involving invasive delivery techniques and the separation of mother and child if the baby is premature and has to be cared for in an incubator are traumatic and interfere with the natural bonding process. Hudson Allez argues that 'this trauma is one that the infant remembers and stores in preverbal somatic and emotional memories, and the longer the period between the separation and physical reunion between mother and baby, the greater the potential for attachment and bonding ties to be broken. The baby needs skin-to-skin contact; to hear the familiar rhythm of mother's heartbeat and voice and to smell her smell. To the baby they are still a single unit and mother's absence can feel like a missing limb.' 'The infant will not understand the disconnection with his mother and will therefore develop a loss circuitry based on feelings of the threat of abandonment and fear for survival' (2011, pp. 7–9).

Some people who experienced trauma or severe neglect in infancy get stuck in what I described earlier as 'a-hope'. For them it is not a case of hope being lost or taken away, but of never developing the capacity to hope in the first place. This may be because of never having experienced being held in mind by a parent who could look forward to things, who believed in their potential and could dream dreams on their behalf (Bromberg, 2011, p. 93).

It may be because the individual's nervous system is dominated by survival responses and the neurological and emotional building blocks for flexible and imaginative thinking are not in place. And it can be a combination of both. When we encounter someone who is stuck in 'a-hope' there is a dead quality which contrasts with the frustration or distress evident in someone who has lost hope and feels helpless, and we can struggle to find any sense of direction or purpose to the work. If we are used to looking forward to things, it can be hard to empathise with such people. We can feel flat and unmoved, somehow at a distance from the client, but also surprised at some of his or her responses. I recall feeling shocked when Sandra, the client mentioned in Chapter 4, said flatly, 'hope isn't a word I use'. It felt like a blow. Something so painfully finite and yet said with no affect. I needed time to take in the enormity of a life where hope is not a possibility. Although Sandra was by no means as lost as the severely deprived, depressed, non-hoping children described by Alvarez (1992), for she had managed to develop a self-reliant persona, this masked a pervasive state of depression and a fear of being with other people.

As a distinction between states of hopelessness and 'a-hope', compare Sandra's 'hope isn't a word I use' with another woman's 'better not get your hopes up'. The latter came from repeated experiences of knowing there was something to aim or hope for, but either not being given it or of good things being taken away. For instance, one of Pam's earliest memories was of being told by a foster carer that she would be given a teddy if she did not wet the bed. Pam recalled trying hard to earn this treat and her devastation when after several dry nights in a row her foster mother seemed to have forgotten her promise. I am not, by the way, saying that Sandra did not set herself things to aim for. She was driven by academic and professional goals. But there was nothing relational in her aspirations. With Pam there was. More important than the teddy was to receive a smile, to be greeted with warmth and love rather than being 'treated' to angry shouts or, at best, a mechanical form of care which had been all she had known in her birth family. She described knowing that she needed to make her foster carers smile and be pleased with her, which suggests a child who believed that if she tried hard enough she could make something happen. Sandra, by contrast, seemed to have no belief or hope that she could have an impact on her preoccupied, emotionally unavailable mother or her strict, domineering father. Pam formed her resolve when she was 2 or 3 and had some language. But infant observation tells us that from birth we do instinctively try to evoke a smile on the faces of our caregivers. We are primed to elicit care and in terms of pre-hoping it is as if we begin life with a wordless, as yet unthought-about level of hoping and aspiring for a loving, attuned response to our communications. When this does not materialise the default is to slip into despair and detachment or a rigidly self-reliant way of being.

In many ways, Pam's start in life would appear to be far more traumatic than Sandra's – for instance, her Mum was a drug addict and she was taken into care at about 18 months old – and many of her later experiences certainly were traumatic. But what strikes me is that she did seek out people and she also found hope through fantasising about very different futures. Sandra, however, lacked a lively imaginary world which could have provided both a retreat and a springboard to forming hopes for the future. I have worked with other people too who, whilst appearing successful and self-reliant, feel hollow inside and struggle to know how to be with others. For them life can feel joyless; they have no vision of something different. They would prefer not to exist. As with Sandra it can be hard to identify what might have been traumatic for them in their earliest days. But in each case I sensed an absence of any life-promoting 'inner objects' and found it impossible to imagine them being held by a lively, encouraging mother who could present a world of things to be hoped for. Not surprisingly, none of the clients in question appeared to hold much hope that therapy could help them and they allowed me only fleeting moments of contact with a hidden, fragile and desperate self.

Autonomy versus shame and doubt

Trauma and humiliation during Erikson's second stage (18 months to 3 years), can injure a sense of healthy autonomy and lead to shame, guilt and difficulties with self-regulation. As well as the major changes that are going on in the brain, this is the period when a child is mastering locomotion. As he learns to stand then walk independently, psychologically he begins to 'take a stand' and assert his will. It is the 'I can' mentality which characterises the optimistic personality. The responses of the toddler's caregivers to his triumphs, failures and self-assertion are important in terms of personality development and a sense of agency. Sometimes inadvertently or deliberately what they say and do squashes the toddler's triumphant excitement and evokes a state of shame.

Shame is one of several distinct emotions that arise during this period. Alan Schore (2003b, p. 154) has described shame as an 'arousal blocker',[8] a brake which modulates high-arousal states such as interest, curiosity, excitement and the elation which we feel when mastering something new. As a brake, this deflation of arousal is important at a time before we have developed a conscience and still depend on external regulation to avoid going too far. The emergence of shame is the first step in developing an internal monitor and being able to think about and modify our behaviour. But shame also has a toxic element. A mis-attuned, critical or humiliating response from a caregiver when the child is feeling grand exercising a new skill or if he suddenly falls is likely to evoke shame. Imagine, for instance, the toddler returning to Mum excited by whatever he has mastered or discovered and wanting her to share his mood. But if there is no smile and joyful response this can trigger 'a sudden shock-induced deflation of positive affect, and the infant is propelled into a state that he/she cannot yet auto-regulate' (Schore, 2003b, p. 155). Ideally, the sensitive parent helps the deflated child to recover, perhaps by empathically soothing his distress and, when calmer, encouraging him to try again. As a result the child recovers from the blow to his confidence and pride and the attachment system is reactivated.

Repeated reparative experiences help children to develop their own ways of coping with emotional stress. But some parents fail to do this. Shouting or laughing cruelly at a child intensifies shame and fails to alleviate the underlying emotions, whether fear or sadness or frustration. Indeed, shaming responses are more likely to activate defensive systems. For some children hypoaroused, submission-based strategies become the default: hanging the head, averting the eyes, trying hard not to be noticed, accommodating and being good. For them not hoping becomes adaptive. Other children might default to rage and aggression in response to any hint of rejection or humiliation.[9] Later in life they are more likely to adopt a cynical attitude to hope and a determined, self-reliant approach to the future.

An example of a shame moment was related by my client Adam. His unmet yearning was for his Dad to be proud of him. When he was 3 he recalls seeing his older siblings giving Dad prettily wrapped birthday presents and he

realised he had nothing to give. He ran to his bedroom and came back clutching a battered toy. He thrust it at his father who looked scornfully at the offering and said 'is that all I get for looking after you!' Even with the distance of
decades Adam flushed with embarrassment and his body seemed to shrink
inwards. All children need parents to delight in their gifts and achievements,
and for a while Adam kept hoping that one day Dad would say 'well done'.[10]
He worked hard to excel at sport. He kept asking his father to come and watch
him play. Dad rarely did and as one disappointment followed another Adam
gave up not just hope, but also in a 'spiting himself' way, the act of trying. As
an older man he now deeply regretted what might have been had he pursued
his evident talents.[11]

Initiative versus guilt

Trauma experienced between the ages of 3 and 5, Erikson's stage of initiative
versus guilt, can lead to a loss of initiative and purpose and, Wilson argues,
to a loss of connectedness from self and others (2006, p. 86). Not only do
some pre-school children experience the horrors of sexual abuse or witnessing or being the victim of violence, but in this and the following stage we
are entering the territory of what has been called the trauma of 'disconfirmation' or of 'non-recognition'. Philip Bromberg has a particular interest in such
developmental trauma. He argues that 'a person's core self – the self that is
shaped by early attachment patterns – is defined by who the parental objects
both perceive him to be and deny him to be'. If they relate to their child 'as
though he is "such and such" and ignore other aspects of him as if they don't
exist' for Bromberg this is traumatic because it is relationally non-negotiable
(2011, p. 57).[12] The disconfirmed attributes, interests and talents of the child
cannot be shared and may become dissociated from the self as well. Bromberg distinguishes the trauma of disconfirmation from 'big T' traumas such as
the 'gross invasion of mind and body associated with mental, physical and
sexual abuse' or with horrific events such as 9/11 (2011, p. 57). People can,
and often do, experience both. But I agree with Bromberg that at some level
non-recognition is an inevitable part of everyone's early life and that we all
carry developmental wounds which shape our expectations about ourselves
and our futures.

Shaw, another therapist from the analytic tradition, talks about 'the trauma
of non-recognition, when a child is punished for her efforts to assert her separate subjectivity, but rewarded for a willingness to serve as the parent's object'
(2013, pp. 5–7). Instead of being cherished, validated, appreciated and loved,
the child can feel shamed for being who she is and increasingly despairing of
her initiative ever being recognised. Shaw argues, 'children will go to great
lengths to keep their parents good and ... will often present themselves to the
parent as what the parent wants them to be'. This is what Adam tried to do
for a while and is a survival strategy that is particularly true for children with
frightening or narcissistic parents. 'From this position, the sense of *personal*

agency and desire is atrophied, replaced instead with anxiety, and underlying resentment about satisfying the demands and expectations of the other' (2013, p. 7. My italics). I find it interesting that the two authors capture both a passive and a more active element to the survival strategies adopted by the disconfirmed child. On the one hand there is a splitting off and dissociation from what is unacceptable to others. On the other, there is an active attempt to become what the other wants – the 'false self' or adaptive child.

One man, who came to see me because despite being a successful academic he struggled to take the initiative to promote himself, had experienced repeated disconfirmation by his father. Dad was a headmaster. He was a temperamental, intolerant man whose shifting moods and contradictory statements left his son unsure how to position himself. He could never be sure what Dad would like or what would annoy him. Roger learned to play it safe and his career moves had always been somewhat accidental. He avoided challenges that interested him because of beliefs about not being good enough or being found out as a fraud. It emerged that the real 'fraudulence' was directed towards himself because the person he had become was not who he really was. Because of this, Roger's life always felt incomplete and he lamented never really knowing what he wanted to do. The psychological work Roger needed to do was to notice when Dad's voice got in the way, to challenge his fears about risking something new and to slowly find his authentic self.

Industry versus inferiority

During latency, the period between roughly 5 and 10, trauma and developmental injury can also impact initiative and self-esteem and, if extensive, lead to pervasive states of futility. Neurologically, during this period there is another growth spurt in the right brain beginning at 6 or 7 for girls and 8 or 9 for boys, and what Panksepp calls the 'lust system' starts to come on line. This provides a template for the child's later adult sexual relationships. Hudson Allez points out that 'vandalisation' of the child at this stage can interfere with normal sexual development, but so too can other aversive experiences (2011, p. 77).

For my client Bill the stories he told about his childhood and his tendency to collapse into depression, lose motivation and view himself as worthless, suggest that this life stage was particularly relevant. It was also a critical period for a woman called Trudy involving bereavement, trauma and the repeated disconfirmation of her reality. Trudy became a 'little Mum' after her father died when she was 6. Her mother was preoccupied with her own grief and the need to manage the family business as well as three children. It had been drummed into her that it was babyish to cry. So she decided that being upset was a bad thing and that she must never complain. She was often put in charge of her younger brothers. If they squabbled or cried it was her fault. When one of the teenagers next door molested Trudy, for a long time she didn't tell Mum in case it upset her or she was cross. Her first attempt to say she didn't like going to the neighbours for tea was met with a telling off for being ungrateful. 'It's my fault' became a familiar script and Trudy often spoke about how demoralised and lonely she felt battling with long-term depression and how hurt she was when people were judgemental about why she didn't work and often failed to complete tasks. When she discovered that the depression was caused by a rare auto-immune disease, Trudy felt relieved to realise that always being tired and struggling to do things others took in their stride was really not her fault and that her apparent lack of 'industry' was not, as she had long believed, because she was inferior or useless. But it took time to stop comparing herself with others and to face the anger and sadness evoked by these insights.

Identity versus role confusion

As said earlier, towards the end of the latency period and during adolescence the second critical period of neurological development occurs, and this process can be compromised by exposure to traumatic events. Adolescence is a time of preparing for adulthood through experimentation and of re-negotiating our relationship with ourselves and others as we adapt to physical changes and their social meanings (Anderson and Dartington, 1999, p. 3). The changes and anxieties of this period can evoke the intense experiences and anxieties of earlier life stages. Trauma experienced during adolescence, or recalled because of a life event, can intensify identity struggles and lead to a loss of coherence, self-sameness and continuity (Briggs, 1999, pp. 30, 31; Wilson, 2006, p. 86). It can lead to a profound mistrust of the adult world and a reluctance to go there. As Hudson Allez pointed out, securely attached teenagers will become proactive about planning their futures. But this is much harder for those who are insecurely attached and especially if they have had an abusive history and are prone to amygdala-driven fear states (2011, p. 86).

For some young people living in a context of ongoing danger, for instance in a home where there is domestic violence or ongoing abuse or in a country torn by war, it may not even be safe to have an adolescence, meaning being able to experiment with one's identity and ways of relating. Sexual abuse can leave a young person feeling like an adult in a child's body and lead to profound anxieties about closeness and growing up (Briggs, 1999, p. 31.) Other examples of being prematurely catapulted into more adult demands to cope, be self-reliant or look after others include being sent to boarding school or for some other reason separated from one's family or country, or needing to deal with the critical illness or death of a family member. Meanwhile, an adolescent who personally experiences severe illness might become frozen in a more childlike dependent state and lose ground with his peers. Other traumas experienced during adolescence include being bullied or physically or sexually attacked and witnessing violence or the hostility between parents who separate in acrimonious circumstances.

The consequences of such traumas and losses can be exacerbated if attachment figures fail to protect and support the young person, a failure which can be viewed as an attachment betrayal. For one 17-year-old the fact that his father rapidly remarried after his mother was killed in a fatal accident felt like a profound betrayal and left him with no one to turn to as he struggled with his own shock and grief. Harry lost both a mother and a family and home as he knew it. He began to avoid going home after school, fell in with a group that took drugs and gave up trying at school. For Nial it was his headmaster who failed him. When he risked telling him that the school priest had abused him he was told not to talk about such things. Nial was left feeling that he had done something awful in speaking out, and was very confused by the mixed messages of his elders. How could the priest do something so awful, yet talk about sex as sinful? Alongside this, Nial felt ashamed and confused about his sexuality. He tried to do what the headmaster told him and buried himself in work. However, it was at a cost and whilst at university he had a breakdown. Anti-depressants helped him through, but the underlying issues re-surfaced when Nial's son was born and it was this that persuaded him to seek psychological help. The stories of Harry and Nial are not unusual. Sadly, we know that all too many teenagers are exposed to some sort of trauma and probably an unquantifiable number experience some form of loss during these formative years.[13]

Intimacy versus isolation

Wilson suggests that trauma in early adulthood leads to detachment and estrangement from others. The dividing line between adolescence and early adulthood is a tenuous one. There are overlaps in the issues and challenges to be addressed and, I would argue, in the ways that trauma and loss can impact the individual. However, if we think of this life stage as the entry into the world of work and for many, but not all, of acquiring a home and family of one's own, then not being able to follow the path of one's peers can indeed lead to a sense of alienation. At one level, early adulthood offers a vista of many choices and opportunities with, hopefully, the secure knowledge that we have lots of time to try something out, make a mistake and start again. As we get older each new choice means that alternative options have to be foregone. We don't have the luxury of retracing our steps and taking another path.[14] But trauma inhibits exploration and choice making. Moreover, at this point in life some people face the harsh process of relinquishing childhood dreams. This could be because, like my client Luke, the limitations of an illness or disability make it hard to engage in the adult world of training and then work.

Luke was a highly intelligent young man who had been involved in mental health services since his mid-teens because of depression and self-harm. The structure and predictability of home and school had just about cushioned Luke when he was younger. But once he left home he found it increasingly hard to function and became very dependent on rituals and self-harming behaviours to manage his intense anxiety and obsessive worries. He would often say to me sadly that, although a recent diagnosis of Asperger Syndrome helped him to understand why he had always found so many things bewildering or frightening, he could no longer keep hoping that things would change and that, as others often well-meaningly said, 'he'd grow out of it'. Some things were there for life. Luke realised that his dreams of going to Cambridge to study maths might never happen and he became increasingly depressed and demoralised as his peers and his sisters went to university, found partners and jobs and began to settle down – the things that had been mapped out for him since he was a child. It was far from easy to keep the candle of hope alight for Luke and I was aware of my own sadness and despair when I observed his increasing detachment from people and from activities that, whilst always engaged in with the obsessive, single-mindedness that characterises an Asperger passion, had nonetheless provided Luke with a measure of happiness and stimulation.

For other young adults, encountering difficulties in conceiving a child or losing a baby, sometimes in traumatic circumstances, is another example of how the destruction of childhood dreams can challenge the sense of self. To face multiple miscarriages or repeated cycles of IVF treatment can erode a couple's beliefs about the future as these cycles are accompanied by oscillating hope and despair. Raphael-Leff points out that 'the psychological trauma of prolonged infertility has an emotional impact which in the past culminated either in acceptance of childlessness or adoption', whereas today's new interventive technologies of fertilisation have 'brought in their wake new hopes and a new syndrome of psychological disturbances' (2012, p. 206). Facing repeated miscarriages or failed treatments can evoke primitive, raw emotions and magical thinking – for instance, investing hope in the 'baby-maker' experts or looking for indicators of something one might be being punished for. Raphael-Leff describes one woman's story and 'its menstrual cycles of waiting and wanting, hope and despair, elation-deflation and treatment stops and starts' (2012, p. 209). It highlights how for the infertile woman the dance between hope and despair is intimately bound up with time: the keen awareness of the body cycle; the painful awareness of anniversaries of losses or a birthday that should have happened; and the awareness of time passing by whilst others more fortunate celebrate their children's developmental achievements.

Raphael-Leff's client's own words illustrate the desperation faced by someone in this situation and resultant magical thinking. At a point when she still believed she could conceive naturally 'Eve' wrote: 'This baby does not exist except in my own mind but when we make love I feel such a powerful rebirth of hope that surely out of longing and closeness our child will connect up and grow to be real', and a little later, 'I'm afraid if I stop waiting all will disappear. I have to hold onto the desire and hope and disappointment all the time, like grieving, otherwise it won't come true' (2012, p. 212). Once a natural conception was ruled out she described it as 'like a funnel. When we started having a child, the options were wide open. Over the years they have been stripped away ... all our energies are concentrated on this last hope at the bottom of a narrow funnel.' This is the territory of hope eroded which I shall discuss in the following chapter. Some of Eve's comments also speak of the detachment and estrangement that this form of trauma engenders: 'I don't feel very in touch with life at all, odd experience going home on the train, seeing people at work living ordinary lives. Inside I feel very separate from it.' 'Having kids is so commonplace, so natural, that if you're not part of it you feel singled out, excluded from all common assumptions' (2012, pp. 221, 223). There is also a risk of feeling disconnected from past and future generations for both men and women who are unable to give birth. When someone well-meaningly said 'but you can always adopt' to another young woman she was angry. She refused to give up trying IVF, even though the cost was causing a massive rift between her and her partner. 'I want to be pregnant', she said. 'I want my genes to be carried on. Adopting just wouldn't be the same.' Paradoxically, her need for a sense of connectedness and ongoingness was creating estrangement from the person she loved best as well as from friends whom she no longer felt able to identify with.

There are other situations in early adulthood – certainly far more than those noted here – which can erode a sense of optimism and excitement about the future and lead to feeling separate from one's peers. For instance, a similar pattern of try/fail, hope/despair is the lot of an increasing number of young adults trying to get into the job market and in time they can also feel increasingly alienated. If their interests were disconfirmed and their efforts dismissed earlier in life, it is all too easy to give up and inhabit the mantle of someone who is useless and a failure. Other young adults, both men and women, can be stripped of a sense of ongoingness and connectedness with others and themselves because of experiencing trauma in their capacity as military personnel or front line workers or as the victims of violence or sexual assault. For such people what should be a natural and ongoing process during the years of late adolescence and early adulthood of 're-negotiating dreams, choices and hopes, whether self-generated or from without' and 'beginning to tolerate opportunities lost and roads not taken', is rudely forced upon them as a result of overwhelming trauma or loss (Waddell, 1998, p. 159). Some people find a way to grow after enduring such traumas or repeated cycles of hope and disappointment. Their relationships might strengthen.[15] They might find a new life-path which brings meaning and fulfilment. They are able to engage with and learn from emotional experience, a capacity which Waddell argues is a marker of maturity (1998, pp. 171, 176). Sadly, others, and in particular those who have experienced trauma or emotional wounding at earlier stages in life, get stuck in lives which no longer hang together and offer little meaning, hope or genuine joy.[16]

Generativity versus stagnation

In middle age, trauma or events that evoke memories of earlier traumas can lead to 'a loss of an inner sense of aliveness' which compromises generativity and leaves the individual depressed, demoralised and often grappling with shame and self-disgust (Wilson, 2006, p. 86). One situation I have often encountered is when people have worked, been effective parents, managed daily life and then because of a traumatic event or an event which served to bring to the foreground repressed memories or emotions about previous traumas, they suddenly crashed into illness. They found themselves subject to intrusive thoughts and flashbacks which kept them in a state of fear and alertness and made it hard to be with people or to go out. They had to stop work and began to avoid social events. Such dramatic changes left them confused and frightened about what was going on. They compared life now and before falling ill and struggled with guilt about no longer being the person they used to be. Typically such clients present with a combination of depression and anxiety and sometimes additional somatic problems. What they and others don't realise is that their 'symptoms' are not shameful or mad, as they sometimes fear, but owe their presence to the way that evolution has shaped our physiological responses to danger.

Anna was someone whose story typifies how frightening and confusing it is to be suddenly hijacked by trauma memories and how devastating it is to lose touch with one's former coping self. I mentioned Anna in Chapter 3 when discussing how trauma constricts exploration and leads to a focus on potential danger rather than the more mundane or pleasurable aspects of life. Because of her acute anxiety and hypervigilance Anna's life became increasingly restricted. She lost her job and a rich social life, but worse, she lost confidence in her judgement. Thinking about her life before the assault evoked intense sadness because of all that she had lost. On one occasion Anna described looking at old photos and said sadly, 'it's as if all the colour has gone out of the pictures. I don't seem to be able to access happy memories any more.' The future looked bleak because of her anxiety that something terrible would happen again, and because the trauma had left her effectively unable to differentiate past and present, it was very hard to enjoy the present moment.

In Anna's case the trauma occurred when she was an adult, although her story also included significant developmental injury. For another woman who also experienced a sudden and frightening crash into illness which necessitated giving up work and spending a number of periods in hospital, an attachment event 'cracked open' previous traumas.[17] She became haunted by intrusive flashbacks and body memories. They completely dysregulated her and she became increasingly agoraphobic. She was also incredibly ashamed of being like this. With her world turned upside down, her mind full of images that terrified and disgusted her and with little sense how she could get back to her previous way of life Megan became increasingly hopeless and suicidal. I will say more about her in subsequent chapters.

Integrity versus despair

Finally, we come to old age, the period of integrity versus despair and one which brings specific traumas of its own. Wilson argued that trauma in later life can alter the individual's capacity for meaning and result in a sense of disconnectedness from life. The trauma could be an accident or illness, surgery or loss. Alternatively, it could be the cumulative effect of years of struggle or a series of losses and illnesses. Earlier in life, with more robust health and buffered by a wide social network, such events might not have such impact. There are still things to hope and strive for. However, with advancing years shocks and losses can be experienced as disorienting and confusing, a sudden uprooting of the self. They can call into question one's trust in the world and sense of reliable ongoingness, one's faith and old beliefs and values. Again earlier forgotten traumas might be evoked. There can be a point when one knock or loss too many plummets the individual into despair. He or she loses the will to fight and retreats into a state of despair and shut down.

Long-term studies of the survivors of Nazi persecution or prisoner-of-war camps have shown that some people display late-onset PTSD in later life, despite having seemingly adapted well for decades. Although it has been argued that losses or illnesses can play an important part in this and assumed that mental and physical resilience decrease with aging, Aarts and Op den Velde have challenged these hypotheses. They point out that although stressful life events may trigger or exacerbate PTSD symptoms, they are not a sufficient cause in themselves and that there is no empirical evidence that coping mechanisms and affect regulation necessarily deteriorate with age (1996, pp. 364–7). Instead they argue that posttraumatic states and the specific developmental problems belonging to old age interfere with each other. First, they highlight the commonalities between the crucial developmental tasks of aging and the tasks involved in recovering from trauma. Both include mourning, assigning meaning to and accept one's experiences, re-establishing self-coherence and self-continuity and achieving ego integration. Unresolved grief, guilt and anger may be reactivated by the losses occurring in later life. If someone has been unable to work through traumatic experiences, then it may be far harder to come to terms with the changes and challenges of aging (1996, pp. 368–74).

A similar point, but from a different perspective, is made by the psychoanalyst Margot Waddell. In a book which explores personality growth across the life span she argues that 'a person will be able to face up to and undergo middle and old age insofar as it has been possible, all along, to embrace the complexity of his experiences and to integrate the painful with the pleasurable, rather than to seek to avoid, or to deny the hard bits and to clutch onto the right to be happy' (1998, p. 197). She continues, 'if a person lacks an internal container of feelings, one that is sturdy enough to withstand new or renewed challenges to his peace of mind and sense of self, he may have recourse to earlier patterns of functioning, ones mobilised in the service of avoiding pain.' As a result, when facing the losses and struggles of later years the individual may 'shallow out' or give in and succumb to feelings of demoralisation, failure, emptiness, pointlessness, envy or meaninglessness (1998, pp. 199–200). The social context, our attachments and affiliations; the nature of or lack of supports, plays a significant part in whether someone is able to heal and grow after trauma or whether he or she slips into states of demoralisation, futility and despair, and in the later stages of life the atrophying of social networks further contributes to states of loneliness and despair. Alternatively, the last chapter of life can be a place of calm, acceptance and gratitude for a life well lived and for hopes and dreams fulfilled, and for some people the hope of something beyond this life sustains them.

Conclusion

It would take far more than one chapter to name the many ways that trauma can invade and disrupt people's lives at different life stages, but hopefully enough has been said to show how traumatic events can interfere with stage-specific developmental tasks. Trauma and attachment injury in the earliest phases of life, which includes pre-birth, may mean that the individual never learns basic trust or the language of hope. Trauma in older childhood and adulthood can destroy or certainly mute an optimistic outlook. Trauma experienced or recalled in old age can lead to emptiness and despair. It should not be forgotten, however, that after encountering the horrors of trauma some people grow in amazing ways and are able to find a new and surprisingly rich direction in life. As professionals we should never give up the hope of transcendence and posttraumatic growth, something captured in many world myths and fairy tales of those who escape from the grip of evil enchanters or descend to the underworld and emerge reborn.[18]

Notes

1. When we feel safe and are socially engaged, the metabolic demand to defend is reduced and this facilitates health, healing and growth (Porges, 2012). Coe et al. observed that long-term separation of infant primates from their mothers produced varying degrees of immunosuppression (1985, cited in de Zulueta, 2000, p. 54).
2. The 'emotional, or 'survival' brain comprises the midbrain and limbic system. Of particular importance within the latter is the body's early warning system, the amygdala.
3. Trauma-related disorders are disorders of integration (Ogden et al., 2006, pp. 4, 36, 182).
4. Of these structures the orbitofrontal cortex is particularly important in regulating emotions. Its maturation is highly dependent on our attachment relationships (Schore, 2003a, pp. 13–16).
5. The former include depression, anxiety, social phobia, dissociation; the latter oppositional and impulsive behaviours. As adolescence progresses these traits can become exacerbated and cause serious problems at home and school (Ford, 2009, p. 41).
6. Survival brain dominance lies behind the main symptoms of PTSD and other trauma-related disorders – namely the oscillation between hyperarousal and numbing, and the resultant avoidance of reminders of the trauma.
7. This can include infanticidal thoughts. Even without being told that their mother contemplated abortion, some people know it implicitly.

8. It rapidly shifts us from Sympathetic to Parasympathetic Nervous System functioning.

9. Nathanson's 'Compass of Shame' provides a helpful outline of four typical responses to manage shame (Kluft, 2007, p. 306).

10. According to Erskine one of our eight relational needs as a child is to be able to express love and gratitude (1999, p. 148).

11. See Shabad on spite (2001, pp. 193–209).

12. Bromberg quoted Ronald Laing's point that 'the confirmation of one's identity does not depend on the others' approval of you, but on their recognition of you, that is, their accurate perception of you as you experience yourself' (2011, p. 57). It is that experience of accurate, contingent mirroring that is so essential in infancy.

13. A random survey of 1245 American adolescents showed that 23% had been the victims of physical or sexual assaults as well as witnessing violence. Of this group, 20% went on to develop PTSD (van der Kolk et al., 1996, p. 5) Another random survey of 2000 10–16 year-olds found that almost half the boys and a third of the girls had been subjected to some form of violent victimisation (Boney-McCoy and Finklehor, 1995).

14. Interestingly, the word 'mistake' comes from an old Norse word meaning a 'mis-take' or taking the wrong path.

15. After some painful ruptures en route, the attempt to make a baby eventually brought Eve and her husband closer (Raphael-Leff, 2012).

16. Erikson observed that the war veterans he worked with had lost a sense of identity, sameness and personal continuity. He wrote: 'they knew who they were; they had a personal identity. But it was as if subjectively their lives no longer hung together – and never would again' (Wilson, 2006, p. 77).

17. Attachment events which can precipitate being flooded by trauma memories include the birth of or significant ages of one's own children, the deaths of significant people, relationship breakdowns which trigger feeling abandoned, and the loss of roles. Other events that may echo or serve to remind about a past trauma include an unexpected encounter, media events, an assault, a medical operation and a current experience of feeling helpless or trapped.

18. See Kalshed's (1996) excellent exploration of the trauma-linked symbolism of fairy tales.

6

When Hoping Keeps People Alive: Non-Mentalised States and the Need for Illusions

---

If I hadn't been hopeful all the time I would have died.

(Pippa)

This chapter continues the theme of the impact of trauma on the individual's relationship to hope and expands on the discussion about the differences between realistic and illusory hope. I will draw on material which speaks about the lived experience of trauma survivors, as it is through listening to the stories of people who remain haunted by the past and feel trapped and overwhelmed by their current circumstances that we really learn about the dance between hope and despair.

The importance of hoping: Mae's story

I shall begin with an example which illustrates how early trauma and neglect shaped one woman's view of herself and her 'anticipatory models' and how hanging on to hope, even if false hope, can keep someone going. Mae also taught me how it can sometimes be adaptive not to hope and how earlier experiences of hoping and of hopelessness can be re-enacted in the present. One of the stories Mae told me has particular relevance to the theme of illusory hopes and it has stayed with me as a graphic illustration of how for a child the need to hope for something different can be crucial. When we are little and cannot change or escape a frightening situation, unaided fantasies of 'rescue' help us get through the day. Such fantasising is adaptive, not regressive. Indeed, as Pippa's words above emphasise, sometimes illusory hoping can keep people alive.

Mae's story is of a young girl standing at a gate waiting for her mum to turn up. Mae was of mixed race. Her father left shortly after her birth. Her mother drank heavily, had an evil temper and abandoned her four children when Mae was 7. They were put into care 'just until Mum comes back'. But 'just until' took 7 years and for all that time Mae stayed hopeful, always waiting. Her last image of Mum was of her walking down the drive in the rain. To cope with the loss she held on to the comforting fantasy of Mum returning with bags in hand as if she'd just popped to the shops. No one ever explained anything to Mae. They simply told her to be patient. Mae ended up in a boarding school run by a harridan who picked on Mae because of her colour and for being a 'Social Services brat' and kept telling her that she would 'come to nothing'. At weekends when other children went home Mae was one of the few left behind. But each Friday afternoon she went to the gate to watch and wait. She would stand there for hours and when teachers tried to call her in she argued that she didn't want to miss her mother if she turned up unexpectedly. 'I had to hope', she explained. 'I had to believe that I'd get away from that place. I had to believe Mum was OK.'

When Mae's mother finally did turn up it was not the happy reunion she had dreamt of. Her mother offered no explanation or apology, no expression of delight at seeing her daughter again. She had a new partner and 18-month-old twins in tow and was preoccupied with them. It was as if she had not been away and was simply collecting Mae at the end of the day. When I asked how she had felt Mae admitted to fury at being displaced by Mum's new family. 'I didn't understand why she'd bothered to come and find me.' But she was aware that she could not let anyone see her anger. 'If I lost that relationship', she explained, 'it would have meant all I'd been through for seven years was wasted'.

Significantly, the theme of hanging on to hope and waiting was re-enacted in a current relationship with a man who took advantage of Mae's tendency to rescue people. Clive would show up when he was struggling, convince Mae that he really loved her, but before long would be off again. Mae knew that he would never make a commitment, yet kept hoping that one day he would change. As we processed the memories about her mother Mae suddenly realised the parallels. 'It's like with Mum. I can't let him go. I keep putting up with things – but really I'm furious.'

The theme of hope and disappointment also entered the therapy itself and occasionally rocked our relationship. For instance, on one occasion I had to cancel our appointment because of an urgent dental appointment. I left a message of apology and knowing Mae could not make the following week said I would call her if an alternative time came up. However, my attempts to find a space did not work. In retrospect I wish I had called to tell her and at least make some contact because the next session Mae arrived announcing that she'd had a terrible fortnight. An appointment with an orthopaedic surgeon had also been cancelled because of an administrative error. Mae was angry and tearful. 'I thought I'd be able to find out what's really wrong and that he'd work out what will stop the pain. I was pinning my hopes on the appointment. Now I feel let down. No one cares. I can't go on like this. I don't want to be here anymore.' She stormed for several minutes then quietened when I said maybe the fact that I didn't call her also felt like 'not caring' and that this was hooking in old feelings about being let down when she really wanted help. Mae admitted that when I didn't call she thought I didn't care either and had angrily decided not to contact me as she sometimes did.

I empathised with the fact that of course she felt angry with me and about her orthopaedic appointment. Hoping it would provide a solution had kept her going for several months and now that hope had been cruelly dashed. Mae agreed. She had slipped back into hopelessness. 'If no one cares and no one's going to help, then why should I bother', she announced. Everything, including therapy, felt pointless. But Mae was prepared to talk about how unbearable it felt to wait and wait and feel hope draining away. She had waited expectantly for me to call. She had already endured a very long wait for treatment for her back problems. She spent months waiting for Clive each time he went travelling with vague promises about coming back when work permitted. And there were the countless hours as a child when she waited in vain for Mum to come back and greet her with the love she craved.

'I can cope if I know what's at the end of the wait', Mae said, 'and if I understand what's going on.' But as a child there was no clear end in sight nor anyone who could tell her what had happened or why her mother had treated her with such cruel neglect. As the session evolved Mae kept shifting states, one minute hopeless and giving up, the next complaining about non-caring professionals and like a sulky child claiming she 'didn't care'. But gradually she allowed me to see and share the sadness that lay hidden behind these familiar coping strategies, and as we explored Mae's feelings, especially about the perceived let down on my part, she returned to a more thoughtful, adult place – sad, but no longer seeming so resourceless and dependent on others.

These past and present examples illustrate how hanging on to hope, even whilst a part of her knew that some of her hopes were unrealistic, provided Mae with a source of comfort as a child and an adult. A more realistic form of hope, which was neither rooted in magical thinking nor dismissive of her capacities and the genuine attributes of others, began to emerge slowly during the therapy. This meant gently challenging Mae when she put herself down, empathising when she slipped into despair and repeatedly validating all her small achievements so that slowly over time she could risk doing more and, crucially, replace self-denigration with the thought that she was doing her best. From this place Mae started to assert herself and set boundaries with Clive. She risked saying no to him and to others and began to challenge her preoccupied ruminations about this man. By the time we ended our work Mae had decided that she was comfortable living alone. She had her children, her grandchildren and her much loved dogs. They were enough. She had also joined a church group and developed a couple of solid friendships. And, crucially, Mae now knew how to take care of the inner child who had for so long been hoping and waiting for the missing experience of unconditional love and care.

On hoping and not hoping: some typical responses after trauma

From my work with Mae and other survivors of overwhelming trauma and loss I have identified a number of typical trauma-based responses to the future and attitudes to hope. For some people caught in unbearable, frightening situations it can be lifesaving to cling to hope at all costs. Sometimes this fosters the determination to not give in and keep trying. But at times it can take the form of a more passive type of hope and a reliance on magical or 'if only' thinking. This, as explained in Chapter 2, is what mentalisation theorists call teleological mode (Bateman et al., 2004). For other people meanwhile it can be adaptive not to hope or expect too much. And some people's experiences evoke so much terror and despair that eventually any shred of hope is destroyed. I am going to use the Hope Scale as a framework for the following discussion. As chronic hopelessness and a-hope were mentioned in Chapters 3 and 4 they are not covered here. The third column of Table 6.1 shows some linked theoretical concepts.

Table 6.1   The Hope Scale: Trauma-Based Responses to Hope and the Future

Realistic, creative and flexible hoping	Aspirations and belief in future possibilities, but a capacity to accept and adjust in the face of thwarted hopes. "Live as well as I can in the circumstances"	
Faith and trust That all will be well		
When hoping keeps the self alive	Mentalised or non-mentalised hope?	Teleological Mode Pretend Mode
	Realistic or illusory?	The Self-care System or Waiting for Care
	Active or passive?	
		Turning Passive into Active
	Self-reliant or relational?	
		Reversal Magic
		The Self-care System
Adaptive not to hope	Don't trust or risk being hopeful	Protector/Persecutor Parts of Self
Chronic hopelessness	Shut down Give up	
Hope destroyed	Despair	
A-hope	No capacity to imagine, dream or hope	

When hoping keeps people alive

Let us look more closely at how hoping can keep people alive in the sense of ensuring that they don't collapse into a state of profound despair and detachment from life. They may hold on to a generalised hope that somewhere, at some point there will be a way out if they just keep going. The hope may have a relational aspect. For Mae it was that her mother would eventually appear. For many children abused by a parent some comfort can be found in the fantasy that they have been adopted and just need to wait for their 'real' parents to turn up and take them away. We often learn about this fantasy when it gets replayed as clients elicit strong caretaking responses in us. This is the transference/countertransference dynamic of the entitled child and the idealised, omnipotent rescuer which has been eloquently described by Davies and Frawley and to which I shall return in Chapter 8 (1994, pp. 178–81). Alternatively, the individual may depend on a more self-reliant form of hope: 'I will survive!' 'I shall get through it.' 'I'll find a way.' Last but not least, for some people faith in something greater than the self shores them up and provides a quiet sense of trust that all will be well. It enables them to transcend the trauma and to find a way, as Viktor Frankl emphasised, of finding meaning even in extreme adversity (2004).

Whatever the object of hope, we could argue that there is often a dissociative quality to hoping against hope and that whilst a part of the mind stays hopeful, another part knows about being helpless and hopeless. At first, as I explored this theme I struggled to find a clear distinction between someone clinging to magical solutions, in other words to non-mentalised hope, for instance the child who refuses to let go the belief that 'one day I'll find a nice Mum' and, let's say, the survivor of torture who said 'something told me that I would eventually be free' yet who always held in mind the horrifying reality of his situation and the slim chances of survival. Hours could be spent debating the differences. But now I find it more helpful to think about degrees of mentalising and about a fluidity in the extent to which someone might split off the knowledge of things being hopeless or be honest with himself about the chances of the hoped-for solution materialising.

As markers of the extent of mentalising we might ask: 'does the object of hope become the only possible solution?' and 'does clinging to it not only stifle other alternatives, but also necessitate splitting off thoughts and emotions that might, if owned, jeopardise the wish?' For instance, Mae developed an internal world in which anger with her neglectful and emotionally abusive mother was dissociated. The same was true with Sonia, another victim of childhood abuse. One part of her knew that her mother was aware of her stepfather's visits to her room. This 'self' was furious that Mum never protected her. Another part of her protected Mum, whilst a third part yearned for Mum to love and look after her. Maintaining the illusion of a good Mum and clinging to the hope that one day she will acknowledge the child with love has serious costs, perhaps the most damaging being the way that the child develops a shame-based personality. 'To keep you good I have to be bad.' However, what needs to be emphasised is the lifesaving nature of hoping in extreme situations, whether the solutions are indeed 'magical' ones or hold at least the seeds of possibility, and this is especially true when you are a child living in a frightening world. I have encountered many people who, like Mae, stayed 'alive' because of a capacity to hope even though the objects of their hope could be viewed as illusory ones.

Waiting for care

If one distinction we can make concerns the level of mentalising that accompanies hope, another is between passive and active forms of hoping. Mae's story illustrates the former. Her 'refuge' was the thought that someone would come and do something that would change the situation. It is what Danielian and Giannotti call 'loyal waiting' (2012, p. 45). For other people for whom hoping keeps the self alive this has a more active quality supported by a resolute belief that they will survive and find a way through. For one young woman her belief was that by using her intellect she could find a way to surmount any problem. But as she struggled with an increasingly disabling illness she had to face the painful reality that this was not enough. Another woman, who like Mae was also highly traumatised, had taken an 'I can' position from early in life. 'I've always been optimistic for me and other people', she told me. She believed that if she was determined and worked hard enough she could do anything she put her mind to, and as I worked with Pippa it became clear how important this belief had been over the years. Indeed on one occasion she told me, 'if I hadn't been hopeful all the time I would have died'.

In a paper on trauma, the body and memory Goodwin and Attias (1999) illustrate how the body can be drawn into this dialectic between passive and active in subtle ways. They identified two types of somatic response. First they describe people who present in similar ways to Mae with puzzling, seemingly impossible to treat medical symptoms and a tendency to cling to idealised figures and magical solutions. Their hypothesis is that people in this group dissociate from the memory or emotional meaning of a traumatic event but retain the pain sensations, and they observed that 'the focus on the body in pain coupled with the effort to silence the real meaning of the pain sends the patient on an unending quest for a diagnosis' or for the 'perfect' doctor or treatment (Goodwin and Attias, 1999, p. 229). This dissociative strategy helps protect the self from overwhelm and enables a degree of normal 'getting on with life', albeit hampered by pain. It also confers 'a sense of specialness and offers some hope, if spurious, of controlling the body-self and its feelings through medical means'. There is also an important relational aspect to this pattern. The patients they studied had not only experienced some form of abusive assault in childhood but, critically, the natural emotional/relational sequence which should occur after a child is hurt: to cry out for Mum who, hopefully, comes quickly and offers restorative holding and mirroring, does not occur (1999, p. 227). When there is no comforting Mum or worse a mother who blames and humiliates, 'the attack moment merges into an abandonment [or shame] moment'. It is a moment of helplessness. The emotional and physical pain becomes too intense to be contained or integrated. Something has to be split off and the child is left feeling hurt, humiliated, isolated and bad about him or herself. We could speculate that he is also left with the seed of a hope which grows over time that one day a nurturing mother will arrive to comfort the hurt self (1999, p. 231). As Mae's story highlights, it is this magical hope which is hardest to relinquish.

An incident mentioned by Mae that stuck in my mind because of its shocking brutality provides a good example of the absence of the natural emotional/ relational soothing sequence. Mae described how one night her mother's current boyfriend flung her to the bottom of the stairs. She lay there in the dark, terrified and convinced that her back was broken. But she dare not call Mum. She was scared that the man would get even angrier and hurt them both and that Mum would also be cross with her. Instead she lay there all night, perhaps, one hopes, helped by her brain's natural ability to dissociate.

When I heard of this I thought of Mae's chronic back pain and how none of the tests and interventions that had been tried had succeeded in identifying the cause or bringing long-term relief. My speculation was that the pain spoke the language of traumatic memories and endorsed a child's belief that she deserved whatever 'got thrown at her'. It was interesting that when we explored Mae's responses to attachment events the pain often flared up. On one occasion, for example, she had been complaining about Clive announcing a plan to visit friends in America which meant he wouldn't be able to go on holiday with her after all. I asked Mae's response on hearing this. She said 'I couldn't breathe and my back went into spasm. I felt so let down.' Then a few days later she realised she was furious with him. I asked her to notice what was happening as she admitted to being angry. 'It's happening again', she said, 'everything has tensed up and my back hurts'. As we talked about anger making her anxious, about her efforts to hide her true feelings and about a childhood belief about not deserving good things, Mae noticed that her muscles had relaxed and the pain abated. It evoked her curiosity and the connection between thoughts, memories, responses to others and her body became something for us to explore in an ongoing way.

Goodwin and Attias's second characteristic response to relational trauma entails distancing from the body and silencing its message of pain by depersonalisation, ignoring, attacking or pushing oneself unrealistically, or alternatively trying to create an invulnerable, ideal body (1999, pp. 24, 231). People in this subgroup are often resolutely self-reliant and claim not to need anyone and that nothing is wrong in order to avoid facing the fear of seeking help and being rejected. They fit the characteristics of an avoidant attachment style, whereas people in the group that somatise are better described as anxious ambivalent, and people with a disorganised attachment style can display both ways of relating to the hurt body-self. The authors sum up their discussion by arguing that people in both categories may 'have developed a profound fear that without the pain-self or the invulnerable-self no one will be interested in connecting with the fully embodied self or in valuing and loving the person', and they suggest that recovery demands working through the body to access the memory of both the attack, the hurt and the abandonment by the person who should have cared (1999, pp. 235–6). This fits my own belief that for real change an approach which integrates mind, body and emotions is needed.

The self-care system

Another way to conceptualise people who are self-reliant, avoidant and hang on to grandiose beliefs about what they and their body can manage until, at some point, the bubble bursts and the child – or now adult – has to face the awareness of his or her limitations, is in terms of what Kalsched called the 'self-care system' (1996). He argued that it serves as an alternative to a needed attachment relationship and evolves as a way to protect the self in traumatic environments when the attachment figure is dangerous or unable to adequately protect the child. According to Howell, the self-care system provides two important things: 'an imaginative use of omnipotence to purvey hope and a self-structure that provides an automatic, effective, and often lifesaving coping strategy in a frightening or abusive interpersonal environment'. Through the use of dissociative strategies it 'generates a sense of psychic stability by creating illusory sources of protection and comfort'.

On the Hope Scale we could see this strategy as a more active, self-reliant form of non-mentalised hoping. The problem with the self-care system is that it is a closed one and the illusions, whether of personal self-sufficiency or of an omnipotent protector, 'are only temporarily helpful and must be continuously replenished. Without a benign enough connection to the interpersonal world, hope cannot last' (Howell, 2005, p. 221). The last point is important to my theme. For people who rely on 'if only' thinking the pursuit of the wished-for solution can be endless. This is often the territory of the addictive and the driven personality. The description of the self-care system will also resonate with anyone who works with people with dissociative disorders who has observed how tough, 'don't-need-anyone' parts of self often shield more vulnerable selves which hold the emotions and traumatic memories.

Let me return to the client who said if she hadn't been hopeful all the time she would have died. Pippa's 'closed system' began to break down in her 30s when she had her first child and disturbing memories began to break through the dissociative amnesia which shielded her as a child. Her generally benign connection to the interpersonal world, because she was someone with a good network of friends, became increasingly challenged as people and situations which held some echo of the people who had abused her between the ages of 2 and 5 began to trigger intense reactions. Pippa became fearful of those out-of-control moments. After one difficult, but certainly not unsafe, meeting with a challenging line manager, she came to therapy in distress. With tears and a hint of fear, she said 'the hopeful part of me has gone. I always thought I could do anything. Now I know I can't.'

Having empathised with how devastating that must feel, I asked if she could remember the moment when she vanished. Pippa thought, and said when her manager told her she did not think it was worth applying for a more senior position it felt as if hope died inside her. Then in a more childlike voice she said 'she took it away'. My hunch was that this was related to an earlier 'taking away of hope' – perhaps the result of an experience that suddenly plunged Pippa into helplessness or because of experiencing the confusion of abusers who were sometimes nice, but sometimes very frightening. However, it was not the right time to go deeper and ask who the manager reminded her of. Instead I reflected how what she had said had really knocked her and shared my belief that her hopeful self might not have gone entirely, but for some reason had gone into hiding. In Chapter 11 I shall return to Pippa's story and describe how my optimistic conviction was proved right. Now, however, I want to turn to a another example which illustrates the lifesaving nature of hoping and of a passive relationship to hope, but goes further in discussing one way in which the trauma survivor might try to turn passive into active.

Turning passive into active: using other people's hope

Eileen, a woman in her fifties, had been put in care from infancy, was adopted when she was 5 and then had a stormy relationship with her adopted parents.[1] She had 'gone off the rails' in her mid-teens after discovering alcohol and drugs. She ran away from home on a number of occasions and finally left for good at 16. In seeking places to stay she often ended up in abusive relationships. In her late twenties Eileen sought help. She went into rehab and slowly began to build a new life. She met her husband whilst there and they married quickly and had three children. At first Gerald seemed to be all that Eileen had ever wanted – someone who cared for her, who was strong and protective, who helped her set up a 'proper home'. But he slipped back into addiction after several periods of redundancy and became increasingly volatile. The illusion of the longed for 'happy family' began to crumble.

The focus of our discussions often centred on the conflict Eileen felt between a desperate wish to leave her husband because his violent outbursts scared her and an equally strong fear of living on her own. On one occasion I asked 'what keeps you going back? Is a part of you loyally waiting for Gerald to change?' Eileen responded by saying, 'I've always had hope. It's kept me going and to let go of hope with Gerald would be like cutting off a limb.' I said something about the difference between true hope and magical hoping. It was one of those 'too much in my head' comments because what I failed to take on board was how, as with Mae, as a child hoping kept Eileen going. Eileen's response, perhaps in protest at my lack of understanding, was to say that sometimes she used other people's hope.

What did Eileen mean by this? It was not clear at the time, but the phrase struck me and I have speculated on a number of possible meanings. It made me think of Bromberg's idea that first we see our potential in the eyes of others. *They* have to believe in it (Bromberg, 2011, p. 93). In the same way, perhaps people without hope need to see hope in the eyes of others and to hear it in their voices before they can internalise any sense of optimism about the future. I wondered who in the past might have inspired hope in Eileen, certainly no one in her birth or adopted families, and in the present, I specu- lated whether the musicians and artists Eileen hung out with offered some inspiration through their energetic approach to life. However, what also struck me was that the phrase 'I use other people's hope' suggests an attempt to turn passive into active. It would have felt very different if she had said 'so and so inspires me', in the sense that we can catch the energy and passion of another person and feel energised and motivated in turn. But this had an adhesive quality to it and made me think of Margot Waddell's distinction between the capacity for introjection – namely, being able to take in and identify with good and thoughtful aspects of our parents – and adhesive identification, where a child learns by way of imitation so that what is taken in has no lasting impact on the personality (1998, pp. 95–9). The latter is more likely to occur if a child has had limited experience of being held in mind by someone able to contain and make sense of his emotions – something which I am sure was lacking in the first years of Eileen's life. It reminds me of a point made by Shaw about the importance of experiencing oneself as a subject, rather than being objectified as a result of abuse and/or chronic failures of recognition. 'A sense of oneself as a subject', he writes, 'means knowing desire, and experiencing oneself as an agent capable of meaningful and productive action' (2013, p. 19).

Having a sense of herself as a subject who knew her own mind and could not just believe but feel in an embodied way that she was capable of mean- ingful and productive action was something my client Margie also struggled with. I talked about her earlier when discussing the distinction between a manic defence and a small sign of growth. If you recall, I had begun to notice a pattern of taking on new projects with excitement and enthusiasm, most of which sadly she could not complete. Each time what seemed to drive Margie, at least in part, was that she admired someone associated with that particular world, including me. I was aware of a struggle whenever she announced a new project between staying interested and encouraging, but also wanting to chal- lenge what seemed a naive confidence that she would succeed. I did not want to stifle her enthusiasm nor her hope. But I felt concerned about Margie biting off more than she could chew. In Chapter 4 I put forward the argument that there was a developmental need for me to see Margie as a woman who could be successful and that to have offered any cautions would have squashed these signs of something more alive and hopeful emerging. From the lens of the current discussion I might argue that we could think of this as another example of using other people's hopes as much as a need to be encouraged and believed in. We could also conceptualise Margie's ambitions as a form of 'pretend mode', a non-mentalising state in which there is no bridge between inner and outer reality. Feelings and ideas (and hopes?) are experienced as totally symbolic and have no implication for the world outside. Thus, Margie could dwell in her dream, and, interestingly, the active part of it was to read lots of 'how to' books and then talk to me about this enthusiastically. But what was lacking was much thinking about the journey between plan and outcome. My pragmatic (or spoilsport?) questions might have been: 'but how will you manage this when ... ?' 'Will it be tough?' 'What if things go wrong?' and 'how do you imagine your life at the end of the journey perhaps with a new qualification or role?' In the later stages of our work Margie did begin to question what she wanted to do with the rest of her life in a more thoughtful way. She also noticed that she had at that point become stuck in comparing herself with a friend who had also recently re-entered the world of study. With surprise it dawned on her that her journey did not have to follow the same course. For my part, it now felt possible to ask questions that I had held back, such as 'where would you like to be in five years' time?' and 'what do you need to do to get there?' and Margie responded thoughtfully as if owning the possibility of her own dreams for the first time. There was still a fluidity in her capacity for mentalising, but it felt as if Margie was now engaging in more realistic, creative and flexible hoping and imagining.

Reversal magic

The last example of non-mentalised hoping I want to mention is what Shabad calls 'reversal magic'. It represents another attempt to turn passive into active by moving from the role of victim to that of aggressor rather than, as in Margie's case, of identifying with an admired other. Shabad argues that if we see trauma as a disruptive wound to a person's continuity of being, then 'revenge seeks to undo the profound disillusionment of that insult and to regain the illusion of life flowing smoothly, as if it had never stopped'. It holds the illusory hope that the traumatic experience can be undone and the victim can begin again. However, he stresses that unless we confront the 'gnawing reminders' of our frailties and vulnerability, such fantasised solutions get repeated over and over again (2001, p. 106). 'It is not through the undoing of trauma', Shabad concludes, 'that one finds a sense of the real. It is only by securing a credible witness to one's experience that one can acknowledge finally the reality of the trauma and secure a new beginning' (2001, p. 108). This is an important point to which I shall return in Chapter 9, and it also reminds me of what Herman said about the trap of revenge and forgiveness fantasies. In her view both are attempts to gain a sense of power after experiences of complete helplessness. But rather than bringing relief, to dream of revenge actually exacerbates the victim's feelings of horror, whilst the fantasy of forgiveness becomes a cruel torment as it remains out of reach of most ordinary human beings. Herman argues that both also hinder mourning, a crucial stage in recovery (1994, pp. 188–90).

As is true of the self-care system, the fantasy of revenge keeps people in a closed system and can push them even further from that 'benign enough connection to the interpersonal world' that is really needed. For instance, as therapists we can struggle to feel empathy for someone who is constantly looking out for slights and talks about what he or she would like to do to attack back. Whilst we can feel shocked and outraged to hear about the ways in which, as a child, the client was wounded and genuine in supporting someone to become more assertive and challenge inappropriate treatment, we often feel pushed out when he or she persists in the wish for revenge. Trying to stay curious about how this might be a way to manage feeling overwhelmed and vulnerable is often the best way to stay present and compassionate. We, at least, don't have to neglect the scared, wounded part of self.

When it is adaptive not to hope

Not hoping can also protect the self. This seems a particular theme with clients who were severely abused or deprived of love and care as young children. As Napier explains, for some people hope can be a signal that bad things are about to happen or a reminder of being tricked, for instance like the little girl excited about being invited to a party by the kind man down the road until she discovered that at this party children got abused (1993, p. 194). If being noticed, doing well, relaxing, getting close to someone or having positive emotions got you into trouble in the past, it makes absolute sense to avoid them and never risk hoping for too much. Being aware of the risk in hoping can help us to understand and anticipate the way that with highly traumatised clients there is often a sudden backlash after moments of progress and hope. Such backlashes might include a dramatic dip in mood, an escalation of self-harm or suicidal feelings or some other form of self-sabotage or attack on the therapy. To the clinician, perhaps heartened by signs of improvement, this can lead to frustration, weariness and puzzlement unless we understand the reasons why someone might guard against hope. Davies and Frawley explain this from a psychodynamic perspective. 'Rather than waiting for the inevitable disappointment to occur, patients with sexual abuse histories', who they argue are generally terrified that good things cannot last and believe that promises will always ultimately be broken, 'often intervene in the build up of anxiety that accompanies hope by assuming control of the situation and shattering what they are convinced is only an illusion anyway' (1994, p. 174). They see these reversals and attacks on hope as an identification with the abuser. It repeats a pattern common in particularly sadistic forms of abuse and torture when the abuser deliberately offers grains of hope then cruelly takes that hope away, as was true for one neglected child who was given lovely presents on Christmas morning, only to have them taken away that night and never seen again.

Intersubjectively the therapist can end up being the one to be cruelly taunted whilst internally there may be a voice which repeats the taunting, dismissive voice of the abuser with phrases such as 'you're a loser', 'so you think you're smart huh?' Whilst this verbal onslaught undermines confidence and self-esteem, functionally what some trauma theorists call a 'protector/persecutor part of self' is trying to shield the hopeful, creative self from further disappointment (Howell, 2005; van der Hart et al., 2006; Shaw, 2013, p. 8). Even if not with these words, it is saying 'don't believe in yourself. Don't risk hoping. You'll only be hurt again.' As one woman reminded me, 'if you allow hope it hurts worse'. The repetitive cycle of hope/no-hope can certainly include elements of self-attack. However, I would argue that it need not be an identification, but simply a repeat of an ingrained pattern – Siegel's 'anticipatory models'. For instance, it could echo how the abused child experienced periods of hope when the perpetrator was surprisingly kind or stopped abusing for one reason or another and then was massively disillusioned when things changed for the worse. Perhaps initially respite would enable the survival brain to go offline and the child could rest or play freely. But over time he would learn to be hypervigilant, perhaps especially during periods of calm. Silence or smiles can become signals for caution. If we think of this in terms of neural patterns, hope and excitement can be paired with mounting anxiety and hence stimulate the fear rather than the care or pleasure circuits in the brain. With this in mind it makes sense when our clients sometimes behave in counter-intuitive ways.

There is a survival logic in the severely abused child learning not to trust or to hope. From my experience, the same is true when a child, for whatever reason, had to go into care or was adopted.[2] Remember the poignant story mentioned earlier of how Pam learnt that it was 'better not to get her hopes up' as a result of the experience of not being given the promised teddy. But this is symptomatic of bigger let downs experienced by children in care – of hoping that each new foster home would provide the 'forever family' or of finding one's birth parents or, having made contact with them, of being welcomed back into their lives, then crashing into despair or bitter anger when these hopes were not met. Pam was certainly not the only adoptee I have worked with who was cynical about hoping for anything from others, and this makes sense given the devastating wound of that first betrayal.

Another type of early environment that can foster the strategy of eschewing hope is one in which the child is disconfirmed. Bill, the man discussed in Chapter 3, was certainly all too familiar with hopelessness after a childhood where he was not seen and prized for the creative child that he was and after a number of debilitating episodes of depression as an adult. As our work progressed he became more optimistic and energised about future plans. But it was a snakes and ladders process. One week, perhaps 10 months into the therapy, Bill arrived excited. Things were going well, but he said that it felt odd and asked how he could cope with being happy and accept this as OK. We agreed to be curious about Bill's tendency to discount his achievements and he realised that when I encouraged him to celebrate his successes his first thought was, 'but that's a bit conceited'. 'Whose words are those?' I asked. 'Mine' he replied, 'but it comes from all the times I heard people saying "you'll never amount to much" or "if you're not careful, you'll end up like uncle Bob"' – the black sheep of the family. When I invited Bill to notice what happened in his body when I repeated those words back to him he realised that he felt sick then angry that anyone should say such things to a child. We talked about children's need for encouragement and how that motivates us. Rather sadly, he said that he never expects much because of those early messages. 'How do you think not expecting much helps?' I asked. Bill replied: 'if you minimise your expectations, you don't get disappointed'. I agreed, 'it protects you from the pain of disappointment. But might not hoping also cause problems?' He looked thoughtful as if appreciating something for the first time. 'If you don't expect much, you don't try to achieve.'

Ilse was another client who was not recognised and cherished for who she was as a child and who, in contrast to Bill's more collapsed, depressed view of the future, presented as deeply cynical and emotionally avoidant. It was rare for her to show much emotion other than anger, but one session sticks in my mind because she allowed herself to cry and risk being more in contact with me. I had noticed how several times Ilse had mentioned having nothing to go back to after a social event and asked if that was also true as a child – to have no one to go back to and share what she had been doing? Rather angrily she retorted 'who'd have listened!' Then more thoughtfully Ilse told me that when she was six she won a school prize. She ran home eager to tell her Mum. Mum said 'that's good'. But she did not look at Ilse or ask to see the prize. Instead she turned her attention to Ilse's brother and proceeded to ask him about his day. I shared my sadness and shock that Mum didn't share her excitement and between tears Ilse explained that she had thought that this time Mum would be pleased. It was then she decided that she was never going to try again. 'Once you've realised however hard you try care doesn't come, you give up, and even if sometimes you do get attention, because it's too painful to have a tiny bit of it, you decide it's better not to have any at all.' I now understood why Ilse was always pushing people away and was so rejecting of my empathy. Sadly, the position of not expecting much and deciding that a 'tiny bit' is worse than nothing is all too familiar for many troubled and desperate clients who have had numerous setbacks in relationships, in their attempts to create a better life and on the road to recovery.

Hope destroyed: despair and the wish to die

Hope was my friend. I trusted her.
With hope as my companion I thought I could do anything I wanted.
Then they stole my hope.
With one withering glance they knocked her flat.

Their words – that one sentence – crushed the life out of her.
And I discovered that the worst torture of all is when people kill your hope.

Let me turn now to the last position in Table 6.1. For some people there comes a point when, like a candle flame, the hope they have clung to for so long gutters and dies. Hope atrophies when people feel utterly trapped by their situation; when they have tried and tried, but encountered blocks and setbacks; when they have been badly let down yet again or have endured cumulative losses. As one woman lamented, 'how can bad things keep happening to me? Won't they ever give me a break?' Hope can be destroyed early in life as a result of overwhelming traumatic experiences and losses and it can be eroded by later life traumas and adversities. Remember Bowlby's sequence from protest to despair to detachment (1989, p. 48). When hope has been destroyed what I have observed is that people fluctuate between states of painful despair and numb detachment. If the pain becomes too much, then shutting down mind and body enables the individual to carry on a little longer in a mechanical, shadow-like way. Being with someone in either state challenges our own hope and confidence, especially when this goes on week after week. We begin to parrot lame reassurances and scrabble around for ideas about what might help. We too can feel very alone and, like our client, find ourselves with few words to describe what this is like.

In this section I shall draw again on examples from my work in an endeavour to give words to states that often defy language. I also refer to written material which has helped me to conceptualise the state of Hope Destroyed and the links between the loss of hope and suicidal thinking. Before going further it is worth reiterating that to experience horrific events can leave people helpless and hopeless 'as they perceive a random and chaotic world where nothing is predictable or safe' and can lead to a 'loss of sustaining faith' and 'sense of hopelessness and despair' (van der Hart et al., 1993, p. 23; Herman, 1994, p. 121). This was certainly true for Sonia. Her hope had been eroded by the cumulative effect of abuse, witnessing domestic violence plus repeated shocks and experiences that could not be assimilated. This included responses from others that led to lasting feelings of shame and rejection. For instance, when Sonia tried to tell her mother about the abuse she slapped her and yelled that she was a slut. On another occasion she told a neighbour to keep an eye on Sonia because of her 'sleeping around'. Sonia was left with an indelible belief that something was wrong with her and that she must be inviting the abuse. From Sonia I learned that intensely shaming, rejecting experiences like this compound the loss of hope because in those moments the individual feels utterly abandoned. Sonia's story also included a series of bereavements, from her father onwards, of the few people to whom she had allowed herself to become attached. In the second year of our work her youngest son was killed in a car crash. Sonia became reluctant to get close to anyone ever again and as a result became increasingly isolated. One day when we spoke about hope Sonia said 'I gave up hope a long time ago.' Hoping frightened her.

Another thing I have learned from Sonia and other survivors of childhood abuse is how horrific it is to be plagued by intrusive flashbacks. Even when her external circumstances seemed a little better, Sonia would be haunted by vivid visual and sensory reminders of what had happened to her. Many were the times when she asked, 'why can't you get rid of them?' Like other trauma survivors, because of the brain's failure to fully process and store traumatic memories, she had become trapped in an endless present in which the past refused to go away. Imagine the content of your worst nightmare and not being able to shake it from your mind. Imagine what it must be like to be unable to look at faces without seeing the taunting eyes of the person who terrified you as a child; to be haunted by images of the sexual depravities that you were forced to witness; to be unable to eat certain foods without gagging because of what was stuffed into your mouth when you were small. Imagine jumping at unexpected sounds; sweating profusely when you encounter men of a particular build; feeling small and scared as soon as night falls or needing to avoid certain places because of the memories they evoke. My list could go on because for the trauma survivor very ordinary objects and activities are laden with meaning. And all the time she is trying, as best she can, to live a normal life – often deeply ashamed of the images and thoughts that trouble her and desperately trying to hide the fact that anything is wrong. 'How could I tell anyone?' 'They'll think I'm mad.' 'They wouldn't want to be with me.' Thus shame compounds what already feels unbearable. That such people pin their hope on miracle solutions, use intoxicating substances to obliterate their suffering or turn to thoughts of death as something that *could* make a difference is understandable, and because psychotherapy does not offer a 'quick fix', helping them and ourselves retain a measure of hope as they move between states of unreachable detachment and suicidal despair can be a challenge.

Suicidal despair and the wish for something to end

Let us look more closely at suicidal despair. Jayne Haynes (2007) wrote a particularly moving and honest account of her relationship with a chronically suicidal patient. Reading their conversation about 'Miss Suicide's' last and unexpectedly transformative attempt to take her life, I was struck by the parallels between what she said and my own desperate and at times suicidal clients. For instance, after describing how agonising it was to get through each day and longing for the moment when she could legitimately drug herself to sleep, Miss Suicide said, 'I remember sitting on the sofa thinking, what can I do? You know, and waiting for the magical cure – the Road to Damascus – this is what I need to get better or whatever.' She described spending a small fortune consulting clairvoyants. 'I just wanted them to talk to me – all I wanted was reassurance.' Here note the desperate relational need for someone to offer some hope, both in a comforting way, but also in showing her how to climb out of the abyss of depression. Later Miss Suicide spoke about her state of mind before the overdose. What strikes me is both what this says about being trapped in an endless present and that a suicide attempt often represents not a wish to end life, but to put a stop to unendurable suffering. 'I knew ... that I could not stand it any longer. I can't handle it. I can't live like this, this existence forever.' 'I didn't want to kill myself ever. I just couldn't stand the pain and isolation' (Haynes, 2007, pp. 160–2, 172).

I believe it is important to keep asking the meaning of suicidal thinking and to explore the suicide fantasy or narrative. Otherwise we risk responding to one non-mentalising state with another (Holmes, 2010, p. 136; Little, 2009). Our responses to clients who have seemingly no hope and want to give up will be discussed in Chapter 8. If a client trusts that we will not panic nor reject him he will often let us know how suicide – the 'escape hatch' or 'get out of jail card' – has always given him comfort.[3] Sonia, for instance, told me that in her teens the thought that 'if it gets any worse, I'll kill myself' helped her to survive. She explained she was not afraid of dying. 'It means that I'll find some peace.' She would have agreed with Nietzsche's words: 'the thought of suicide is a great comfort. With it a calm passage is to be made across many a bad night' (cited in Holmes, 2010, p. 135). This need for comfort is even more crucial if you are a child feeling very alone and afraid. As Napier pointed out, 'for children who are overwhelmed by trauma it's almost inevitable to believe that to die would solve everything. It's as though thinking about suicide becomes a source of soothing, a safety valve or insurance policy that says that at least you have the power to stop it all if you choose' (1993, p. 151). Despite the emotional pain she lived through, Sonia had never tried to take her life. The image of peace *was* her hope, the imagined better future. Would she have tried if she did not have children she cared about? I don't know. As life became bleaker with the loss of her son, she would often say 'when no one needs me anymore, then it will be time to go'. Sonia gave no impression of resenting these ties. But for some people the reasons why they can't die add to the sense of being trapped and to their despair. 'Even that way out is barred!'

Holmes argued that 'in every completed suicide or serious suicide attempt there is still the hope of survival, however miniscule' and he assumes that 'all seriously suicidal people somewhere in their deepest being, have not entirely given up on hope' (2010, p. 136). It may be the hope of peace, or for reassurance or for the long-yearned chance to be seen and loved for who they are. For example, I knew that Sonia still secretly hoped that one day her mother would renounce her stepfather and say she was sorry: in other words, that she would finally show love to her dutiful daughter. However, as Sonia allowed herself to face the reality of the latter's ongoing narcissistic demands and to acknowledge her anger, she began to slowly let go this long-held dream. When we feel ourselves to be slipping into despair about a client, it is important that we hold in mind that a hidden part of the client may still hold hope or that, as Holmes says, her hope may have been 'temporarily located in us for safe keeping'. If we also take on board his point that 'suicide is triggered by a disturbance or collapse in an individual's attachment network' and bear in mind that somewhere there will be a relational element to the suicidal thoughts, this can also bolster our faith that what we are offering, simply in being there, is far from useless (2010, pp. 150, 136). It can help us to stay connected to our clients and their suffering and to avoid falling into the traps of 'I've got to do something' or 'I'm going to give up because there's absolutely nothing I can do.'[4]

The paradox that people who contemplate suicide can simultaneously be hopeless yet still hold hope and the connection with a relational element is interesting. I noticed this with another client who had known the wish for suicide for as long as he could remember. Rees recalled how at boarding school he would hide in a locker room crying and wishing he could die. It was a school with a sadistically bullying culture and Rees was mercilessly picked on. He found it hard to make friends. He was desperately lonely. His repeated calls to his parents begging to come home were not listened to. Rees's father was strict and believed you should 'man up' and get on with life. Sometimes he also bullied Rees. His mother was always preoccupied and never seemed to have space in her mind for her only child. There seemed no way out for Rees. By the time he came to therapy Rees had already made several unsuccessful suicide attempts and had been on medication for depression and severe anxiety for years. The first occasion was when, in his twenties, he felt trapped in a job where he was repeatedly ignored by colleagues and criticised by the manager. He believed everyone was laughing at him and the more he tried to connect, the more inadequate and isolated he felt. Everyone seemed to know what was required to make friends. Rees had no idea.

Physical problems compounded Rees's misery. He developed a degenerative eye condition which meant that the few things that gave him pleasure like photography and reading became increasingly difficult. In his forties Rees was diagnosed with rheumatoid arthritis. By his fifties any physical activity left him in pain for days. There seemed to be less and less to live for. 'I can't go on.' 'I've had enough', were words I often heard. Then one day Rees arrived looking curiously happy. 'I've found a way to die', he said with a smile. 'There's a place where people understand why you want to and help you.' He had heard about Dignitas and looked it up. I asked Rees how that left him feeling. 'It would feel so different to die with someone there – not alone in a goddam hole.' I felt very connected to Rees in that moment and deeply sad to appreciate yet again the depths of his aloneness. 'You so want someone to be there for you don't you?' I said. 'That's something you've always been seeking.' His eyes welled, but he smiled. 'It's odd, you know. Knowing it's there ... maybe I don't want to go just yet.'

What Rees said is significant. It is as if the thought that he could be supported whilst dying, should he reach a point when life became unbearable, gave him enough hope to continue. Why should this be? In an article about assisted suicide, Catherine Jackson (2014) presented a spectrum of views from professionals who work with the dying. The theme of being able to determine and control one's own life and death stands out. For instance, Rachel Freeth, a psychiatrist and person-centred counsellor, commented on people who stockpile medication. 'It gives them a sense of control. They feel there is a way out. They do have the means.' This is something I have also observed. Freeth also believes it is the lack of control that perpetuates feeling hopeless and which lies at the heart of mental disturbance.

Another therapist, Judy Parkinson, who works with the terminally ill, said 'some people who are dying want to feel in control of the process. They feel that they have lost all control, or a lot of it, of their physical body, their relationships, that they are not in charge of their daily life anymore because they are so ill. Therefore anything that gives them a sense that there is something they can do to be in control might be important to them' (Jackson, 2014). The same could be said of people with chronic, severe mental and physical health problems, including PTSD. Because of survival brain dominance, the legacy of trauma can also entail feeling that the body is out of control and getting through the day can be a nightmare.

It seems significant that of those who access Dignitas and go through the process of assessments and counselling, only 14 per cent go on to the stage of assisted suicide (Jackson, 2014). Like Rees, Sonia and people who hoard medication, perhaps they feel some comfort knowing it's there as an option if things really get too bad. But perhaps more than that, is it that their long-held, secret wish suddenly becomes 'relationable' – something that can be spoken about with another human being? And if one of the things that has progressively driven someone to the depths of suicidal despair is a profound sense of aloneness, then this is hugely important. But in the telling there is risk. Might the listener be angry? alarmed? panic? withdraw? perhaps say that he should be sectioned? Or can the response be empathic and open up dialogue, rather than closing it down? Again this is why reflecting on our responses and trying to avoid the traps of giving up or being pulled into action is so important.

When one young woman, Magda, went through periods when, in her words, there was no fight left in her and she just wanted to die, I caught some of her despair. I had tried everything I could think of to help her manage the intense anxiety and obsessive thoughts which plagued her. But nothing seemed to work. I could see how hard it was for her to get through an hour without resorting to self-harm or compulsive rituals, let alone a whole day. I also knew how demoralised she felt at the seeming impossibility of completing her studies. Sometimes I fell into teleological mode and got busy trying to 'find solutions'. I clung to 'if only' hopes. At other times I felt at a loss and useless. Yet I held in mind what Magda said after one prolonged phase of suicidal despair: 'I don't think I'd have got through the last few months if you hadn't been there.' It reminded me of something far more important than responding to the pull to act – of the need for us to 'go into the fire' with our clients, to demonstrate our willingness to understand and bear the pain with them.

There is an unbearable loneliness about suffering something endless whilst trying to keep up the appearance of an apparently normal life. This was something familiar, but in different ways, to Sonia, Rees and Magda. And as 'beings-in-relationship', we can gain some comfort if we know that we are not alone, that someone understands or that others have been through this. But what if this is not the case? With another woman our connection felt more tenuous. I knew there were parts of her that really could not trust me. This was understandable because Melinda had been the victim of ritual abuse for the entirety of her childhood. So I worried when occasionally she went off for days, knowing that a suicidal part of her may have taken over. However, I also knew she carried around a picture I had given her. It was a small stick figure – me with my arms held out reaching to pull her back.

I recall a profoundly sad and shocking moment when Melinda had been denying that she had horrifying flashbacks and frequently dissociated. 'It's not real', she pronounced. 'It's just me. I'm crazy.' 'What would be the worst thing if this was real?' I asked. After a long pause she whispered, 'it would be that those things really did happen to me'. 'And if you were to accept that terrible things happened to you as a child, what would be the worst thing about that?' I continued. 'Then there wouldn't be anything that was normal – not then or now'. Melinda's words punched the silence. I was aware of a strong impulse to point to certain aspects of her life and say, 'but look, this is normal and this ...', because it was unbearable to contemplate a life where nothing had ever been 'normal', and perhaps one of my not quite conscious hopes for Melinda was that at some point she could enjoy a life that was more humdrumly ordinary. But I said 'thinking there's nothing that's normal must feel very lonely'. Melinda nodded. I then spoke of my impulse, but added that I knew that the most important thing was for us both to bear the sadness of those unbearable truths. And the more I work, the more I appreciate that something shifts when we stop trying to make things better, for to feel truly understood offers a bridge to a more relational world. Robert Hobson wrote: 'in loneliness we are inarticulate. There are no words. That is the agony. We cannot speak our loneliness.' He also observed, 'we can feel helpless as we apprehend the loneliness of another' (1985, pp. 267, 271). In that moment with Melinda I believe that there was an implicit shared moment of helplessness and loneliness and that owning my impulse was as important as sharing my understanding of the enormity of facing a world in which nothing is normal. In such a world no wonder our deeply traumatised and troubled clients cling to magical hopes and desperate solutions.

Notes

1. It is interesting that Eileen also had ongoing physical complaints that had no clear cause.
2. Such children may, of course, have also experienced some form of abuse – sometimes by their birth parents and sometimes in their new foster or adopted homes.

3. There may also be more aggressive aspects to the suicidal fantasies, for instance, one part of self wanting to kill off another despised, vulnerable part or the hated body. But again there is a hope of an idealised state beyond this (see Little, 2009).
4. I am not implying here that we do nothing when it is imperative for a client's wellbeing. We always need to be guided by the principles of beneficence and non-maleficence.

7

Despair, Dissociation and Shifting Self-States

Which version of you will come through my door today? And who will leave?
Which of my different selves will stir as you tell me your pain? How many
times must we dance together through hope and despair? And if I'm willing to
face the entirety of myself, will you – one day – find who you truly are?

I ended the last chapter by relating a small, but important, interaction between myself and a woman who had been repeatedly and brutally traumatised. As I got to know more about Melinda's troubled inner world and to encounter some of the 'not-me' parts of self that held memories and emotions which had to be dissociated in order to survive and manage daily life, it became clear that different 'parts of self' were more or less hopeless. With other deeply traumatised and dissociative clients I have also observed that there are distinct hopeful and hopeless parts of self, and even people we would not think of as being dissociative often have multiple relationships to hope and can move between the different positions outlined in this chapter. They may oscillate between clinging to a hoped-for solution and then denying hope within the space of a few moments, or the shifts might occur across longer expanses of time. The fluctuations may be dependent on mood and state of mind or they may, I suspect, often be influenced by what is going on relationally.

In this chapter the focus is on how the fluctuating dance between hope and despair gets played out internally. I want to expand upon the argument that we can all have multiple relationships to hope and that when life events overwhelm us in some way we can move between the different positions on the Hope Scale. I also intend to explore the interconnectedness between hopelessness, vulnerability, blame and shame and to discuss how for some highly traumatised people these emotional states are held by discrete parts of self. Sometimes we defend against the feelings of vulnerability and inadequacy that are frequently associated with dashed hopes and stuckness by resorting to blame – blaming others and implying that it's their responsibility to do something; locating fault in ourselves and savagely attacking our perceived frailties. Sometimes, as earlier examples have illustrated, hopelessness shifts rapidly into shame. My discussion will be based on my experiences working with people who move rapidly in and out of dissociated parts of self, and I will draw on two models to make sense of this multiplicity as well as referring to the work of experts in the field of trauma and of relational analysts such as Mitchell and Bromberg who approach the subject of multiple self-organisation from a different standpoint.

Dissociation in the service of preserving hope

Before going further let me outline my understanding of the concepts of multiplicity and dissociation, which is based on a synthesis of several helpful, but differing in emphasis, definitions. We now have a far greater appreciation of how normal it is to shift states of consciousness. As Mitchell notes, 'because we learn to become a person through interactions with different others and different interactions with the same other, our experience of self is discontinuous, composed of different configurations, different selves with different others' and he cites Sullivan's suggestion that 'we operate in "me-you patterns", never singularly, always in relation, and we tend to form very discrete "me-you patterns" in different circumstances'. We have an illusory sense of continuity. But 'we are all composites of overlapping, multiple organizations and perspectives' (1993, pp. 104–6). These different versions of self, Mitchell continues, 'may not only be encoded in different language systems, but ... may be accompanied by and experienced in different physiological states as well'. Thus 'happy [hopeful] versions of self are often distinctly different, emotionally and physically from depressed [hopeless] versions of self' (1993, p. 105).[1] I have added my own words in parentheses because this accords with my argument about distinct hopeful and hopeless parts of self. I should also emphasise that our shifting self-states are not only deeply embedded in relational contexts, but the body itself contributes to our multiplicity. For instance, it is not just that different states manifest with different physical presentations, but that if we are unwell, in pain, tired or very hungry we can easily move into one of our least coping and less hopeful selves. I cannot be alone in inhabiting a more childlike me if I am physically out-of-sorts and I know that both positive and negative body experiences can alter my mood and self-state.

Our capacity for multiplicity enables us to enact the different roles we have in the world and adapt to a constantly changing environment (Howell, 2011, p. 32). Usually, despite the discontinuities we can still 'recognise all these differences as versions of a more or less invariant myself' and, as Bromberg so beautifully put it, are still able 'to stand in the spaces between realities without losing any of them' (Mitchell, 1993, p. 107; Bromberg, 1996, p. 274). However, standing in the spaces is far harder if one's earliest experiences are of a traumatic world in which others are frightening, frightened and contradictory. Rather than a fluid shifting of self-states, a closed self-system can evolve in which there is a lack of integration between mind and body and different systems of memory, and connection between self-states is impeded (Howell, 2011, p. 33).

Although chronic dissociation is problematic, as a process dissociation is one of the ingenious and highly adaptive ways that our nervous system has evolved in order to survive extreme, overwhelming situations, whether this be unendurable pain or states of terror which threaten the integrity of the self. It entails a rapid alteration of consciousness and the splitting off or compartmentalisation of aspects of our experience into isolated fragments. Although dissociation enables people to escape mentally from traumatic situations when actual escape is impossible and to carry on afterwards in an apparently normal way, the disruption of normal integrative processing makes it difficult to experience things as a coherent, ongoing self. Certain aspects of experience become separated off into 'an alienated, not-me domain' and remain unassimilated or unformulated (Allen, 2001, p. 185). In consequence, the borders between reality and fantasy and between what is external and internal become very blurred.

Although it used to be generally thought that dissociation was primarily a defence against extreme stress and trauma, recent research on disorganised attachment indicates that the caregiving context is likely to play a bigger role in habitual dissociation than previously thought and that a disorganised attachment style increases the likelihood for dissociative reactions to later traumas (Liotti, 2004; Lyons-Ruth et al., 2006). It offers a vulnerability model showing how when a mother offers highly contradictory responses to her infant's attachment cues this sets up multiple internal working models. In other words, the child will have one mental blueprint of how to respond when Mum is like this and another when she acts like that.[2] The child cannot integrate a coherent sense of self or of others. This impedes the development of adequate capacities for emotional regulation and for mentalisation – indeed how can you contemplate the contents of another's mind when there is no logic for how that person responds? I would argue that it also impedes healthy imagining and hoping as opposed to being stuck in a pre-symbolic form of fantasising and non-mentalised hoping.[3]

The most charged situation is when a caregiver is both the source of and the solution to the child's alarm and the defence and attachment systems are simultaneously triggered. Putting this into more subjective language, the infant's experience may go something like this: *'I'm feeling uncomfortable. It's getting overwhelming. I need Mum. Eventually she comes when I cry. But her face, which a few moments earlier was smiling, suddenly frightens me. It is a look of fear (or anger). I feel even more overwhelmed. The feeling is unstoppable. There is nothing I can do except look away and switch off.'* Repeated experiences of feeling scared of, yet desperately needing to turn to, a caregiver for support can lead to habitual states of what Bowlby (1989) would have called detachment, but we can now view as some form of dissociation or fragmentation of experience.

From the perspective of current theories about dissociation, Howell argues that in the phase of detachment what is defended against or kept sequestered from the rest of consciousness is the experience of the 'lost, terrified, abandoned child' (2005, pp. 57–8). To appreciate how areas of experience can become sequestered is, I believe, crucial to an understanding of why people can have multiple relationships to hope. It can help us comprehend how clinging to illusory hopes can protect our traumatised clients from really facing the pain of loss or getting in touch with the self who was terrified and helpless. Not hoping also makes sense when considered through the lens of dissociative splitting because to risk hope and venture towards something new also demands acknowledging and grieving the childhood that never happened. Our psyche needs an 'emotional circuit breaker' which shuts down and shuts out emotional states that threaten to overwhelm us. What is understood less is that dissociation can also help to preserve hope. At one level we could think of this as like keeping a tiny treasure deeply hidden until it might be safe enough to bring it out, and as therapists I believe that we are deeply privileged when the survivor of trauma trusts enough to tell us the secret of a fantasy that gave him solace on the darkest days.[4] At another level we could argue that if the 'bad' can be excluded from consciousness and the body-mind is insulated from being overwhelmed then the person can face the world and its challenges, albeit in a constricted way.

The internal dance of structural dissociation

A model I find helpful to make sense of multiplicity is that of structural dissociation – a trauma model based on the underlying premise that we all shift self-states according to context, both external and internal, but that the more traumatic the experience the more out of awareness, fragmented and rigidified these shifts can be. At its simplest, structural dissociation entails a splitting into two mental systems: First, there is what some writers call the 'apparently normal personality' (ANP) but I prefer to call the 'getting on with life' or 'daily-life' self, which appears to manage everyday demands, but has failed to integrate the traumatic experiences (van der Hart et al., 2006, pp. 46–57). Then there are other 'emotional or traumatised personalities' (EPs) that hold split off memories and feelings. The daily-life self may remember nothing about the trauma or have only partial memories and is likely consciously and unconsciously to avoid anything that might lead to remembering. When people are in daily-life mode, although they may present as efficient and business-like, they can be chronically numb; lack in optimism, enthusiasm and imagination and lead a rather constricted life. A habitual numbing of awareness, sensation and emotion enables the survivor of childhood trauma to go to school, college and later work as if nothing was wrong. However, because fragments of traumatic memory often intrude through the dissociative barrier, such people can also grapple with hyperarousal, hypervigilance and intense anxiety which can lead to avoidance of many aspects of the social world including an avoidance of intimacy and emotion. An example of this is a client who in daily-life mode had always worked hard, but in very routine ways and with limited social contacts. His life was typified by his habit of keeping his head down when he was out and never looking directly at others. In this way he missed seeing things that were interesting or might give pleasure but also, crucially, signs that could update his survival brain with new information – information that 'now' was very different to back then; that people's faces could be neutral or kind rather than hostile and ridiculing. Because of this failure to orient to the present the man was often triggered and could rapidly slip into a more dissociated state. However, not all trauma survivors have such avoidant daily-life selves. I have also encountered people, like Pippa for example, who appear highly optimistic and energetic when in getting-on-with-life mode, people who get things done and are sometimes very active campaigners which is perhaps a sublimation of their own unmet needs and hopes as a child, and I would contend that in such cases it is likely that as well as horror, pain and vulnerability being split off, so too are states of hopelessness and helplessness.

Whilst the daily-life self remembers too little, the 'emotional personalities' remember too much. These sequestered parts are stuck in the past; experiencing things and acting as if the traumas and relationship failures are still happening. This is because operationally they are driven by the defensive action systems: fight, flight, freeze, submit and attach for survival,[5] which are hard-wired into the brain as part of our evolutionary heritage (van der Hart et al., 2006; Panksepp, 1988). Remember my point in Chapter 3 that when the defensive systems are 'on line' the daily life systems will be inhibited. This evolutionary, psychobiological perspective can help us to understand the logic of splits and conflicts between parts of self devoted to performing the functions of daily life and others designed to promote survival.

Another way to consider the segregation into self-states is to adopt a relational perspective. Each part of self will operate in terms of certain 'me-you patterns' or internal working models which are based on how we have learnt to be with others from birth onwards. In addition to being associated with particular defensive and relational patterns, the different EPs often have very different views about the world and the future and take contradictory positions on the Hope Scale. Some parts appear more hopeful, others more hopeless and helpless. Whilst generalisations fail to capture the uniqueness of each individual's story and the ways he or she learned to adapt, a hypothetical schema is provided in Table 7.1.

The dominant 'me-you pattern' of 'fight' parts is one of mistrust, defensiveness and self-reliance.[6] They can be hostile and denigratory towards others, quick to take offence or cynical and self-righteous. They may be very cynical about hope or cling to dreams of compensation and revenge. Intrapsychically, they can be judgemental and persecutory towards other parts of self. For instance, this is the critical voice that pours scorn on perceived weaknesses – a voice which many traumatised and troubled clients know all too well. Vulnerability of any sort cannot be tolerated. Attachment needs and emotions are

Table 7.1 Structural Dissociation and the Hope Scale

	RELATIONAL STYLE	RELATIONSHIP TO HOPE	POSITIONS ON THE HOPE SCALE
Getting on with life self	Relate through tasks and roles Detached	Detached, pragmatic and may lack enthusiasm and imagination or be highly optimistic	Non-mentalised hope Self-reliant
Fight	Mistrust Hostile Self-reliant	Hopes for revenge or is cynical about hope	Adaptive not to hope
Flight	Avoid intimacy and commitment	'If only' solutions. Pin hopes on substances or exit strategies	Non-mentalised hope
Freeze	Terror of others	Terror destroys all hope	Hope destroyed
Submit	Fit in Please others Caretaker role Shame based Compare self unfavourably with others	Chronic Hopelessness 'I don't deserve' Identification with hopes of abusers	Adaptive not to hope or Hope destroyed
Attach	Cling to others	Hopes for a rescuer to take care of me. 'One day I'll get the love I crave'	Non-mentalised hope Passive Relational

derided as being weak. Meanwhile 'flight' parts, as one might expect, tend to be avoidant of intimacy and of emotions. They dislike commitments and can back off if others, therapists included, get too close. On the Hope Scale they are more likely to adopt a non-mentalised position and go for magical 'if only' solutions, but unlike attach parts, these are less likely to be relational hopes. For instance, when flight is dominant people pin their hopes on substances or exit strategies. 'If I could only get out of this relationship, job, house ... life, then things would be better.' Here bear in mind that suicidal thinking often represents a wish for change. 'If I could kill this body, then I'll find an easier life.' Bear in mind too that 'if only' thinking is part of human nature and on a spectrum we all engage in fantasies about how much better things might be if only we could escape or be rid of certain aspects of our lives.

When we encounter a 'freeze' part it often feels as if we are in the presence of a terrified and desperate child. This self generally holds the most frightening memories, which emerge in the form of nightmares and flashbacks, and has learned to be incredibly wary of others. A word or gesture on our part can throw the client into a state of mute, catatonic terror. In a moment he or she can feel very unreachable. My belief is that for this self terror has destroyed all hope. When caught in freeze, time becomes an eternity – as if the self is cast adrift, exiled in the vastness of space. There is no belonging; no 'bigger, stronger, wiser, kind' adult to hold onto for understanding and security – and so how can there be a future?

'Submit' parts are also trapped in the subjective experience of not belonging, but in a different way. Here shame is the dominant emotion rather than fear, and shame leads to a wish to hide and not be noticed. When in this self-state the individual tends to be compliant, always trying to please and rarely asserting himself or saying no. He tends to compare himself unfavourably with others and is always on the lookout for potential disapproval. Submit or minimising harm, as pointed out in Chapter 3, is an immobilising defence which leads to shut down, depressed states – remember Bill – and either to a lack of motivation or to working hard but in a 'going through the motions' way. Things might be achieved, but inspire little joy or interest. Chronic hopelessness is the territory of this self and it is exacerbated when the individual oscillates between shame and terror. There is so little energy or imagination to hope for something different and when something potentially new does emerge beliefs about 'not deserving' can sabotage pursuing the goal. Because of their fine-tuned capacity for compliance children who needed to resort to submission in order to survive may also have identified with the hopes and beliefs of their abusers or narcissistically disconfirming parents. Like Bill they will have internalised messages about 'not amounting to much' or that they will only be worthwhile if they are like their parents or loyal to the family culture.

Turning to the final category, attach is the part of self that clings to the hope of one day getting the love and care so long yearned for. This is the child who, like Mae, found comfort in fantasies of rescue and loyally waited for a loving Mum to turn up, and even if other parts of self are cynical and mistrusting of others, as adults the rescue fantasies can break through. When someone is in attach mode he or she can appear childlike, appealing, needy and dependent.

The survival logic of attacking, blaming states of mind

To sum up what has been said so far, a fundamental lack of safety and repeated experiences of being alone, terrified and helpless lie at the heart of the structural dissociation of the personality. The individual adapts in the best ways he or she can to prevent further harm, to avoid potentially overwhelming emotions and to maintain a semblance of 'normal' life. In some cases this leads to fragmentation into discrete parts of self which coalesce around very different ways of relating to the world and strategies for protecting the self. A key aspect of structural dissociation is that it leads to inner conflicts and confusion. The protective strategies and beliefs of different parts of the personality can be so at odds that survivors of severe trauma often lack a coherent, ongoing sense of self. They find it hard to know their own minds and who they are.[7] Moreover, because the traumatised EPs can hijack the daily-life self and his or her endeavours and because these conflicts and intrusions can feel 'crazy', for some traumatised and troubled clients this leads to despair and, in extremis, to a wish to end such a troubled life.

One thing I have noticed is that the conflicts between parts of self frequently revolve around the interlocking themes of hope, helplessness and vulnerability, blame and responsibility and shame. To resort to blame when we feel helpless and hopeless is all too human and so the dance between hope and despair is often accompanied by oscillations between blame and shame. Blame which comes from a place of desperation seeks to find a cause, an explanation for why something has gone wrong; why things feel stuck and why we are reeling from something so unpleasant internally. It is also an 'evacuation'. In blaming we are unconsciously trying to make someone else – or another part of self – feel this discomfort. When blame is directed outwards the refrain we frequently hear is: 'It's your fault, his fault, their responsibility!' This will be one of the topics in Chapter 8. But with many traumatised and desperate people, and especially those who tend more towards hypoarousal, the attack is directed inwards. Here the refrain is 'I hate myself. I'm useless, pathetic, weak!' Although what we hear is an attack on a singular 'I', what may be less apparent is that, from the perspective of multiplicity, internally some parts of self may be 'persecuting' others including the ANP.

Fight parts can be particularly scornful of other EPs that hold hope and punitive towards attach parts that turn to others, including therapists, as the hoped-for solution. Here bear in mind that when the client starts to trust and rely on us this can be destabilising for the inner system and the client may intensify self-attack. As Janina Fisher emphasises, all too often instead of being the answer, 'we and the therapy pose as much threat as hope to the client' (2011). But, however scathing, savage and self-attacking fight parts are, if we can become curious about how they are trying to help, we find that they are usually trying to protect the individual from further harm.

Logistically, it makes sense to get in before someone else criticises or humiliates you or to 'stand over yourself with a whip' to ensure you work as hard as possible if achieving was one way to appease a hostile parent or gain needed attention as a child. To some extent we probably all find ourselves using both of these strategies at times. But the logic of what Kalsched aptly called 'protector/persecutor' parts goes deeper than this. It is not so much a transient and normal self-critical phenomena, but a protective, procedurally learned system that, as Howell argues, evolved because 'there never was enough real protection, only in fantasy'(2005, p. 222). This is Kalsched's self-care system mentioned in the previous chapter, which, like the immune system of the body, actively attacks 'what it takes to be foreign or dangerous elements'. Kalsched argues that vulnerability is seen as just such a dangerous element and is attacked accordingly. What the protector/persecutor is trying to defend against is ever being so helpless again. It attacks other parts of self to keep them from 'hoping for life in this world' because 'each new life opportunity is mistakenly seen as a dangerous threat of re-traumatisation'. As a result, even though the individual wants to change and tries to improve life or relationships, 'something more powerful than the ego continually undermines progress and destroys hope' and drives the patient more deeply into fantasy (1996, pp. 4–5. My words in parentheses.).

This is the backlash phenomenon that often follows change and therapeutic growth. We need to constantly bear in mind the relationship between safety and hope – recall the Tibetan word *re-dok* which combines the words for hope, *rewa,* and fear, *dokpa.* Fear not only destroys hope, but for the survivor of complex trauma hope can evoke fear. It simply does not feel safe to hope too much. Bromberg offers an excellent description of what I have in mind. He writes that the dissociated horror of the past fills the present with affective meaning so powerful that no matter how 'obviously' safe a given situation may be to others (or indeed to the adult part of self who rationally knows that nothing bad will happen here), 'a patient's perceptual awareness that she is safe entails a risk that is felt as dangerous to her stability of selfhood'. The risk is due to the fact that 'the safer she feels in the relationship the more hope she starts to feel, and the more hope she starts to feel the less will she automatically rely on her dissociative mental structure to ensure hypervigilance as a "fail-safe" protection against affective dysregulation. Consequently, the parts of self that are dedicated to preserving affective safety [often the protector/persecutor parts] will monitor and oppose any sign that the patient is starting to trust feeling safe' (2011, p. 21).

Another way to view hostile self-states which complements Kalsched's argument is in terms of a procedurally encoded identification with or imitation of the abuser. It is not, as originally conceptualised by Anna Freud, 'that a part of the aggressor's identity has literally become part of the child, but that the child [or adult victim of severe and ongoing abuse or torture] mimics out of intense attachment and dissociates out of sheer terror' (Howell, 2005, p. 166. My words in brackets). According to Frankel, this form of identification demands getting into the aggressor's mind 'to know just what he is thinking and feeling in order to anticipate exactly what he is about to do' and therefore know how to maximise the chance of survival.[8] This is usually through 'a precisely attuned compliance with the attacker', which can include feeling what he wants us to feel or what he himself feels (Frankel, 2002, pp. 103–4). One's own experience has to be dissociated in order to do this and this means not just dissociating from what is unbearable, but from what might be dangerous. As Frankel explains, feelings that may pose a threat if they were to be expressed need to be selectively split off. Fear, for instance, might intensify the attack if noticed and because simply feeling fear carries the possibility of showing it, the emotion has to be dissociated. Anger also has to be 'air-brushed' from the mind and 'fight' has to go underground in homes where to protest or defend oneself might enrage the abuser. Frankel concludes that 'identification informs us which of our feelings are dangerous in the present situation, and dissociation banishes these feelings from aware-ness'. 'You feel what you must feel in order to be convincing in the role that will save you' (2002, p. 109). This is an interesting expansion of the concept of dissociation and one which, given that the identification can become part of procedural memory, can aid our understanding of structural dissociation. For instance, as Howell points out, 'the child orients around the aggressor from the victim position, yet as a result of trauma procedurally learns the aggressor position' (2005, p. 166). He develops two complementary but rig-idly segregated internal working models. In the aggressor position, not only are the abuser's punitive voice and attacking behaviours taken on, but also his or her hopes and goals.

I shall briefly return to Mae to see how these theories help make sense of a part of her that attacked hope and tried to sabotage any small signs of success. In the previous chapter I discussed her long-standing pattern of hanging on to hope and how this had provided her with a source of comfort for years. From the perspective of structural dissociation because Mae's hopes were so relational, repeatedly waiting for and depending on others, we could surmise that it was an attach part of self that held the hope. Sometimes it was this needier self that turned up for therapy; sometimes it was an angrier, persecu-tory version of self. This took the form of a highly critical inner voice which interestingly stepped in after any hint of change. In a mocking way the voice kept putting her down and reminding her of things from the past that she regretted. She said this voice never went away and, significantly in the light of my argument that sometimes it is adaptive not to hope, that took away all her confidence and hope.

On one occasion I asked Mae how she thought it helped to have a critical part always ready to step in and put her down and, even though I guessed it was protective, was surprised by her immediate, insightful response. 'It reminds me – "don't ever risk hoping that things could go well or that you could succeed!" It keeps me indoors. It stops me applying for jobs or joining things and getting to know people.' As we explored the survival logic of such an undermining self it became clear that Mae had learned at school to sup-press any ambition or hope of praise because her headmistress drummed it into her that she would never succeed academically. If she got good marks or triumphed at sport her success was immediately dismissed with warnings not to get above her station or insinuations that she had cheated. There was something tragic about this annihilation of any belief in her own capacities or hope of future successes. In the light of the theories discussed above we could think of Mae's critical voice as a 'protector/persecutor' and as an imita-tive identification with not just her sadistic headmistress but also her mother who, much earlier in her life, frequently launched into hostile, humiliating verbal attacks. An important part of the work with Mae, as with other clients who are beleaguered by scornful fight parts, was to invite curiosity about the functions of that self and to slowly develop more compassion for the self that had and still suffered.

Idealised wishes, hopelessness, shame and blame

Acceptance and self-compassion demand facing vulnerability, sadness and shame and, in the language of structural dissociation, achieving some degree of integration between different parts of self. But one of the things we can all find hard to tolerate is the awareness of our own inadequacy and helplessness. To adapt a quotation from Sinason, 'it only matters feeling little and helpless if there is also another self who is furious at not being all-knowing [or in control]' (1992, p. 32. My words in brackets).[9] We adopt all manner of strategies to avoid encountering any reminder of our vulnerability because knowing it makes us feel ashamed – hence the fury. We feel ashamed of being helpless and dependent on others, of having needs and strong emotions, perhaps even of some of our hopes because we fear they are too grandiose or presumptuous. Once more we are conflicted.

In a book which explores the connections between ideals, presenting symptoms, anger, self-righteousness and shame, Danielian and Gianotti discuss different ways that splits can occur within the self. They use a heuristic they call the Four Quadrants Model which, to my mind, integrates well with structural dissociation.[10] Of particular relevance here is their concept of 'Loyal Waiting'. This was a 'fantasy construction, originating in the imagination of a child in an attempt to compensate for a depriving, inconsistent, or unsafe home environment' and in adulthood encapsulating unrequited wishes carried forward from childhood (2012, p. 45). What is waited for includes the 'perfect other' to make up for all that was lacking in childhood, to provide unconditional love or rescue from pain and suffering. The individual might also hold magical wishes for happiness and salvation, praise or absolute answers and assurances. In the language of structural dissociation these are all things that are yearned for by 'attach' parts of self. When what is loyally waited for does not materialise or when people fail to meet their own ideal standards, the feelings about this, including shame, can get split off and masked by symptoms such as depression, somatic complaints, suicidality, addictions and eating disorders (2012, pp. 42–4). An alternative strategy is to resort to anger and blame in the face of these inevitable disappointments. What Danielian and Gianotti call 'Revenge Enactments', which include self-righteousness, contempt, complaints about injustice or self-sabotage and self-denigration for imperfections or for 'being stupid enough to pin one's hopes on others' – fits with what I said earlier about our tendency to blame when we feel helpless and hopeless (2012, pp. 47–9). It is a position which is consistent with 'fight' parts and can manifest both intrapsychically and as I shall discuss in Chapter 8, interpersonally.

The problem for anyone who keeps switching between the positions in the Four Quadrants Model or, in the language of structural dissociation, between parts of self is that he or she exists in a closed system. The need to cling to unrequited, illusory hopes and to avoid or defend against helplessness and despair can keep people stuck in something endlessly recursive – a dance between hope and despair or between shame and blame. But this is where our curiosity and compassion is so important. If we can avoid getting pulled into the dance and relating solely to one part of self or being pulled into the reciprocal roles demanded of each quadrant and if we can avoid shaming our clients, then new 'me-you patterns' can emerge.

To illustrate the theories discussed and provide examples of the interactions between the helpless self and more shame-based or furious parts of self let me turn to two examples.

Pippa: from 'ridiculous hope' to realistic self-care

Pippa, the woman discussed in Chapter 6, spoke of knowing that she can be 'ridiculously hopeful.' From a structural dissociation perspective my sense is that sometimes her hope was held by the more adult, daily-life self, and most people who knew Pippa would probably have described her as optimistic, very active and pioneering. However, I suspect that there was also a child part that believed in a less mentalised way that she could do anything she set her mind to and that in owning being ridiculously hopeful a wiser self was aware that this was not always based on firm foundations. In order to get on with daily life it was vital that, as a child, Pippa split off all feelings of terror, sadness, hopeless and vulnerability. These emotions had to become 'not-me' and I think this was for several reasons. First, that they were too overwhelming to be experienced. Witnessing how overwhelmed and scared Pippa became if she touched on these emotions in even a small way helped me to appreciate that. But thinking of Frankel's thesis that certain feelings pose a threat if expressed and noticed offers another perspective. Something Pippa eventually acknowledged was that she still feared that her abusers would find her and kill her. She could tell herself this was irrational. But as with many children subject to particularly sadistic forms of abuse she had been shocked into believing that if she ever told anyone, they would kill her. With this in mind I wonder whether she had selectively dissociated any emotions that might cause concern in her parents – such as anxiety, sadness or distress.

Internally, this meant that certain parts of self stayed deeply hidden. But in time they started to appear fleetingly in therapy sessions. I came to think of one as the 'terrified child' and another as the 'hopeless child'. Pippa could rapidly dissociate and go into a state of freeze if she thought about her childhood, and in this state it felt as if I was literally sitting with a terrified little girl. She cowered, shook and fixed wide staring eyes on me or covered her face in her hands as if to shut out something terrible. Sometimes she winced or moaned as if she was being hurt. Whenever Pippa froze I did my best to bring her back to the present with reassurances that 'it's over – it's not happening now' and calls to listen to my voice, look around the room or see if she could move her fingers and toes. It could take time before she regained her adult, coping self. Sometimes, before this happened, a more hopeless and tearful self briefly emerged. Pippa would usually pull herself out of this more collapsed and helpless state with a joke at her own expense or self-criticism for being silly. She would quickly deny it if I ever commented that she had appeared sad or upset.

It was a breakthrough when Pippa began one session by saying that she'd been feeling sad and realised that she rarely acknowledges sadness. She mentioned a dream in which she was watching a desolate child curled up in a corner. The child looked like a limp doll with no hope, no fear and no energy. When I asked Pippa what she thought the girl in the dream most needed, she replied that she had learnt that it was pointless to have hopes or wants or opinions. She had given up. Pippa also observed that my question had evoked panic because she 'sort of knew this was her, but didn't want it to be'. She explained that occasionally she had the feeling that she was much younger and it was like a cloud of sadness and hopelessness hanging over her, but added that she tried to ignore it. I was curious about the panic and reflected that maybe that sad, hopeless part of her had learned that it's not safe to dare to wish or hope and especially to hope for something from another person. Haltingly Pippa agreed and said, 'I hate that part of me. I try to push it away. But I don't think this really helps.' I suggested an alternative approach: 'how about if we tried to give some kindness to that sad, hopeless part and to listen to what she has to say?' My thoughts as I suggested kindness were of that natural emotional/relational soothing sequence mentioned in Chapter 6 which should occur after a child is hurt. This was something gravely missing in a childhood where no one noticed that anything was wrong and Pippa had to repeatedly dissociate her experiences and develop the self-reliant, optimistic persona that had achieved so much.

Another more hidden part of self that Pippa eventually owned was the one that held what she called 'unsafe thoughts'. This self was often triggered when the hopeless part was around. Although adult Pippa was scared of this part, she came to appreciate that at various points in her life the thought that 'if it gets really bad I could kill myself' led to a tiny amount of hope and actually kept her going. It was her 'bail out card'. Pippa had other 'flight' strategies as well. Sometimes she escaped from uncomfortable states of mind by throwing herself into her work. She was also literally a runner and often ran marathons. She had always pushed herself to train several times a week, often disregarding her body if she felt unwell, and when I questioned this she said that somehow she always felt safe when she was running and it calmed her down if she was worried. The other part of self that often appeared and we came to call her 'caretaker' self provides a good example of turning passive into active. Pippa was always doing things for others and seemed to have an intuitive sense if they were distressed. She said tellingly, 'I hate hearing anyone say that they're feeling hopeless. I always think surely there's something we could do.' Significantly, as Pippa began to face hidden feelings and memories she realised that she actually craved time to herself. She reduced the time spent running, and

Table 7.2   Pippa's Multiple Relationships to Hope Viewed on the Hope Scale

Realistic, creative and flexible hoping	Optimistic by nature
Faith and trust That all will be well	'I just knew things would get better'
	'Ridiculous hope'
When hoping keeps The self alive	'I can do anything'
	Active
	Self-reliant
Adaptive not to hope	'I don't need anyone' 'Don't trust others'
Chronic hopelessness	Hopelessness and vulnerability stay hidden
Hope destroyed	Fleeting moments of suicidal despair

discovered that she did not miss it as much as she had feared, and she became more realistic about how much she could do for others. I will say more about Pippa's transformative journey in Chapter 10.

Megan: from shame and self-loathing to anger

In Chapter 5 I mentioned a woman who suddenly became unwell when intrusive memories began to break through after a very difficult family event. The flashbacks haunted her and because of their content made Megan feel deeply ashamed. She became very dysregulated and, because she had to give up work, increasingly hopeless and sometimes suicidal. As I got to know Megan I realised that although she had done well for most of her adult life, it was a 'getting on with life' self that had managed work and parenting. However, in the wings were a number of traumatised parts of self which had been firmly hidden behind a dissociative barrier until the 'crash', but which from then on began to hijack her in increasingly distressing ways. Both the structural dissociation and the Four Quadrants models helped us to understand the logic of her different selves and how they had been trying to help.

Megan was like many other trauma survivors whose need to shut down left them desperate and full of shame. Freeze and minimising harm were her dominant survival strategies. The 'freeze self' was scared of any attention and especially being looked at, ridiculed or hurt. The 'minimising harm part' was chronically depressed and hopeless. When I talked about this 'hopeless self', Megan said she was scared of feeling so depressed and what she might do. 'I feel such a failure. Often I wake up and I just don't want to carry on.' Her words fit with what I said earlier about the characteristics of 'submit/minimising harm' parts, but fail to convey how agonising it was for Megan when she got stuck for weeks at a time in a depressed, hopeless state of mind. This usually occurred after she had worked hard to change something and it had not worked or if a family event or triggering encounter re-evoked the terrifying nightmares and flashbacks which haunted her. Megan really did lose hope at such times. She would often numb herself with alcohol, and now and then, fortunately less as time when on, attempted suicide.

On another occasion when this more desperate and very lonely self had overdosed, Megan said she was scared that she might never be able to have a real and lasting friendship. This reminded me of Loyal Waiting. Megan desperately wanted friends, but was scared to reach out to others in case they rejected or hurt her. 'If they found out what I'm really like', she explained, 'they wouldn't want to know me'. She was deeply ashamed of herself because of what she had experienced as a child and because, in her opinion, of 'being so useless'. She anticipated that others would see her as she saw herself – disgusting, worthless and bad. She was also frightened of anger, whether directed towards her or her own anger. Because of all that she had witnessed and experienced at the hands of her father and grandfather, anger meant danger. If anyone let her down Megan's default was to ask 'what's wrong with me?' But, like Pippa, Megan had hidden parts of self and occasionally an angrier self burst out. Her anger was usually directed towards herself and my guess is that self-blame protected her against hopelessness and shame. More deeply hidden was the fact that this angry self was furious with the people who had hurt her, and, significantly, when Megan eventually started to express some of this anger her symptoms began to abate. As in many cases, although the 'fight' part had a self-destructive quality which manifested through self-harm and vitriolic self-criticism, a positive aspect of this fiery energy was Megan's determination. Her determination to keep going and work as hard as she could to change her life motivated her commitment to therapy, even though it was such a 'snakes and ladders' process. I often remarked how important her 'determined self' was. But I also pointed out why being kinder and less attacking towards herself could be helpful.

I worked with Megan from an experience-near sensorimotor perspective, prioritising developing strategies for emotional regulation and using psychoeducation to normalise her responses to her experiences. Because Megan engaged with the language of parts of self, I often used objects and diagrams to help her understand and feel compassion for her shifting self-states. Figure 7.1 represents a shared attempt to understand the strategies and concerns of these different parts of self. What strikes me looking back is how important understanding her habitual responses was to Megan. 'When I understand something, it gives me hope', she explained, and some of the most moving and remarkable moments in our work occurred when Megan discovered the logic of her dissociative strategies. In shutting down she protected herself from further harm; in numbing her emotions she avoided feeling overwhelmed and also the risks

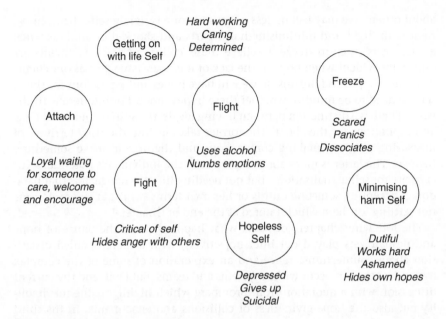

Figure 7.1 Megan's Shifting Self-States

associated with showing sadness or anger. This made sense because she needed to prioritise safety and dissociate her hopes and dreams in order to survive in a world where her family controlled everything she did. Thankfully – and this was also true of Pippa – Megan retained a secret dream – to do an art degree — which stayed dormant until it became safe enough to allow herself to hope and contemplate something new.

I mentioned earlier that people like Pippa and Megan who have learned to use splitting and compartmentalisation to manage overwhelming affect often lack a coherent, ongoing sense of self, and not only do they sometimes act in very contradictory ways, but they can appear physically very different according to which version of self is present. This lack of coherence means that our experience of such clients is also constantly shifting. We can feel confused, wrong footed, pulled to react and, depending on our own stories and attachment style, it is likely that we will respond in different ways to different parts of self. We are no less multiple than our clients and although we can hope for a stronger capacity to 'stand in the spaces', retain a sense of our core self and reflect on what is going on, we are certainly not immune from slipping in and out of the different quadrants. This is especially true if what is emerging evokes our own sense of helplessness or shame. Our different selves can collide with or enmesh with those of the client. We can be pulled in by attach parts and lulled into an idealising transference or draw back from someone who is helplessly beseeching us to do something. We might feel uncomfortable or angry with fight parts or get drawn into colluding with self-righteous complaints about others. We may feel useless when someone is rigidly self-reliant; impatient with flight and minimising-harm parts and shocked or anxious when a client gets stuck in freeze. I believe these 'collisions' and enactments are especially evident when hope or the lack of it is a key issue. Just as our clients have their hopes and dreams, so we will have hopes and aspirations for them. But we need to be mindful whether these hopes support or interfere with the work. There is a distinction between having ideals, the stuff of Quadrant One, and aspirations for the client. The former takes us into the risky territory of measuring progress, making comparisons and the urge to make something happen. The latter is more about recognising the individual's potential – his capacity for self-actualisation – but not needing him to change. It is that paradox of accepting someone on his or her own terms, whilst at the same time not settling for them which I noted at the end of Chapter 4.

The following chapter considers what happens when the dance of hope and despair gets played out intersubjectively, with a more detailed discussion about countertransference and an exploration of some of the complex dynamics that can occur within systems and teams. But I will end the current discussion with a quotation from Bromberg which highlights the inevitability but also the hope-givingness of collisions and enactments. In his third book Bromberg uses the metaphor of the shadow of the tsunami to capture how past traumas continue to haunt people. They can get replayed within the therapeutic relationship through enactments, but this reliving can also lead to healing and growth. The relationship he argues 'is not a vehicle to get rid of the tsunami – as if the past were an illness', – one of the magical hopes that so many traumatised clients bring to therapy, – 'but a means to live together in its shadow, allowing it to shrink a little bit at a time'. This process of living together within the shadow of the tsunami will of necessity involve dissociative processes in both client and therapist and evoke intrapsychic and intersubjective clashes between different self-states. But if the relationship is 'safe but not too safe' then Bromberg believes this can free 'the patient's natural capacity to feel trust and joy' in human relatedness along with a greater capacity for relational affect regulation (2011, pp. 6–8, 16–19). From my reading of Bromberg, I suspect that he would agree with me that it can also free our clients' natural capacity to hope.

Notes

1. It can be helpful to consider which version of self comes to therapy, which version leaves the room and how different parts of self conflict.
2. The contradictory responses include when parents present as frightening and frightened; suddenly dysregulate the infant but fail to modulate his distress; and when they consistently display competing, contradictory and disrupted communications such as intrusive behaviour, withdrawing having invited contact, smiling when the infant is distressed, or role confusion.

3. Here see Alvarez (2012) on children's play and different levels of symbol formation.
4. Some cultures have negative superstitions about jinxing or ruining the possibility of good fortune by revealing a hopeful thought or wish or exposing happiness (Shabad, 2001, p. 183). With the same superstitious logic some people can be very reluctant to share their hopes and dreams with us 'just in case ...'.
5. Whilst it can be helpful to label different 'parts' in terms of the defence systems, using language which works for each individual client is important. For instance, what I conceptualise as a 'fight part' I might refer to as 'that tough part of you' or that 'critical, judgemental self'. Some people who are structurally dissociated may not present with all the types listed in Table 7.1. In other cases there is an even greater degree of fragmentation. For a detailed account of different levels of structural dissociation see van der Hart et al. (2006).
6. I am indebted to Janina Fisher from whom I have learned so much about working with highly complex, structurally dissociated clients and using the language of 'parts of self'.
7. I want to stress that whilst structural dissociation can help us understand people with what might be labelled as a dissociative disorder, shifting self-states is not exclusive to our more severely traumatised and complex clients. Some degree of structural dissociation probably occurs after any traumatising circumstances which take people to a place of shock and terror.
8. Here recall my points in Chapter 3 about the hypervigilant 'figure-it-out' part of the personality that I have observed in a number of victims of childhood abuse.
9. Sinason was writing about people with learning disabilities, a group for whom the theme of hope and despair is also relevant, and many of whom have also experienced some form of trauma. Her remark makes me think that for anyone facing circumstances that bring some form of vulnerability and sense of inadequacy, there is always likely to be a comparison – a perceived better state or way of being, and this cannot always be tolerated with good grace.
10. I like how the model can be depicted visually with Four Quadrants surrounding shame at the centre. Quadrant One captures 'how I view myself' – in other words, the individual's ideal standards. Quadrant Two depicts presenting symptoms. The third and fourth quadrants represent 'Loyal Waiting' and 'Revenge Enactments'. I also value how, like the structural dissociation model, it is not static. Both show a fluid shifting of states of mind as people respond to the nuances of interactions with others.

8

Systemic Perspectives: Our Responses to Getting Stuck in Cycles of Hope and Despair

> *Strong affects challenge a therapist's identity, both personal and professional. ...*
> *A trauma therapist whose work is based on his capacity for hope in the face of his client's despair may be shaken when he finds himself joining with the client's hopelessness in an unconscious transference reaction.*
> (Pearlman and Saakvitne, 1995, p. 138)

For a moment I am going to invite you to pause and simply notice your responses when you read the following words:

- *'Nothing's working. What's the point in coming?'*
- *'I can't carry on. I don't want to be here anymore.'*
- *'I'm stuck. I've tried everything and nothing's changed. It's hopeless.'*
- *'You don't care. Nobody does. I might as well not exist. Everyone would be better off without me.'*
- *'I feel so depressed and useless. I couldn't do any of the things we talked about last week. All I wanted was to stay in bed.'*

What happens in your body? Does your energy level change? What thoughts and emotions come up? Do you feel a pull to do something or to back off and avoid when faced with a hopeless and helpless client?

For therapists and other professionals working with people with chronic, seemingly incurable mental and physical conditions,[1] whose daily lives are hampered by pain and disability or who are plagued with obsessive thoughts or horrific, intrusive flashbacks, there is an inevitability of periods of empathic strain. Under such strain, as Pearlman and Saakvitne point out, the clinician's hope can be shaken and her faith in her skills and capacities undermined. It can also be a challenge to resist the contagion of hopelessness, the urge to act or alternatively to give up unless the practitioner is well resourced, well supported and has adequate time for reflection.

In this chapter the focus is on the ways individual therapists, care professionals, teams and systems can get pulled into the hope/despair paradigm and develop defences to deal with states of powerlessness and hopelessness. I identify some typical scenarios when strong countertransference responses can lead to enactments and potential rifts in the alliance. One is when we catch the emotional tone of a chronically hypoaroused client. It can feel as if our energy gets sucked out of us and our heart can literally sink at the thought of seeing someone who, after our best endeavours, still seems so stuck and hopeless. The second scenario can occur when individuals or teams work to defend against acknowledging the painful truth that there is no cure or solution to the problems of the people with chronic, disabling illnesses with whom they work. We can also end up feeling helpless and hopeless as a result of working with persistent self-destructiveness and clients who sabotage progress. Finally, with clients who have experienced multiple traumas which have left a legacy of an out-of-kilter nervous system, a range of competing survival strategies, enduring relationship problems and a disturbed, impoverished sense of self the therapeutic journey is often one of 'snakes and ladders'. Both therapist and client will feel awakening hope at a sign of progress then a crash into despair when the client takes a couple of steps backwards. After repeated cycles of 'up a ladder' then 'down a snake', it can become progressively difficult to retain a sense of optimism.

In the following discussion my overarching questions are:

- *How do we as therapists or other practitioners in the caring professions protect ourselves from feeling overwhelmed by what we learn of the endless and disturbing nature of our clients' experiences?*
- *Or from what we witness of their pain in non-verbal ways?*
- *Or from what can get lodged in us via projective mechanisms?*
- *And, how do we buffer ourselves against the contagion of hypoarousal and retain our capacity for optimism and hope?*

It is inevitable that sometimes we will have strong reactions and find it hard to walk what Wilson and Brwynn Thomas call 'the balance beam between empathic attunement and empathic strain' (2004, p. 67). It is also likely that we will oscillate between using what might be termed 'appropriate defences', in other words, the conscious attempts we make to protect ourselves from stress, or turning to more 'pathological defences' in order to deny or dissociate from a painful reality (Dartington in Obholzer, 1994). The latter can include shifting into blame and in my discussion I will expand on what I said about blame in the previous chapter.

Before going further, however, let me outline my understanding of the terms countertransference, enactments and empathic strain, as they are concepts which I find helpful when trying to make sense of our responses to getting stuck in cycles of hope and despair. The emerging discussion is intended to apply to people who work within teams or multi-disciplinary systems as much as to therapists working alone.

Conceptualising and making sense of our reactions

Countertransference

Of the many definitions of countertransference I find the following helpful: Countertransference reactions are 'the therapist's affective, somatic, cognitive and interpersonal reactions [including defensive] towards the client's story and behaviours' (Wilson and Brwynn Thomas, 2004, p. 20). However, there are different types and varying degrees of countertransference reaction. Sometimes our response is mild and barely, if at all, noticeable. Sometimes the reactions call our attention. They are what Donnell Stern calls 'snags' or affective 'chaffing'. 'The alerting signal', he says, 'is often small and subtle. It often has a mildly bothersome quality. One feels an emotional "chafing" or tension, an unbidden "hint" or "sense" that something more than one has suspected is going on in the clinical encounter'. Stern uses a lovely metaphor to capture this. 'Therapeutic work is often the equivalent of walking along a forest path in a wool sweater that snags now and then on a branch or twig. When it does we stop, investigate and disentangle ourselves. We note some kind of change in our feelings, ask ourselves about it, and find that we are responding to something about the analysand that we have not yet explicitly noticed. A new perception comes about.' Stern argues that we should try to open our awareness to whatever 'affective clues drift our way' (2010, pp. 81–2, 104). However, sometimes our reaction is much stronger and longer lasting. One of my own metaphors for this is that we find ourselves at risk of drowning in a lake. What we most need is to be able to get out onto the bank. Once there it is easier to reflect on what might be going on.

One of the first to identify different types of countertransference was Racker in 1968. His first category is when we are induced into feeling what the client feels or how he experiences himself. We can have a 'mirror reflection' of our clients and unwittingly and unconsciously take on the same defensive armour (Wilson and Brwynn Thomas, 2004, p. 24). Racker termed this 'concordant' countertransference, but I am going to call it a 'me-like-client' state. As an example, with a very detached client we might also feel strangely numb and detached. This detachment protects us. But at the same time it limits our capacity to notice, stay attuned and be flexible. There is also the risk of dropping into futility mode. The work we entered into, full of hopes and aspirations, can begin to feel unrewarding and interminable and, like the client, we might start to question the point of what we are doing and even secretly long for a 'way out'.

Alternatively, we can be induced into reacting to the client as significant others have done. Racker called this 'complementary' countertransference. As an example of this 'me-like-other' state, the therapist may unwittingly be pulled into feeling and responding like the client's acutely depressed, psychically numb mother who was effectively 'dead' to her little child's reaching-outs and the ebb and flow of his emotions. In the room with the client we might find it hard to feel anything or to respond in a lively way. A third position is when we are swayed by our 'blind spots', the unresolved past and present issues that we bring in from our life which can cloud our view and may mean numbing or dissociating from certain aspects of the client's story or being pulled into some form of enactment.

These three forms of countertransference: concordant, complementary or 'neurotic', as it used to be called, are how therapists have traditionally viewed our responses to a client.[2] We are either picking up something via a projective mechanism or dealing with something personally unresolved or disavowed. But the increasing emphasis on what goes on in the present moment in therapy has given us a greater appreciation of how a strong reaction to a client can be a genuine and 'normal' here-and-now response as we momentarily, or more long term, become dysregulated by learning about his story or being with him in the room. In other words, in this situation *anyone* would be impacted by hearing such a horrific tale or witnessing someone in such intense distress. Likewise, anyone might feel hopeless when nothing seems to work or feel bored or irritated hearing the same complaints over and over again. However, once dysregulated, how we deal with this may involve old defences and patterns. And the more out of our window of tolerance we become, the greater our need to defend against it in order to regain a sense of internal control.

Enactments

Along with the growing interest in working at 'relational depth', increasing attention is being paid to enactments. Fonagy comments on a shift in emphasis from 'countertransference-as-feeling' to 'countertransference-as-enactment'. With the former we tend to look at countertransference in isolation from transference. But there is an artificiality in this because they are like two interlocking strands in the dyadic relationship, always interacting and influencing each other. The latter, meanwhile, acknowledges that we are participants in a shared activity or what Bromberg calls a transference-countertransference field 'characterised by its vividness and its immediacy' (2001, p. 124; 2011, pp. 16, xxvi).

But what exactly do these writers mean by an enactment? For Bromberg it is 'a shared dissociative event' and an 'unconscious communication process' in which out of awareness areas of both client's and therapist's self-experience collide and influence the interaction in subtle or dramatic ways (2011, p. 16). Meanwhile, Donnel Stern talks about a dissociative strategy designed not to defend against any single feeling, fantasy, thought or memory but against a state of identity. In other words 'what moves us to unconscious defence ... is the need to avoid assuming a kind of identity. The unconscious purpose is to avoid the creation of a certain state of being or "self-state", for instance of someone who is disappointed, bereft, frightened, humiliated, shamed or otherwise badly hurt and threatened' (2010, p. 13). As I shall discuss in Chapter 9, our attempts to make sense of our part in the interaction and to identify where strong reactions to a client might have come from can be pivotal in facilitating change. As Mitchell says, 'some of the most important work done in impasses and stalemates is in the countertransference, in the analyst's struggle to regain his own sense of the meaning and value of his understanding, despite its limitations' (1993, p. 214).

Empathic strain

Empathic strain is defined by Wilson and Brwynn Thomas as 'factors in the therapist, in the patient, *or in the dyadic interaction* that impair or limit or adversely impact the therapeutic process'. They argue that these factors 'significantly affect the capacity for sustained empathic attunement'. If it is recurrent or unexpected, empathic strain can lead to countertransference responses that risk rupturing the therapeutic relationship (2004, pp. 21, 43). Maroda says something similar when she writes, 'to keep enough distance in order not to completely feel our patients' depression, we run the risk of rejecting and alienating them'. However, if we are so close to them that we feel their powerful affect, and this perhaps stimulates recollections of our own pessimism or despair, 'we may be catapulted into another form of distancing' (1994, p. 144). So our challenge is to cultivate the capacity to stand both inside and outside of the unfolding process.

Empathic strain can manifest in various ways. It can cause a fleeting loss of empathy and micro mis-attunements which are quickly forgotten or repaired. Alternatively, to use Maroda's words, it can catapult us into a charged, out of proportion response before we have had a chance to re-collect ourselves and reflect what is going on. This in turn might evoke an equally strong response from our client and derail or rupture the working alliance. Empathic strain can also build up over time because of the impact our clients have on us emotionally and somatically. For instance, we might be aware of treading on eggshells each time we meet in an attempt not to dysregulate or enrage someone. We might brace ourselves in readiness for complaints and attacks. We could find ourselves worrying anxiously about someone during the night. Our bodies can also warn us of empathic strain both during or after sessions. For instance, we might experience increased heart rate, shallow breathing, trembling or suddenly feeling very hot or cold, sleepy or nauseous. We might be troubled by digestive problems, headaches, muscle tensions and inexplicable pain, and more generally, sleeplessness, susceptibility to colds and other illnesses. When empathic strain becomes significant and persistent it can shake our capacity for hope and give rise to 'a sense of anxiety, uncertainty or confusion about professional efficacy or the right course of action' (Wilson and Brwynn Thomas, 2004, p. 105). Over time empathic strain can lead to compassion fatigue and vicarious traumatisation and both work and life may suffer.[3]

Making sense of countertransference reactions

One way I monitor and conceptualise my own process is by using the following diagram based on a dialectic model from Wilson and Lindy (1994). The first dialectic honours the potential normality of our responses, which I would argue can include concordant and complementary countertransference. For instance, if we experience strong empathic identification and/or feel and react like significant others, then so surely might any therapist. Yet it also invites consideration of our personal 'hooks' which may evoke a stronger or more out of proportion reaction than average. We need, therefore, to keep questioning whether we are being hijacked by unresolved personal issues or by some form of identification with the client and what it is that might be creating a 'fit' between us at the subjective level.

The second dialectic illustrates the type of reaction we and others might have in response to contacting our clients' pain or encountering something overwhelming or 'heart sinking'. In a state of empathic strain we might slip into more avoidant, numbing strategies or into some form of over-identification and enmeshment, what Wilson and Lindy call Type I and Type II countertransference reactions (CTRs). Within a team one can often see both at work. Some people might go for a distancing, down-regulating strategy, whilst others might up-regulate and in some way become over-industrious or over-involved with the client. At the level of the individual there is often a swinging between the two extremes. We might withdraw in some way from

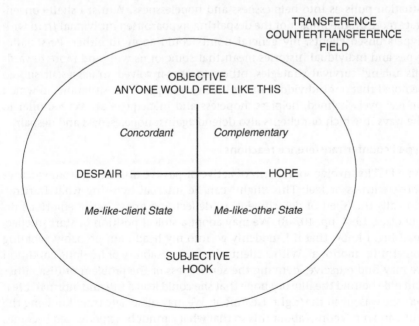

Figure 8.1 Countertransference Responses

the client. This can be both overtly and more subtly, for instance in secretly wishing that he would not turn up or would decide to end therapy or in finding we have doubled booked his time. Then we feel guilty and overcompensate by swinging to the opposite pole. In a counter-phobic way we try harder. We rescue. We give more not less time and get stretched beyond our boundaries until exhaustion or frustration at being taken for granted or nothing changing takes us back into withdrawal and detachment. The challenge is to monitor when we are pulled out of our range and to stay somewhere in the middle.

Although the model was designed to make sense of trauma-specific countertransference reactions, I believe it can be applied more generally and is especially useful as a guide when we get stuck in a polarised position and our responses feel out of proportion. To guard against getting entrenched in some form of unmentalised enactment the following questions are useful to consider:

- *Would anyone feel like this in response to this person right now? Or is there a subjective 'hook'?*
- *Am I doing too much or too little?*
- *Would a colleague be troubled by similar thoughts and do what I am doing? Or am I being influenced by my own story?*
- *What is it about my client's story or affective state that makes it so unbearable?*

In what follows I identify some characteristic countertransference reactions which we can all resort to in order to re-establish a sense of internal control when working with people who are stuck in a trough of despair, and whose situation pulls us into helplessness and hopelessness. Whilst I shall concentrate more on the impact of the despairing hypoaroused individual than with hyperaroused clients, my general points could apply to either. Personality types and individual histories mean that some of us will tend more towards 'distancing' survival strategies, others to over-involved strategies. It should be noted that our individual and collective 'escapes' from situations in which we feel overwhelmed, helpless, hopeless and inadequate are very similar to the ways in which our clients also defend against hopelessness and despair.

Type I countertransference reactions

Type I CTRs involve some form of active or passive distancing from what we know, witness or feel. This 'flight' can be internal by using what Dartington calls the 'shell of detachment' to deflect and anaesthetise emotions (in Obholzer, 1994, pp. 107–8). We may adopt a stoical position or start intellectualising. I know that if I suddenly go into my head I am probably avoiding something emotional. With a client who has a disability or life-long condition we may find ourselves denying the seriousness of the problem or disabilities and hide behind the illusory hope that she could lead a full and 'normal' life *if only* she was given the 'right' treatment. We may dissociate from knowing the truth and our feelings about this so that what cannot be experienced becomes a 'not-me' or 'not-us' domain (Bromberg, 2006, p. 154; 2011, pp. 5–6, 69–70).

For some professionals their 'flight' strategy might manifest in hiding behind the desk or behind a task. As psychotherapists the equivalent of the desk could be to retreat behind a 'blank screen'. Alternatively, our avoidance might include a rigid reliance on technique or structured methods or protocols, or becoming preoccupied with outcome measures and other forms of psychological testing. In these task-centred ways we effectively depersonalise the client. We focus on the 'disease', the treatment and results, but not on the unique and suffering individual in front of us. More subtly, we might experience a sense of relief when the client does not turn up or a wish that he'd decide to end. But then such 'unacceptable' thoughts get pushed away rather than stimulating curiosity about what they might tell us.

I would also add blaming others to the list of Type I CTRs. By blaming and assigning responsibility to others – the language of 'if only he, she, they did this or stopped doing that, things would be better' – we can avoid facing our sadness or anxiety about the client's predicament and dissociate from the shame or inadequacy of temporarily not knowing what to do and having no tools at our disposal to make things better. The other side of the coin is to blame ourselves. But because this usually entails becoming hyper-responsible I see this as a Type II CTR. In their different ways and to differing degrees these avoidant strategies could all be seen as forms of 'psychic numbing' (Lifton, 1967), and once we have protectively numbed ourselves to our own and the client's emotions, this limits our capacity to notice, stay attuned and be flexible. Moreover, Wilson and Brwynn Thomas argue that prolonged use of psychic numbing can result in fatigue, exhaustion, somatic complaints, dysphoria and a loss of sensuality and interpersonal sensitivity – in other words to burnout (2004, p. 124).

Type II countertransference reactions

Type II CTRs include various forms of over-involvement and over-identification with the client. The clinician may feel overwhelmed by the client's story and deeply affected by his despair. From a place of hyper-responsibility she may become preoccupied thinking about her client and how to help, spend longer than usual writing notes or contacting other professionals, perhaps fired by anger or protectiveness on the individual's behalf. She begins to expand the boundaries of the contact time, drifting in an un-negotiated way into extra phone calls, longer sessions or additional sessions in the week. And then comes the risk of more serious boundary violations which blur professional and personal relationships and in extremes cause considerable harm. Alternatively, the 'doing too much' may be a counter-phobic response to feelings of frustration or boredom with the client which can get disguised under a façade of busyness and 'chronic niceness' (Speck in Obholzer, 1994, p. 97). An important question to ask in order to avoid such defences is 'in what ways do I treat some clients differently to others?' Then we should consider what feelings are possibly being dissociated.

The clinician might also slip into the role of the 'omnipotent rescuer', the 'good mother', the one who never lets the client down, the only person who understands and can possibly save her (Davies and Frawley, 1994). This can either be a reciprocal response in a transference-countertransference drama, where we get hooked in by a part of the client that is desperately seeking attachment or because of unresolved personal issues. Either way it is a manifestation of unmentalised hope. The hook may be particular to a specific client. For instance, perhaps a chronically depressed woman reminds the therapist of her own mother and of a similar feeling of helplessness as a child to do anything to help, and so, out of awareness, she gets pulled into a 'special mission' to make the other better. The 'rescuer' or 'caretaker' role may also reflect the therapist's personality traits and interpersonal style. For instance, one of the five personality types identified by Wolstein in a study of psychotherapists is 'overprotective nurturing', which he argues originates in a personal unmet need to be cared for (Wilson and Brwynn Thomas, 2004, p. 125).

The rescuer role often emerges when working with people abused as children. It is also noticed by therapists who work with young people. For instance, in discussing work with disturbed children, Shirley Hoxter talked about the pull to rescue, for instance, the fantasy of fostering the child 'and providing for the child what all others have failed to provide'. She saw this response, born of our own sense of inadequacy and guilt about *only* providing therapy, as reciprocating the child's yearning to find a long-lost idealised parent. But she pointed out that 'the child's fragile high hopes usually disrupt painfully on the first occurrence of some minor frustration and the subsequent antagonism and derisive rejection of the therapist are likely to effectively demolish in the therapist any tendency to self idealisation'. She also argued that encountering the frustrations of this relationship can help the young person to develop more realistic expectations and tolerance that will help him in other relationships (Boston and Szur, 1983, pp. 126–7).

I can recall several troubled young people about whom I had 'fostering fantasies'. It is amazing how seductive the arguments in our heads can be. It seems so logical. 'I have a spare room in my house.' 'I really understand her.' 'She is desperate at the moment and likely to be thrown out of her current home if no one does something.' 'It fits my ethos of supporting those in most need.' Then I have to remind myself that if I want to support people it has to be in other ways and that I need to let go of omnipotent, magical thinking. What I and therapy can give to this young person *is* important. But other people also have important things to offer. I was reminded of the importance of what we *do* offer when one young woman said, 'I want you to be my therapist. I don't want you to be anything else. The boundaries make me feel safer and I can trust that you will keep them.' I suspect that this trust helped her to believe that she too could keep to the boundaries of our relationship, however tempted she might sometimes feel to seek more from me, which from past experience she knew would not be safe.

The discourse of blame: 'the person is not the problem, the problem is the problem'

A countertransference response I find interesting – both because it often emerges when we feel stuck and hopeless and because it can manifest both at an individual and a systemic level – is that of blaming. As argued in Chapter 7, blame often comes from a place of desperation, where we are trying to find a reason why something has gone wrong or make someone else feel how awful or hurt we feel inside. Blame can emerge when people are in extremely hyper-aroused states as well as manifesting as a bitterer, cynical state of hypoarousal. In the former case, maybe subtly in the latter too, I would argue that it often comes from a blend of fear and helplessness. Picture someone who is beside herself with grief having just learned that her husband was killed in a road accident. She rounds on her son and yells 'you killed him! If he hadn't been so stressed about you he wouldn't have gone to the pub and this would never have happened'. In a calmer, more reflective state this woman would probably have been horrified by what she had said. She needed a vehicle for her shock and grief – and maybe too for her guilt at not supporting her husband enough. But for the child it would have left an indelible mark.

In this example the blaming attack was sudden and vitriolic. But we probably all encounter milder versions of this every day – either as the recipient, the onlooker or the perpetrator. Jeremy Holmes provides a delightful example of this (2010, pp. 130–2). He recounts how when his Aga broke down the mechanic shifted from affable on his first visit to increasingly frustrated and irritable with each call out. He ended up blaming the manufacturer, the people who had installed it, the Aga itself – and perhaps, who knows, the owners for doing something wrong to thwart all his attempts to fix it. Holmes' point in telling the story is to illustrate how often we 'blame the victim' when we feel stuck or hopeless in our efforts to help. 'When something or someone … fails to respond to our ministrations, we start, often subtly at first, to blame them, rather than examining our own contribution to the situation or looking objectively at what is happening.' Holmes is writing of people with complex, multiple problems who are often given the diagnosis of Borderline Personality Disorder. 'They can be problematic', he says, because 'they defy the rules of normal medicine [or evidence based, manualised treatments][4] – i.e. to cooperate docilely with whatever is offered, spend a defined amount of time being "ill" and then gratefully recover thanks to the wonders of medical science'. Then, Holmes points out, such people are [sadly] 'often labelled as "disruptive", "manipulative", "antisocial", "self-destructive", "bad news", "heart-sink patients"'.

Holmes' argument can be applied to anyone who, as a result of attachment failures and multiple traumas, presents with a complex array of problems and who cannot be 'mended' like the Aga with one course of treatment. To blame or scapegoat is a non-mentalising position. It reduces things to a more simplistic cause and effect, rather than acknowledging that a situation is complicated and that there may be multiple versions of the truth as well as a number of potential solutions. And our human tendency, when we are stressed, pressurised, stuck and lacking in time and supportive resources, is to simplify. Donnel Stern speaks about the inevitability of blame when there is a deadlock or impasse in the therapeutic relationship and each participant loses the capacity to see or value the other's perspective (2010, p. 66). In this stuck place 'most direct expressions of one participant's feelings or perceptions about the other, or about the situation between the two, contain some variety of blaming; and blaming, obviously, resolves nothing'. Resorting to blame is all the more true in large, complex systems such as hospitals, mental health services, schools and prisons. The priorities of dealing with crises, keeping people safe and alive and battling with targets and paperwork, mean that being able to notice and reflect on our responses to someone who challenges our capacities, or in a team to reflect on the different and often conflicting responses of the team members, is regrettably not often possible.

From a different theoretical base, yet also an inherently mentalising one, a premise of systemic therapy is that one member of the family holds the symptoms and acts as the target for blame. With this in mind, highlighting how 'the person is not the problem, the problem is the problem' is the first step in dissolving blame (Partridge and McCarry, 2009, p. 13). These authors write that, 'when families and agencies get caught up in problems, discourses of blame predominate. Children are labelled as "naughty", parents are criticised, and professionals may be blamed for failing their clients'. They see systemic therapy as 'a shift from blame to appreciation' and help families do this by trying to separate out the person from the problem and to identify and mobilise the resources of family members for the good of all. In this way they maintain that it is possible to decrease blame, increase hope and facilitate a successful outcome. 'But when a problem becomes the sole identity of the person, despair prevents change' (White cited in Partridge and McCarry, 2009, p. 15). The ethos of shifting from blame to appreciation is also helpful when thinking of 'internal family systems'. I believe this is what Fisher had in mind with her concept of dancing with the resistance. If we can stay curious and compassionate about how the problematic, blamed parts of self have been trying to find solutions to the real problem, then over time something begins to heal internally.

Blaming can divide families and teams. I will illustrate this in the examples which follow. But blaming and self-righteousness can also bond people. Rather than feeling the sadness, hopelessness or fear aroused by a situation, there is comfort in banding together in demonising someone or something else such as the problem child, difficult service user or unhelpful department.[5] But the real enemy is the task of getting in touch with painful feelings. When I catch myself with blaming thoughts about how another professional has spoken about or responded to one of my own clients I find it helpful to remember the advice of Shirley Hoxter regarding work with very troubled,

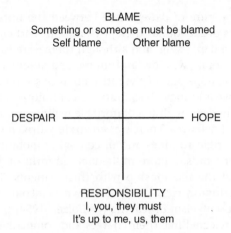

Figure 8.2   Hope, Despair and Blame

deprived children. She observed how 'feelings of injustice, frustration and the wish to blame seem to be endemic in this field of work' – and I would argue within the field of working with vulnerable adults – and how 'sometimes our response to learning about the distress of a young client is of anger – we want to blame someone for not caring enough'. But, she continued, 'as a therapist one cannot allow oneself the comfort of passing the blame on to someone else; in the child's eyes one stands for the adult who is responsible for having failed him and one needs to be ready to receive the child's outbursts of pain and anger if one is ever to be able to help the child to bear with such feelings himself' (1983, p. 127). Ultimately neither blaming nor rescuing helps – even if for a short while we feel better about ourselves. We need the courage to face our own angry side and to bear the client's outbursts – which can include owning the ways in which we probably have let them down. Figure 8.2 illustrates how I conceptualise the interface between the paradigms of hope and despair and blame and responsibility.

Linking theory and practice: working with the 'incurables'[6]

In what follows I shall give some examples in which there is evidence of the discourse of blame and a number of typical Type I and II countertransference responses. These also illustrate some of the scenarios mentioned in the introduction. For instance, let us consider what it is like to work with people with life-limiting, incurable conditions. A supervision case discussed by Roberts illustrates the connections between hope and despair and blame and responsibility within a care unit for elderly people who could no longer live independently (in Obholzer, 1994, pp. 75–83). She observed significant contrasts in attitude and the nature of patient care between the nurses and visiting professionals such as occupational therapists and physiotherapists. The unit wards were bleak and depressing, and although there were high standards of physical care, staff morale was low and illness and absenteeism were high. 'Deprived of both the hope and of the satisfaction of seeing at least some of their patients improve and move back into the community', Roberts noticed that the nursing team dealt with uncomfortable feelings by adopting a number of avoidant Type I defences. There was an anxiety-driven stress on patient safety, which meant rigid routines and discouraging mobility and personal possessions: in other words, a more individualised form of care. This effectively depersonalised the relationship with their patients. The nurses also turned to what Dartington calls the 'breakdown/breakout solution' with a flight into illness, absenteeism or leaving (Obholzer, 1994, p. 107). They felt that they had been rejected like their charges and complained about always being blamed. Yet they blamed others in turn including other professionals, relatives and the elderly people themselves.

By contrast, the visiting OTs and speech therapists were enthusiastic and full of ideas for improving the patients' quality of life in what Roberts describes as a manic defence (Type II). They still held hope and blamed the nurses for standing in their way. Yet significantly in their drive to keep doing something, the therapists tended to forget details and could be careless about record keeping. Could this, I wonder, be viewed as an avoidance of actually seeing the details of their patients' incurable condition? Meanwhile, the nurses avoided real contact with their charges in their routine, sanitised approach and were zealous about administrative tasks that their colleagues neglected. Only by having a shared space in which to reflect on what being with these 'incurables' meant to them, could the two teams notice how they all adopted avoidant or over-involved countertransference strategies, reclaim what they had projected into each other and find a more cooperative, middle ground.

Working with the hopelessness of persistent self-destructiveness

Another scenario that can lead to feeling helpless and hopeless is when we work with clients who sabotage progress and attack themselves and their bodies in various ways. This is something that therapists who work with troubled children know well. For instance, Sue Kegerreis wrote about the frustration and despair for teachers and workers who have seen a child improving then suddenly relapsing into self-destructive behaviour and she asked what is it that makes change for the better so desperately difficult for these children? (in Trowell and Bower, 1995, p. 101). The demoralising impact of witnessing repeated self-destructiveness is also felt by anyone who works with adults who rely on self-harming, addictive behaviours.

The following example illustrates the impact this had on a team of drug and alcohol workers. It also provides an example of the discourse of blame within a system. The support workers struggled to agree how to respond to a woman who suffered spinal injuries and had miscarried after being involved in a car crash. Left in chronic pain, Rosa became depressed and relapsed into drug use. She began to neglect her 20-month-old son Tommie. The GP was worried and involved other professionals. Because of past history – Rosa already had two children in care – the authorities arranged for Tommie to go to his grandmother while Rosa came back into treatment. The interweaving of the themes of hope-lessness and blame were evident in this tragic story. Rosa hated the fact that she had to rely on others for help and could no longer do things she used to enjoy and oscillated between blaming others and herself. She blamed the lorry driver, the hospital for not saving her baby, her GP whom she labelled as use-less and her social worker for never being there when she wanted help. And, of course, the support workers were in the frontline for her angry attacks. Rosa also berated herself for driving on an icy day and for being 'a failure because I can't look after myself'. But underneath her angry tirades Rosa felt hopeless about ever escaping the controlling hold of drugs and making a better life. Sometimes she sat sobbing saying, 'I can't do it anymore.' 'I don't want to be here.'

Within the team opinions were divided. Rosa's keyworker found herself angrily blaming her for neglecting Tommie. It emerged that for her the sub-jective hook was that her own parents had been addicts. A colleague who had also lost a baby kept challenging her for losing her compassion. Another woman, who had worked closely with Rosa on two former admissions to the unit, admitted to despair to see her coming back. 'We put everything we've got into this work. And if they relapse it's hard not to think when is this going to end? Is there any point?' As we talked, everyone in the team admitted that Rosa's scornful dismissal of help wore them down and they got angry with her and each other. They also became indignant about the responses or lack of support from other services and self-righteous about what they were offering.

When asked how blaming themselves or others who might be trying to help, the support workers realised that going into 'blame mode' was masking deeper feelings. They shared how they often felt disabled, an interesting word given the disabling nature of Rosa's injuries, and how they empathised with her suffering and, like her, drifted into hopelessness. They were aware how much Rosa had lost and risked losing, because if she did not complete the programme it was likely that Tommie would also be put into permanent care. Once this was acknowledged they noticed how sad they felt. This sparked discussion about how similar feelings emerged about everyone they worked with. But they rarely talked about it or even let themselves acknowledge their feelings. In supervision we talked about the contagion of helplessness and noticed how 'blame' seemed to move around the system. Everyone – within the team, in Rosa's family and in the wider professional network – seemed to blame someone or something and everyone had moments of feeling it was their responsibility to 'do something' and make a difference.

Writing about another group of professionals in this field, Dartington reflected that the hardest thing to speak about was their resentment towards people who seemed to 'thwart their effort and care' and 'connive at their own death'.[7] She observed that 'our intellectual knowledge often makes very little difference when we are faced day after day with the hopelessness of persistent self-destructiveness in others' and feel deprived of 'any gratification or significance in [our] work' because of not being able to help those we work with get better (in Obholzer, 1994, pp. 106–7). Dartington's point led me to consider how any of us respond when we are frustrated of work satisfaction because someone we work with continually sabotages our efforts to help or keeps attacking him or herself in some way.

To avoid empathic strain and countertransference responses that can, in their own way, also be destructive, our first task is to model self-care. The second is to try and find meaning in the strategies our clients adopt and the dynamics they set up. For instance, returning to the question posed by Kegerreis – 'what makes change for the better so difficult?' – after severe trauma and neglect change can feel dangerous. One reason is that it entails loss. Kegerreis argued that when hope begins to dawn children 'can be thrown into a most painful state'. They 'have to deal with complex feelings about leaving a place which simultaneously symbolises both their problems and the kind of nurturing they needed. They also have a great deal more to lose now. It is far worse to fail a second time around. Whether in special or in mainstream school, children who make a move away from their "problem" status have to wrestle with the burden of having real hope for their future' (1995, p. 102).

Another way to understand attacks on hope is that they reflect desperate attempts to avoid re-traumatisation. In Chapter 5 I argued that for some people hope and excitement are paired with anxiety and stimulate the fear rather than the care or pleasure circuits in the brain. After trauma our 'better be safe than sorry' survival brain is likely to mistakenly see 'each new life opportunity .... as a dangerous threat' which has be avoided or attacked (Kalsched, 1996, pp. 4–5). As discussed earlier, because a sadistic aspect of abuse and torture is to offer a grain of hope then cruelly take it away, people learn to avoid the risk of disappointment and the anxiety that accompanies hope by assuming control of the situation. And what better way than sabotaging progress? At least you know that this is under your control. There can also be a relational element to this including what Davies and Frawley argue is an identification with the abuser. In their view it is crucial for the therapist to experience and enact the role of victim. 'Only in this way can clinicians begin to truly appreciate at a visceral level the terror, paralysis, hopelessness and impotent rage lived by the patient when she was a child' (1994, pp. 174–5).

An example that highlights this and emphasises the potentially re-traumatising dangers of therapeutic change is given by Marsha Hewitt in her account of work with a very suicidal patient (in Willock, 2014, pp. 99–113). She located her client's sabotaging behaviours within a systemic context. Mr M. was stuck in depression, anger, contempt and suicidality. But this was less frightening than giving up his role as the sick one in the family.[8] Indeed, 'to lose his depression would be to lose his identity, his way of experiencing himself and being in the world'. Change felt dangerously destabilising and fear always accompanied any moment of happiness.

Hints of change also jeopardised the therapeutic relationship and when her client began to feel some attachment towards her, Hewitt describes how she became another dangerous persecutor who threatened his core identity as a depressed individual. 'He began feeling pressure to relinquish familiar, grounding despair in favour of disorienting, unfathomable hope that generated terrifying dread and pain' and became persecutory in turn. At times Hewitt felt 'boxed in and helpless' and 'like an emotional hostage, "forced" to relinquish my needs in submitting to the tyranny of his suicidal threats'. Sometimes Mr M.'s savage attempts to humiliate her and overpowering body odour meant she could 'barely stand him' and it was tempting to retaliate to his attacks. Then she felt guilty about having such feelings. She realised that 'we were caught in a repetitive dialectic of often, but not always dissociated, disavowed hate and love, hope and despair that, despite our best efforts was, in the end, impossible to regulate'. And when any of us are pushed to our emotional limits after weathering attacks, fears for the client's safety and repeated downturns after a hint of progress it is all too easy to fall into this dialectic and end up feeling as stuck as the client.

Sometimes I wish it wasn't so crucial for us to feel what our clients feel and join in the dance of hate and love or of hope and despair. But it is – and if we can find a way to see what is happening from a wider perspective than the confines of our relationship, these pernicious cycles loosen their hold. For instance, I know that something changes when I start to see that, whatever form destructive behaviours take, they are what our most troubled clients learnt helped them to manage overwhelming feelings. But problems arise when strategies originally designed to help bring unintended consequences. For example, let us imagine that for Rosa being repeatedly and cruelly rejected as a child led to intense sadness, loneliness and shame so that in the present any hint of criticism or rejection evokes similar emotions. Then let's speculate that as a teenager she discovered that drugs dulled her feelings. But now, the unintended consequence is that others get angry when she relapses and withdraw rather than offering what she most needs – comfort and reassurance. As I try to capture in Figure 8.3, instead of being soothed, the unbearable feelings are intensified.

I doubt if the others involved in such a scenario – whether relatives, friends or professionals – feel good about themselves either. And it is one thing as someone in private practice to be faced with a self-harming, angrily blaming client when there may be time to collect oneself and at some point reflect on the meanings behind what he or she does. But if you work in a setting where this is the norm – for example, a rehabilitation unit, school exclusion unit or care home designed for critically self-harming young people – often what you are doing is trying to survive the onslaught of one incident after the

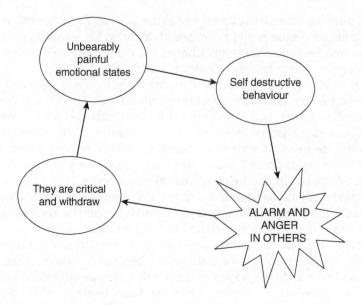

Figure 8.3 The Negative Cycle of Self-Destructive Behaviour

next. There is precious little time to reflect and, hence, consider the meaning behind sabotaging behaviours. And despite the dedication of the staff towards their charges and commitment to promoting change, slipping into Type I and II CTRs is inevitable. Moreover, as Moylan emphasises – a strained, under-resourced team can become 'infected by the difficulties and defences of their particular client group' (in Obholzer, 1994, p. 59). In a drug and alcohol unit, for instance, addictive coping strategies might manifest amongst the support workers; whilst in an eating disorders clinic the staff might find themselves under or over eating. To reduce the risk of enacting what is projected, I believe regular clinical supervision is crucial and that reflection needs to be an integral part of an organisation's culture.[9] But space to reflect can be the first thing to go in under-resourced organisations.

The snakes and ladders phenomenon

The third scenario I want to discuss is when someone's journey towards change is one of 'snakes and ladders', a process which typifies work with clients with complex trauma-related disorders and other severe, enduring mental health problems. This is not only because of the backlash which frequently follows a transformative moment in therapy or step towards change. It is because life crises get in the way. One week we might be working in depth on a traumatic memory, there is a shift in stuck beliefs and the client leaves feeling relieved.

We both feel renewed hope. Then next session he or she arrives in an agitated state because of the arrival of an impossible-to-pay bill, a child in trouble or, even more dysregulating, an encounter with or news about an abuser.

Several people come to mind when I think of this phenomenon and how it can pull me into the countertransference traps of 'I must do something' or 'I feel like giving up.' They include Mark, an intelligent, likeable 18 year-old who had been plagued by anxiety and OCD for years. Mark was an only child and lived with his widowed mother in a rural village. He found it hard to make friends and was very isolated. Because the obsessive thoughts were so overwhelming and interfered with everything Mark enjoyed and wanted to pursue – for instance, he was a gifted pianist and dreamt of going to Music College – there were times when he resorted to self-harm and often contemplated suicide. Witnessing Mark's struggles I had to grapple with a recurrent sense of hopelessness and when he felt most suicidal I was challenged to deal with my anxiety, sadness and anger about his possible death and the tragic waste of a young life full of so much potential. It was inevitable that at times I became embedded in Mark's world. Having space to reflect was crucial and I became curious how everyone in his 'system' – myself, his mother, his support workers – positioned themselves in the dance of hope and despair.

Sometimes we all fell into teleological mode and clung to 'if only .... then' hopes. People become active in trying to make things happen (Type II CTRs). There were meetings and lots of phone calls. It was as if everyone regained energy and renewed motivation when there was a solution to aim for. Sometimes one or more of us resorted to blame – usually, I suspect, when feeling particularly helpless. It was rare for everyone to be in the same place in the dance at the same time and we pulled in different directions at times when thinking and working together was most needed. Some of the hardest moments followed a period when hopes were raised then dashed – for instance, after considerable effort had been spent applying for funding for a more intensive form of therapy than I could offer. This also occurred after some hints of genuine progress. There were periods when Mark began to go out more; he became interested in studying music again and the self-harm diminished. Then, having gone up a ladder, he slipped down a snake again into despair and suicidal thinking. I could see how each setback dented Mark's fragile hope and confidence in his capacities. It was alarming for everyone to see him like this and I was aware of my own shifts from feeling helpless to becoming overactive in trying to find something that might help. Then, having tried everything I could think of to little avail I was back into despair.

The snakes and ladders pattern also typified Megan's journey, and not only was it demoralising for us both, it meant that it was hard to hold a sense of where we were going. When our focus had, of necessity, to turn to what felt urgent and immediate it was difficult to follow up and integrate work done in a previous session, and I found it hard to stay mindful of the overarching themes. In time what I did find helpful was to conceptualise long-term work with traumatised clients like Megan within the framework of the three-phased model that is widely adopted by trauma therapists (Herman, 1998; van der Hart, et. al. 2006; Wright, 2009a). In my experience, we repeatedly move between Phase One work with an emphasise on regulating the client and developing resources to deal with triggers and flashbacks, and Phase Two work on processing memories. And I believe that when we are focussed on dealing with a here and now difficulty, this gives an opportunity to strengthen and refine coping strategies. The problem is that, as a default, our traumatised clients frequently turn to their old survival strategies – to dissociate, numb themselves with alcohol or give in to someone who is hurting or humiliating them. Later, old beliefs about being a failure, useless and bad resurface and with them comes the familiar descent into despair.

For me a personal challenge is to maintain a wider perspective and to hold the phased model more consciously in mind as I work with people like Mark and Megan who unwittingly and necessarily bring aspects of the original chaos and incoherence into the work itself. Work with clients with complex problems cannot be rushed or conceptualised in terms of 'moving someone on'. It is a deeply relational process and, as in all good-enough attachment relationships, development comes because of repeated reparative and containing interactions, not as a result of following a pre-planned schedule.

Conclusions

In this chapter I have emphasised the importance of being able to reflect on our responses to the people we work with. We need to be able to mentalise. But we also need to be mindful therapists – able to track our present moment experience. The two support each other (Wallin, 2007, pp. 326–8). Our embodied countertransference can be particularly informative. If we mindfully tune into our bodies we can catch subtle hints of where we are in the dance between hope and despair and the pulls to withdraw or become too active. For example, I have noticed that if a desperate client makes eye contact and smiles when greeting me my body relaxes, and I feel suddenly energised when someone talks enthusiastically about something they have read or done. On the other hand, to hear someone open with: 'nothing's working. What's the point in coming?' or 'I've had enough. I don't want to be here anymore' my energy sinks. When I fall into teleological mode I know I speed up and tend to sit forwards. My body is tense. Just slowing down and sitting back can help me access a more spacious reflective state. There will be less subtle clues as well – feeling sick, very tired, hyped-up or sudden pain. However, we don't always connect such 'symptoms' with the impact a particular situation or individual might be having on us and it might only be sometime later that the 'affective chafing' makes sense. The non-judgemental stance of mindfulness is also important. As I have illustrated, our individual and collective responses to situations that leave us helpless and hopeless often include judgement and blame. Compassion and curiosity are powerful antidotes. I shall say more about these positions in the remaining chapters.

Notes

1. This might include the terminally ill, the elderly and people with profound learning disabilities and multiple handicaps.
2. The traditional perspective also views countertransference as a distraction that needs to be got under control (Mitchell, 1993, p. 145).
3. Generally, we think of vicarious traumatisation as a response to witnessing or hearing of horrific events. But do we consider the likelihood of a similar cumulative response to prolonged work with helpless and hopeless clients? Pearlman and Saakvitne's definition of vicarious traumatisation is applicable to both, namely 'a transformation in the trauma worker's inner experience resulting from empathic engagement with the client's trauma material', especially when his or her responses are not adequately processed, and this can include a loss of hope, idealism and sense of meaning to one's life (Wilson and Brywynn Thomas, 2004, pp. 19, 23, 197–9).
4. My words in brackets.
5. In his identification of certain defensive positions which mitigate against a group working together constructively Bion called this 'Basic Assumption fight/flight'. The 'assumption' is that there is a danger or enemy and that fighting or running away are the only mechanisms to preserve the group (Stokes in Obholzer, 1994, pp. 20–3).
6. I acknowledge that this word depersonalises the suffering individual and is not a term I would normally use. But like Roberts, I am deliberately using it here as a reminder of how in the past these are groups that might actually have been called the 'incurables' and treated with far less dignity than I hope would be offered today.
7. Dartington was discussing a support group on a liver unit in which the nurses reflected on the patients who kept returning because of alcoholism, and on the number of deaths on the ward despite hours of intensive care.
8. This role allowed the family to maintain a sense of stability, sanity and cohesion by disavowing their familiar and individual pathologies.
9. Jeremy Woodcock offers a compelling argument that for people who work with the survivors of extreme events and trauma, supervision is not a luxury but an absolute necessity (2014, p. 14).

9

Working with Hopelessness from a Relational Perspective

> *Hope is an orientation of the spirit ... an orientation of the heart. It transcends the world that is immediately experienced, and is anchored somewhere beyond its horizons. Hope in this deep and powerful sense is not the same as joy that things are going well, or willingness to invest in enterprises that are obviously heading for success, but rather an ability to work for something because it is good, not just because it stands a chance to succeed ... Hope is definitely not the same as optimism. It is not the conviction that something will turn out well, but the certainty that something makes sense regardless of how it turns out.*
>
> (Havel, 1990, p. 181)

I remember feeling demoralised when a colleague commented: 'people will want to know *how* you work with hopelessness, not just to be told what it is like'. My anxious, unspoken thought was 'but do I *know* how I work with it?' It is not something we can prescribe or manualise. Indeed, being with someone who has lost hope takes us into the territory of *not* knowing what to do and, as the examples in Chapter 8 highlight, all too often encountering our own helplessness and hopelessness. It is not so much *what* we do, but *how* we are with such people – and here I am reminded of the words of Vaclev Havel that hope is 'not the conviction that something will turn out well, but the certainty that something makes sense regardless of how it turns out' (1990). Whilst I certainly believe that there are ways in which we can inspire hope in our clients and free up their capacity to discover hope for themselves (O'Hara, 2013, p. 19), our starting point should be the question: 'how do I manage the tension between holding hope for my client and bearing something that feels overwhelming?' We cannot hold this tension unless we are mindful of our own fluctuating orientation to hope. We need to keep noticing how this shifts, sometimes ebbing in tune with a client's descent into despair, sometimes strong and steady as we connect with things that resource and inspire us.

As I continued to reflect on my colleague's implicit question 'how do you work with hopelessness?' I realised that my second unspoken thought was 'it depends'. It depends on context – on the reasons why someone is feeling hopeless, on his or her assumptive world and attachment story. I would want to consider 'why now?' 'What recent life events or relationship problems might

142

have catapulted my client into a depressed, hopeless state?' or, at a micro level, 'what was it in our dialogue that triggered a descent into futility and despair just at that moment?' In contemplating what might make a difference I would be considering how resourced is this person? Who or what is there for her to turn to when she feels desperate? What strategies does she have for managing emotional arousal? And when less desperate, what other positions does she adopt on the Hope Scale? Maggie Turp suggests something else to take into account with her observation that 'there is a difference between feeling that one is supporting the client's existing capacity for hope and thinking of needing to actively engender or co-create hope. The client may have forgotten his or her initial hopefulness' (2010, p. 37). But how long lost? That is the question. Has a recent difficult life event turned the client's world upside down? Or was his/her fledgling hope eroded very early in life because of trauma and attachment failure? Our approach will be different in each case.

My final thought about how to address my colleague's comment was that it demands two separate but linked responses. I could have listed some of the things I might do during a session when someone slips into a hopeless state of mind, usually a predominantly hypoaroused state, but often with an edge of hyperarousal as well. I could also have spoken about what is important in a more ongoing way when trying to help someone who is stuck in a chronically hopeless place or is prone to repeated episodes of despair in response to life events and setbacks.

So here is the challenge: how do we integrate the *'how we are'* and the *'what we do'* aspects of the therapeutic relationship? Striking the right balance is particularly hard with traumatised, very dysregulated and desperate clients. It is hard because there will always be a pull to do something and make something happen. But ultimately, it is our presence and willingness to welcome and weather all that such clients bring into the relationship that makes a difference. It is how we receive and make sense of the 'if only' demands of someone seeking magical solutions, the blame and accusations when we fail to meet their hopes and the contagious despair when hopes are dashed. However, there are interventions of a *doing* nature which we can make use of in an informed and relational way. In the next two chapters my aim is to speak about both the relational aspects of working with hopelessness and to share some of the interventions I use in the moment and over time to help someone to move through and out of hopelessness and despair.

The first section of this chapter will focus on the qualities of the therapeutic relationship most needed for fostering our clients' capacity for hope whilst also supporting them when hope has vanished. Then I shall go into more detail about working in the moment when people slip into hopeless, hypoaroused states of mind. In the next chapter I take a longer-term perspective and discuss the process of engendering or rediscovering hope from three angles. The first entails developing an 'alternative perspectives mind'. The second is about finding a way to grieve and sometimes rage about past hurts and losses. The third entails letting go of illusory hopes and fantasies in order to come to a place of acceptance. These are all easier said than done and we need to stress this when suggesting trying anything new to a dispirited client. Otherwise we risk triggering more shameful feelings of inadequacy. It is hard for all of us to come up with alternative ideas when we are at a low ebb. If feeling sad or angry makes us anxious, then of course we try to avoid such emotions, and if illusory hopes and fantasies have offered some comfort and kept us going through many a long night, why would we want to let them go? As Germer says, 'the mind has its own natural ways of avoiding distress', and I like his wise acknowledgement that there are times when avoiding serves us better and his invitation to seek a middle way between facing and avoiding our difficulties (2009, p. 26).

Before going further let me recap some of the factors which lead to states of despair. They include being or feeling trapped and unable to take charge of one's life. Our desperate clients may be literally caught in a choiceless, interminable situation or relationship or trapped in haunting memories that make the present feel unsafe. They have tried repeatedly to change things, but nothing has worked. People who have encountered cumulative losses or experience enduring physical pain or a chronic mental health problem such as OCD or an anxiety disorder are also familiar with helplessness and hopelessness. Sometimes bad news, another loss, a perceived failure or a hope-dashing experience catapults the individual into despair. These are 'last straw' situations which can break the spirit of someone who is already struggling. Whatever the external factors that have trapped someone in a web of helplessness and despair, this is intensified by difficulties in managing emotional and physiological arousal. Being persistently on red alert, a common legacy of severe trauma, and fighting against intense anxiety on a daily basis can also erode hope and it is worth reiterating that whilst we associate hopelessness with hypoarousal, people caught in a state of despair are also likely to experience periods of intense hyperarousal.

Writing in the 1950s, Jerome Frank tried to identify what it is about psychotherapy that leads to healing. He argued that the success of psychotherapy depends on the ability of one person to influence another and this influence springs primarily from the fact that the latter looks to him for relief. In a similar way to non-medical forms of healing such as shamanism and religious healing, it is an expectation heightened by the therapist's cultural role and special training. Implicit here is that the very act of seeking out help implies a hope that we can offer relief and that what takes place in a therapeutic encounter will lead to change. It places us in an 'expert' role, although Frank also believed in the importance of personal attributes (1974, pp. 43–4, 76).

On first meeting a client it is certainly important to convey our faith in what we have to offer, and if we suggest activities and experiments en route it has to be with a genuine conviction that, even if we cannot predict exactly what will happen, our suggestions will help. But the situation is far more complicated than Frank believed. Over 60 years after his enquiry we know that it is not primarily our 'socially sanctioned expert role' that leads to change. Indeed, it is often those moments when we have let go of trying to understand or make something happen that are pivotal. All the research on caregiver–infant interactions since Frank's day has taught us about the importance of intersubjectivity, and this understanding, enhanced by advances in neuroscience, has fuelled a growing interest in what goes on at a micro-level between therapist and client. Moreover, today's psychotherapists and counsellors probably see a much broader range of people with more complex difficulties than the patients Frank had in mind. Certainly, anyone with a background of complex trauma will find it hard to trust us and will quite likely have little expectation that therapy will make a difference. Some have learned to be resolutely self-reliant and remain sceptical about fully embracing what we offer. Others – quite the opposite – have unrealistic expectations and reify us as the 'one to fix them'. We need therefore to be mindful that, whatever they say, many of our clients will have mixed feelings about therapy and the process of change.

So, whilst I agree that part of our role is to engender expectancy and hope (O'Hara, 2010), I believe that there are other ways in which we can use the therapeutic relationship to help people out of states of despair and apathy and create a climate in which they might begin to risk investing in hope. As indicated earlier, they involve things we do in a reciprocal way on a moment-by-moment basis – what the Boston Change Process Study Group would call therapeutic actions at the 'local level'– and also over a period of time (BCPSG, 2010, p. 96). Some will be deliberate; others are the result of more intuitive, implicit ways of being with our clients. In what follows I am going to discuss four aspects of the therapeutic relationship which I believe are fundamental: namely, creating safety, offering a different sort of relationship, sitting with despair, and alerting and enlivening.

Creating safety

For change to occur it requires a relational climate in which our clients feel safe enough to explore their world, play with ideas and share their more vulnerable selves and secret hopes. They need to be able to trust that we can hold them through the bleakest moments and that we won't shame or disconfirm them. Only then might they risk letting go of old beliefs and strategies and try something new. Remember what was said in Chapter 3 about the need for a secure base in order to be able to explore. If someone's survival brain is on line for much of the time then far from being able to envisage alternative futures, what he will see on the horizon will be past dangers, rejections and losses. It is this 'negativity bias' of the brain which, although vital for the survival of the species over the course of evolution, can impede exploration and the pursuit of new and more hopeful pathways (Hanson, 2009, pp. 41–2).

Creating safety includes what I think most therapists would agree are the fundamentals of a solid working alliance – clear boundaries, a protected space, consistency and confidentiality. Also important is the physical environment. My training as a Feldenkrais practitioner gave me my first appreciation of the fact that the brain won't learn anything new if the body is uncomfortable or the nervous system is dysregulated and this became even clearer in my work with profoundly traumatised people. Feldenkrais talked about the need to lower the 'background noise' (1984, pp. 20–2). There is a law in physics, the Weber-Fechner law, which argues that the level of a detectable signal is dependent on the 'noise' in the background. For instance, we are unlikely to hear someone whispering at a rock concert or to notice a candle on a sunny day. To get round this, either the signal has to be increased, for example you could light a bonfire, or the 'noise' has to be reduced, for example you could take the candle into a dark room.

For a traumatised client there are many things in the environment which create 'noise' and from the outset we need to be alert to sudden changes in arousal level, posture, eye contact, vocal tone and ego state that might indicate that something in the surroundings or in what we said or did might have evoked the client's threat system.[1] It is not that we can necessarily eliminate all triggers. But we can do things to reduce the noise and help regulate his or her arousal.[2] Like an attuned caregiver, through an informed and an intuitive use of prosody and our own bodies we can help to calm or alert and energise the person we are with (Stern, 1985, pp. 75, 102). There are also practical things we can do, including checking where people would like to sit, or if there is something that could be adjusted in the room that would help them to feel calmer and more present. Creating safety also entails knowing when it is important to put the brakes on and reduce whatever is being attended to. So often someone will arrive wanting to tell us everything that has happened and exactly what they think or feel. They flood us and themselves and risk going rapidly out of their window of tolerance. In such moments a sensitive invitation to pause, step back from what they are describing and orient to the present moment can make such a difference. I shall say more about this later in the chapter.

Being different

Over time the fact that we can be different in some way from the adults who hurt, failed or disconfirmed our clients as children also fosters safety and trust. Being different does not mean that we won't get pulled into repeating the past. Indeed, we need to bear in mind that our most traumatised clients will expect us to be like those adults, but will simultaneously hope – whether this is conscious or unconscious – that we will be different. We won't always get it right. There are a myriad of ways in which we will trigger them and many opportunities for mis-attunement. Moreover, at some point it has to be faced that we can never be the ideal nurturing caregiver who will rescue the wounded 'child' from his or her suffering.[3] But what we can offer that is new are the core conditions, which in my view includes compassion alongside empathy, and a willingness to non-defensively negotiate rifts and ruptures in the alliance.

The territory of ruptures and enactments is where relational psychotherapists locate the source of therapeutic action rather than, as Bromberg argues, our ability to provide a safe environment. In his view, working through enactments is an inevitable and potentially growth building experience. If we can find some way to reflect together after a rupture, this helps the client to tolerate internal conflict – something I shall say more about in the next chapter, and shift out of 'no-way-out' or 'if-only' thinking (Bromberg, 2011, pp. 6, 57, 105, 162). It is 'standing in the spaces together' which demands an openness to observing and reflecting on our own process and idiosyncratic dance between hope and despair, and a sensitively paced and non-shaming invitation to be curious together (Bromberg, 1996, p. 274). This is what Patricia DeYoung calls the 'terribly hard part of relational psychotherapy'. Her position is that 'when things go wrong in therapy, it doesn't make sense to explain it in terms of what the client is bringing in from her past. It makes more sense for the therapist to ask "what just happened? How did I miss you? Where did I misunderstand you? What did you hear in my response to you?"' (2003, p. 149).

DeYoung also observes how 'when either person feels threatened by the other's organising of their mutual experience, interpersonal protective strategies appear. Feeling ambushed, ignored or helpless, the therapist may "diagnose" the client's self-protections as resistance, negative transference, or something more fundamentally wrong in the client's psychological make-up. Then at least the therapist knows what is going on!' (2003, p. 150). This is the discourse of blame I spoke about earlier. How subtly invidious our 'knowing what's going on' can be! And of course, there will be multiple reasons why either or both partners in this 'co-transference' feel threatened. But entangled with those reasons, more often than is perhaps appreciated, I believe that states of helplessness and wishful hoping are playing a part. Along with other relational psychotherapists, DeYoung believes that a way out of these enactments or ruptures emerges when the therapist genuinely wants to hear and understand her client's experience. I agree with her point that 're-experiencing trauma, even in the form of negative transference can't make anyone feel better. Genuine integration and healing happen only when a new experience of relationship allows the old feelings to be understood more gently and thus be laid to a better rest' (2003, p. 152).

The older and, hopefully, wiser I get, the more I appreciate that being different also means letting go the need to change or solve something. If we can focus instead on providing our clients with a new experience and engaging in a more *'being'* approach, then they will be more likely to access what they need for transformation and healing. Porges says something similar from a neurobiological perspective: 'As soon as we attempt to modify a person's behaviour, we tend to overwhelm the client with so much negative feedback emphasizing that the behaviour or feelings should be changed, that the client responds defensively as if they did something wrong ... This changes their physiological state and makes the circuits for social engagement behaviours [and for exploration] unavailable ... If we want individuals to feel safe, we should not accuse them of doing something wrong or bad' (2012, p. 19). We need to bear in mind that each time someone implies that the client needs to change it can reactivate old messages about 'only being loveable if ...', and sometimes even a benign suggestion or enthusiastic comment on our part can be heard by our clients as 'you too want me to be different'. It is easy to fall into the trap of investing in change, and again and again we face the challenge mentioned at the end of Chapter 4 of 'accepting the patient on his own terms, and at the same time not settling for them' (Friedman in Bromberg 2011, p. 93).

In Dialectical Behaviour Therapy this challenge is captured by the notion of 'radical acceptance'; in Gestalt Therapy by the paradoxical theory of change[4] (Linehan, 1991; Beisser, 1970). Another version is Janina Fisher's rather beautiful idea of 'dancing with the resistance' (2012), which entails being curious about the purpose of entrenched patterns and limiting behaviours and reframing them as adaptive rather than trying hard to change them. Let me give an example of this from my work with Anna. To recap on her story, which I touched on in Chapters 3 and 5: After a horrific sexual assault Anna struggled with chronic hypervigilance. She was often hijacked by flashbacks and overwhelming anxiety and used a lot of energy to keep traumatic memories out of her mind. But as she said, 'they are always there waiting to leap out when I least expect it'. Anna dare not relax for fear of what might happen if she was not on guard. She also experienced days of intense sadness when something reminded her of her life before the assault and all she had lost. On other occasions she was angry and impatient with herself.

As the therapy moved between moments of a little more hope and then back into despair, I noticed a pull for us both to work too hard. I was aware of wanting to give some tangible hope that things could change – perhaps coloured by knowing that I was Anna's third therapist since the assault and aware of an internal voice saying 'surely you can make a difference!' I knew how desperate Anna was to get rid of the hypervigilant symptoms, which she said neither medication nor therapy had ever touched, and was aware that character traits she had always viewed as strengths, such as being very self-reliant, preferring not to ask for help and caring for others rather than attending to her own needs, kept getting in the way of healing because she repeatedly ignored her body when it flagged up the need to rest.

Focussing on dancing with the resistance helped me step back from doing too much. I began to realise that change could only come as a result of Anna learning that she could tolerate her memories and the emotions they evoked, and for this to happen I had to manage that tension mentioned earlier between offering hope and being able to sit with her when things felt hopeless. As a first step towards such tolerance we had to both become curious about her familiar survival strategies – about the 'on guard' part of self and a tough, self-reliant part. For instance, could she start to accept, rather than fight, the hypervigilance? Could she also notice when rejecting help or being very busy was masking feeling sad or vulnerable? From a place of compassionate acceptance that she had been vulnerable and still could be, I knew it would be easier for Anna to come to terms with living a life that could never be quite the same.

On one occasion Anna complained how fed up she felt. Whilst on holiday she had not felt frightened and had allowed herself to rest and let other people take over. But once back home she felt jumpy. She realised that she was frightened of feeling frightened and so fell into the trap of racing round doing as much as she could before the fear took over, ignoring tiredness and the wish to stay in the warm and trying hard to avoid thinking and feeling. I commented that a tough part of her was back in 'soldiering on mode' declaring 'I shouldn't need help', and that there was also a protector part around, namely her busy mind, always assessing things and on the lookout just in case anything dangerous emerged.

Anna laughed at the thought of her mind as a protector. She said it gave her a warm feeling inside. I invited her to notice what it felt like to have this warm feeling – to really get to know it and to see if there was an image which captured its essence. I had in mind the idea of embodying a good feeling, and thus creating new memories, and of developing a resource to return to in future sessions. It was then possible to share my thoughts about the dilemma facing us. We both wanted things to change and this led to an urgent attempt to find something to 'fix' the problems and, in particular, to get rid of the 'hypervigilant protector'. Along with this, Anna's self-reliant part kept trying to avoid any hint of feeling sad, lonely or vulnerable. But it was important not to neglect her vulnerable self and to treat it more kindly. Anna was interested in the Buddhist notion of 'pain plus our thoughts about it leading to suffering' and in the idea of trying to alter our thoughts by mindfully noticing them (Kabat-Zinn, 1991). It reminded her of how inspired she was by a disabled friend who seemed able to accept and live in the moment. She then decided that she would carry around a picture of her dog, the image which had come up in association with the warm feeling, and look at it when she felt overwhelmed by anxiety.

Of course, there were many more steps in Anna's particular dance between hope and despair and many moments in our dance together which contributed over time to real change. The BCPSG talk of 'now moments' and 'moments of meeting'. They define the former as 'a special kind of present moment, one that gets lit up subjectively and affectively, pulling one more fully into the present' in which 'the known, familiar intersubjective environment of the therapist-patient relationship has all of a sudden been altered or risks alteration' (2010, p. 16). In these 'moments of meeting' 'each partner has actively contributed something unique and authentic of his or herself as an individual' – something that is not dependent on theory or technique and certainly not dependent on trying to be different or to make something happen (2010, p. 18). They are moments of affective immediacy which slowly and incrementally begin to change our self-with-other patterns and, I would add, our relationship with ourselves.

I believe that what changed for Anna came about because of repeated experiences of being with and surviving overwhelming affect in the presence of another – someone whose responses were different from the dismissive or judgemental responses she expected. My endeavours to create safety were important, but it also demanded that both of us had to find something different from our shared pattern of working very hard – and to do this we had to be authentic.

Sitting with despair

It is in the bleakest moments that it is hardest to resist the urge to do something to change things. As David Malan said, in the face of acute grief and suffering we 'feel compelled to offer comfort, when often no comfort can be given; and the resulting feeling of helplessness is very difficult to bear. Yet the truth is that we are *not* helpless, and the greatest service we can give to people in these circumstances is to stay with them and simply share their grief [or despair]' (2001, p. 140, my words in brackets). I absolutely agree. Sometimes we have to be willing to journey with a client into the abyss and face the despair with her, to be in a place of having nothing to say, no solutions to suggest, no tools at our disposal – just the courage to sit with someone, however unbearable, hopeless and endless things feel. We are in that place of accepting people on their own terms. But we are certainly not giving up hope. For long stretches of time we might be the only person who keeps hope alive and this quiet faith acts as a bridge between the endlessness of the client's despair and the possibility, even if only tiny, of something new. For very desperate individuals this matters.

'You can overcome anything as long as you have hope', a young woman said to me on one occasion, and I believe hope is more sustainable if we feel accepted and don't have to travel alone. As Holmes says: 'if sorrow can be given words, feelings shared and objectified, their power to distress or overwhelm is mitigated' (2010, p. 85). This is a very different place from getting stuck in non-thinking despair. There will be times when the most important thing we can do is to listen to the impassioned words of a desperate client telling us that they can't go on, that things feel unendurable. We are called to face together the unbearable truth of how hopeless and agonising things feel. However, in these 'being with' moments what happens relationally is much more than a sharing of words and because so much goes on at a non-verbal level it is far from easy to describe. In my experience, often neither of us says much. For long periods of time we might share a silence. But it is not silent inside. I am aware of many thoughts, intense feelings and accompanying body sensations. I can feel anxiety, desperation, deep sadness, hopeless and sometimes blank, empty-headed and useless. The emerging thoughts and feelings might tell me what my client is feeling or call up something from my own past. I may find myself doubting my competency whilst simultaneously pressurised by thoughts about needing to succeed. In these time-suspended moments we are called to face our own vulnerability and humanness, and if we allow ourselves to stay in touch with our process something important will eventually emerge. For instance, sometimes images or phrases come which we can hold for a while or fashion into a simple contact statement – a mutative metaphor or brief phrase of recognition which captures how bleak, dead and hopeless it feels inside. We are trying to find what Hobson calls a shared 'feeling-language' with which to bridge the chasm that separates the suffering individual from others (1985, p. 9). We may find our mind wandering to a place that could have meaning or find ourselves envisaging our client as a young child – scared, lost, lonely, frozen or frantic – perhaps along with a shadowy sense of the presence of a caregiver. Alternatively, we may suddenly see an unfamiliar, striking beauty in his or her face or catch an expression or tone of voice that hints at the presence of other parts of self lurking behind the helpless, desperate self. Allowing space for our active imagination and following what takes our attention can guide our responses.

Robert Hobson gives a beautiful example of staying with someone in an isolated and seemingly desperate place in his book *Forms of Feeling*. It illustrates my point how, whilst very little is actually said, an awful lot can happen internally and can be communicated in a few words. Hobson's client was a lad of 15 who had become mute. After weeks of trying to understand what Stephen was experiencing and to communicate this, Hobson admits to reaching a point of giving up. He felt he had run through all his repertoire of techniques. He tried to concentrate, but his mind kept drifting to other things. Then one morning, noticing how Stephen was twisting his fingers, he burst out with 'it's bloody'. This is what I have in mind with the idea of a contact statement which, through the power of the words and how it is said, captures our understanding of how the client might be feeling. 'It's bloody' was probably as much about what Hobson was feeling as his young client, but they freed something up between them. Following his instincts he took a pen and paper and drew a squiggle, casually asking if Stephen knew how to play the Squiggle game (Winnicott, 1990, pp. 10, 121–3). Silently, the boy drew a tiny boat beside Hobson's wave shape and a co-created story began. The final steps are so relevant to my subject that I will quote from Hobson's text. It provides a flavour of how the therapist needs to grapple with his own despair and of Hobson's attempts to cling to hope and how, through a genuine wish to stay alongside someone and develop a mutual conversation, the child or adult's hope can be awakened (1985, pp. 9–14).

By now we are engaged in a very serious playful conversation, and the rest of the picture is completed quickly. Stephen's face has begun to move whilst drawing, but now it is once more mask-like. Yet, as he draws he speaks. For the first time. "A flying-fish." "An octopus", I say drawing [the next thing]. Stephen's shoulders droop as he slowly marks lines. "It is raining" he says with a sigh of sad resignation. Maybe I can't stand it … or maybe. Well I tell myself, "there must be some hope of a game of cricket on Saturday". Silently I draw the sun with its rays conflicting with the rain. Stephen pauses. It seems an age long pause … then he looks at me. Or with me. With a sweeping hand he draws embracing lines. "A rainbow." He smiles. We smile. A moment in and out of time.

With another desperate teenager, Hobson again intuitively found a language they could share when he gave up trying and started to talk about cricket (1985, pp. 4–5). Reading this story reminded me how there are times when staying with a desperate client includes talking about ordinary things. With one young woman, for instance, there were moments when, having acknowledged her despair, we drifted into conversation about what she was reading, the sunset or a storm the previous night, a wounded bird, something heard on the news. Sometimes that was all she could manage, but those real-relationship conversations kept us connected and I believe kept her connected to something beyond her suicidal despair.

For another woman, knowing that I wasn't giving up on her helped sustain her through several periods of suicidal despair. On one occasion I told Lucy that even though she felt hopeless and everything seemed pointless I still wanted to work with her. I used the image of a rope stretched between us and however far away and lost she felt I was going to keep hold of my end. This image was something we often returned to. Sometimes Lucy told me that the rope was as thin as spider's web thread and she could barely keep hold. But it was clearly important to her, and on one occasion she told me that it had kept her going to know that I was holding onto the rope even when she let go. For Margie, the woman mentioned in Chapters 4 and 6, the sense of our ongoing connection through long periods of illness and emotional turmoil was also hugely important. When we ended our work she said appreciatively: 'It was like you were there holding my hand through the darkest, conflicted times.' 'I won't forget that. Nor will I forget that day when you said you were appalled at what had happened to me and you had tears in your eyes.' It was not something I remembered – and it is interesting that we don't always know what has mattered most to our clients. We talked about how this had moved her and how I held feelings for her when she could not do so for herself. 'In the void I didn't have feelings. There was nothing there.' 'Or maybe', I suggested, 'you were too scared to have them. They were too big until you had someone to hold your hand?' 'Maybe', she smiled, 'but I've got them now!'

The more I work with people who get caught in the web of despair – people like Lucy who reach points when they feel utterly defeated after repeated attempts to change – the more crucial the role of someone who does not give up seems to me. And in that conversation with Lucy I was reminded of Havel's words – that hope is not about knowing that something will succeed or turn out well, but 'the certainty that something makes sense regardless of how it turns out'. We do what we do because it matters and we believe in it, not because we know for sure how it will work out. It is a steady determination to keep fighting no matter how hard and endless the struggle and no matter how hopeless and helpless we both feel – and a preparedness to weather all the emotions, doubts and frustrations that go with the struggle. We 'lend' our hope, our resilience and our willingness to think of other perspectives. But more than that, there is something important about facing our own vulnerability that is crucial. If we can do this I believe that, even though we may not openly share it, it helps those we see to face and bear their own wounded selves. One of the conclusions of the Boston Change Group is that 'the more one's experiences are shared with a responsive other, the more one's thoughts and feelings will be experienced as human and "relationable", that is, able to be included in one's relationships with others and thereby with oneself. Sharing of meanings and experiences converts experiences of shame, guilt, or deviance into expressions of a joint humanity. And that convert's one's subjective mental life into something acceptable and bearable, and something that can be included in one's exchanges with important others' (BCPSG, 2010, p. 209). It is Hobson's shared 'feeling-language' and what Holmes called a 'reparative bridge' (2010, pp. 95–6). One of the key features of despair is that it is such an alone state – a state of isolation, alienation and fear that is often accompanied by shame and beliefs about inferiority and uselessness. To share what it is like to be in this place with someone who understands and does not judge – someone who has been there or who is willing to go there with you, helps to convert this experience into something more 'relationable', and from that place, I believe, the seeds of hope can begin to grow once more.

Alerting and enlivening

Having stressed the importance of 'being with' rather than trying to create change, there are also occasions when it is necessary to throw a lifeline to pull our clients out of states of deadening hopelessness.[5] As Greenspan pointed out, when someone is under-aroused 'we need to create a more compelling personal environment' (in Alvarez, 2012, p. 23). In the same way that a mother will instinctively introduce more energy into her voice and exaggerate her facial expressions and gestures to enliven and 'gee up' a flat, rather depressed baby, we also need to adopt a more dynamic, animated mode of interaction to up-regulate such clients. We are wanting to draw people who are chronically detached and shut down into greater contact with themselves, with us and with their surroundings – to attract and keep their attention, to inspire curiosity and, in Alvarez's words, waken them 'into mindfulness and meaning' (2012, p. 13). This is both about drawing the client into the present moment, rather than being stuck in mental time travel or a more dissociated timeless state, and also implicitly communicating through our own energy and commitment that something or someone has to matter (2012, p. 26). This in itself is sometimes the needed 'new' experience.

Inspired by Anna Alvarez's work with very troubled children I am calling these alerting or reclaiming functions. Alvarez appreciated that, depending on the degree of trauma and disturbance and the child's capacity for symbolic thinking, sometimes a therapeutic approach – in her case analytic – has to be modified. She identified three levels of work with her child patients (2012, pp. 12–25). First, there is an explanatory, more interpretative level which demands a capacity for mentalising or what she calls two-track thinking. Alvarez argues that this more traditional approach is not appropriate for all or appropriate all the time. Next is the descriptive level, which aims to enlarge meanings and includes empathic and amplifying comments. Third, and sometimes necessary before the first and second are possible, is a more intensified, vitalising level in which the therapist tries to attract and keep the child's attention. Alvarez adopts this third position when working with children who present with the affectless states of autism or who are locked into a more dissociated, shut-off state due to trauma or chronic neglect. It is a more active way of using oneself therapeutically in an attempt to reclaim profoundly lost, apathetic and despairing children – or in her words making a 'firm pull on the lifeline of contact' (2012, p. 23). Although based on work with a very different client group, I find it helpful to hold these three levels in mind and to be aware that with very lost, desperate adults there may be long periods when we need to stay more at level three – holding firmly onto that lifeline – or during the course of a session slip briefly into alerting, enlivening mode.

What Daniel Stern and Alan Schore have written about the maternal and, by extension, therapeutic role of a 'self-regulating other' or 'neurobiological regulator' has also inspired my thinking about our alerting, enlivening functions. For instance, Stern describes how both partners in the infant-caregiver dyad adjust to keep the infant within an optimal range of excitation (his window of tolerance). In a complex, moment-by-moment dance of facial and vocal expressions, gestures and body movements they mutually regulate the child's self-experience and this includes regulating excitation, arousal levels, affect, somatic states, *attention, curiosity* and cognitive engagement with the world. As a result, the infant starts learning how to self-regulate (Stern, 1985, pp. 102–3, 75). I have highlighted the words attention and curiosity as it links with what I said in Chapter 3 about the importance of the Seeking system and evoking curiosity and what I will argue later about trying to develop an alternative-perspectives mind. What Stern's work so eloquently emphasises is the co-created nature of these tasks. For example, he writes: 'the caregiver's mediation greatly influences the infant's sense of wonder and avidity for exploration', and my sense is that our most depressed, shut down clients have lost or sadly never experienced the wonder and rapt attention of sharing a focus on something beautiful or fascinating.

Let me give a short example of a lovely shared moment in a session with Megan which captures what Stern means by a sense of wonder and avidity for exploration. When Megan arrived she looked grey and exhausted, her hands picking at her scarf, her legs shaking, her eyes downcast. Indeed she did not look at me for the first 20 minutes. She spoke in a faltering voice about how desperate she felt. The nightmares had returned full force. She had started self-harming again, which made her feel a failure. The tasks she had to do were mounting up, but she could not get to grips with anything. It was not the right time to re-engage with memory work and Megan agreed when I suggested that we start with a visualisation, something I knew from experience would help to regulate her. It did. She settled and we were able to talk about the ongoing conflict she felt between really wanting to say no to family demands, some of which triggered trauma memories, and a strong sense of duty and responsibility. When I spoke about our human need for occasional days to ourselves to do whatever we want, she looked at me for the first time and said sadly, 'I don't think I've ever done that in my life'. And it was true. As a young person Megan could not play. It was either expected that she help out in the shop or the kitchen, or alternatively she was hiding away somewhere in an attempt to protect herself from the ongoing abuse. Her survival brain had to be online all the time.

Rather impulsively I said, 'would you like to play with something with me? Would you like to see what I was given this week?' Because of my own excitement I think my voice conveyed the sense of wonder when an adult points out something interesting to a child. Catching a spark of interest in Megan's voice I carried on and took out a small box. 'Look!' I said, 'look how beautifully the box is made. Shall I show you what's inside?' Then without speaking I slowly took out a small singing bowl and carefully laid it on the floor. 'It's beautiful', she exclaimed, her face suddenly alight. I agreed. 'Let's listen' I said, and began to carefully run the beater round the edge of the bowl. The sound built up, echoing, reverberating, and then faded away as I sat back. I handed the bowl to Megan. 'Would you like a go?' It was lovely to watch how from a tentative but wondering start she began to play, the smile on her face, how her eyes sparkled. We listened together. We laughed when, as often happens, the beater jarred against the bowl. We sat together in the sound-filled silence. Then we talked about how Megan might use a singing bowl to calm and refocus when she was troubled by intrusive thoughts. Had we worked that day? No, we had played – and that was the work.

To my mind this was an example of what Alvarez meant by the third level of work, the alerting, reclaiming position, and it was an example of the very active use of vocal tone, pacing, gesture, facial expression and timing – Stern's vitalising affects come to mind here – that may be required when working with intensely hopeless clients. A lot of this goes on at a level beneath awareness. I knew that something was needed that session to bring Megan back into contact, to widen her attention rather than being so stuck in thoughts of failure and futility and to see if, somewhere, we could rediscover hope – something to convince her it was worth carrying on her struggle. But I did not know how that would be achieved and was certainly not consciously planning each relational step any more than Hobson planned to suggest the Squiggle game. It was an intuitive process which built on Megan's responses to my relational moves. Alan Schore talks about listening and interacting at an 'experience-near subjective level' and flexibly and fluidly modifying our behaviour to 'synchronise with the moment-to-moment rhythmic structure of the patient's internal states' (2003b, p. 52). He also argues that this process is helped by our ability to 'enter into the other's feeling state and to modify and contain stressful negative states (which I would argue include states of hypoarousal as well as anxiety, fear, shame or anger) induced in us by the patient's communications of dysregulated negative affect' (2003b, pp. 56, 53). On this occasion I needed first to contain my initial fleeting feelings of hopelessness and anxiety on seeing how dysregulated Megan was on arrival – feelings that had a charge because it was such a graphic reminder of how she used to arrive week after week. I also needed to convey my compassion and empathy – I for one was not blaming her for the downturn – and once she was calmer to become more of the compelling mother/therapist that Greenspan advocates.

Of course, this raises some fundamental questions: when do we contact how hopeless someone feels and stay with it, and when do we work in a more active way to help him or her shift out of the stuckness of hypoarousal? When do we need to calm and when is it important to alert and 'reclaim' our client so that something or someone can begin to matter to him/her? And how do we balance more directive interventions with an attuned, fluid responsiveness to his or her lead? To end this chapter I shall list some of the strategies I use during a session to ensure that people are calm and alert enough to be more fully in contact with the present moment, engage in deeper work and to contemplate anything new. My approach here owes much to Sensorimotor Psychotherapy.[6] Out of context these strategies may sound mechanical and prescriptive. But I endeavour, like other Sensorimotor Psychotherapists, to use directive interventions in ways that are deeply embedded in relationship and should stress that often it is through exploring the moments when something does not work – the surprise responses and the 'yes buts' – that important themes emerge or something begins to change.

Working with hopelessness in the moment: regulating arousal levels

Finding strategies to help regulate arousal levels is particularly important when working with the survivors of trauma, and especially childhood trauma when caregivers were unable to provide a safe haven after any form of fright or upset or to help the child manage overwhelming feelings. It is important to remember that a common legacy of trauma is an out-of-kilter nervous system. The body is repeatedly being flooded by chemicals that mobilise the individual for defensive action or create a state of shut down. As the trauma survivor oscillates between under and over arousal there is little chance for periods of ordinary rest and recovery or for states of more pleasurable high energy. At the same time there is either too much emotion or too little. Over time the individual begins to feel anxious about these overwhelming feelings and sensations – a 'fear of fear' – and to despair about things ever improving. It becomes a battle to get through the day and, as the examples I have shared illustrate, people start to interpret their predicament as indicative of personal failings. With this in mind, helping people to stay in or come back to the window of tolerance is not just a priority before other interventions will have impact. It is an essential part of helping them to manage daily life and eventually begin to expand their horizons.[7]

Our skill in observing or tracking our clients' present moment responses, and our own, is part of the process. For instance, we might observe a sudden drop in energy, dropping the head, glazed eyes or a sigh. Alternatively, our clients might speed up, become restless, change colour, breathe rapidly, clench their fists, turn away from us or become flustered and embarrassed. Whenever we sense that someone is going out of the window of tolerance it is important to put the brakes on and orient him or her to the present moment. As already emphasised, when someone is very flat and presenting as helpless and hopeless we want to invite him into awareness and curiosity and into greater contact with himself, with us and with the world around him. In such moments we may need to introduce more energy into our voice – to be more compelling – and also to find ways to expand the individual's attentional focus. Let me explain what I mean.

We can think of what we attend to in a two-dimensional way. Our 'field of consciousness', or the amount we attend to, can be narrow or wide. The 'level of consciousness' or intensity can be high or low (van der Hart et al., 2006, pp. 102–5; Ogden et al., 2006, pp. 68, 73–4). In a hopeless state of mind the field is likely to be narrow and the level to be relatively low. For example, Bill complained that on a bad day he might go walking, but nothing would grab his attention. 'The depression robs everything of its colour. Everything's drab and grey.' But when the depression lifted he was someone who had a lively, roving attention – excited by things he saw in the natural world and eager to share his focus. In a state of hyperarousal, meanwhile, the level is necessarily high and the field might be very wide – here Anna comes to mind and those 'red alert' states when she was continually scanning her surroundings for any hint of danger – or it could be very narrow – for instance, a terrified child with eyes fixed on the angry parent's face waiting for him or her to erupt.

Helping people like Bill and Anna to develop a more flexible style of attention is important. We all need to be able to shift from narrow to wide, from low to high or vice versa according to circumstances, and we probably all have our preferences. But for some people their attention gets 'stuck' – whether this be because it is drawn like a magnet to potential trauma-related threats or to obsessive thoughts, or relationally to any hint of criticism or rejection, or because of the deadening grip of long-term depression. Sometimes I might try to shift the 'spotlight of attention' in an explicitly relational way, for instance, to elicit a shared focus with invitations such as: 'Could we think about this together?' 'Would you be willing to be curious with me and see what happens?' 'I am noticing ... how about you?' Remember, exploration is easier when we have a safe haven to return to or a trusted companion to travel with. Alternatively, my questions might direct attention to our surroundings and things perceived with the senses.[8] This can be helpful when focussing on the self or on our relationship proves to be too dysregulating. Here my intervention might go something like this (said with a light, interested tone and allowing optimal spaces between each new idea):

Could we pause and spend a moment looking around the room? How many green objects can you see? Or Look at all the different shapes and patterns. Now shift to things you can hear. Notice my voice ... the birds ... a car approaching then fading into the distance. Now let's use touch. Can you feel the chair through your back and your legs? How does the cushion feel to your hand? Is it soft? textured? Warm?

Another option would be to invite my client to alter her position and observe how that felt. For instance:

What would it be like to sit back, put your feet flat on the ground and allow your spine to lift a little? Take a few deep breaths. Do you feel more or less energy sitting like that? And what happens to your breathing? Has it changed in any way?

Here I am offering a menu of things that could be observed, but am trying not to imply that there is a right or wrong response. A client may give feedback at the end, but it does not matter if he does not. We can usually see if there has been a change.

For someone who is agitated, restless and talking rapidly – and remember this can go hand in hand with hopelessness – we want to slow her down and possibly narrow her field of attention. Again an invitation to notice the present environment can help.[9] But with a hyperaroused client I would say less and use a calmer, more neutral tone of voice. For example, I might try a breathing exercise with an element of repetition in my words and again an invitation to be curious:

Could you focus for a moment on your breathing. Notice the in and out breath ... coming and going ... Don't try to change it, just notice... In and out ... In and perhaps a little pause. Out and another pause ... which is longer – the in or the out breath?

In addition to the regulating function of breathing, a few moments guiding attention to a specific focus alters arousal levels. Grounding exercises or movement can also be regulating:

Can you feel your feet? Is it possible to wriggle your toes and feel them in your shoes?

Just open and close your fists for a moment, maybe in tune with your breathing.

How would it be if we stood and walked round the room to help settle that panicky feeling? Now pause a moment and notice how your body has responded.

Alternatively, some people find it helpful to use objects. For example, holding a cushion, soft ball or pebble can be calming and focus the attention, whilst tossing a ball between us is an immediate and playful way to orient to the present and evoke social engagement. I have given a few examples to give a flavour of a Sensorimotor approach. However, what works for one client may not work for someone else or on another occasion and so it is good to develop a repertoire of stabilising techniques. My own list has grown over the years as I learn from my clients and from other therapists.

Another intervention that forms an intrinsic part of the Sensorimotor approach to working with trauma is to use psychoeducation, by which I mean 'teaching' about the impact of difficult events on the brain/body or sharing a model which offers people a different way of seeing their problems. This can be regulating because for a moment we are stepping out of traumatic dysregulation to consider something from a more distanced place. We have shifted the spotlight of attention and, hopefully, in the process engaged the client's Exploration system. Moreover, because psychoeducation offers alternative perspectives it can be incredibly reassuring. To learn that how you have been experiencing something and responding is a normal and understandable response after some very 'un-normal' events and to realise that you are not alone and that other people think, feel and act like this is a challenge to long-held beliefs about being mad or bad. Moreover, through discovering a name for what you are experiencing and that there are ways of working with the difficulties, new hope emerges.

Psychoeducation includes simple comments such as, 'did you know that many people feel guilty about … ?' Or, it could be a longer explanation: 'Would it help if I explained how your survival brain is hijacking you at the moment?' I frequently use diagrams because they stimulate curiosity and take the spotlight off the individual. A quick sketch is worth much more than a handout because it can be elaborated as we talk and helps to form a co-created language. The model I use most, because it is infinitely adaptable, is the window of tolerance. It provides a simple, de-stigmatising way of making sense of a vast range of symptoms, behaviours and ways of being and can be used as a focus for thinking together about the different ways people have learnt to adapt to difficult circumstances.[10]

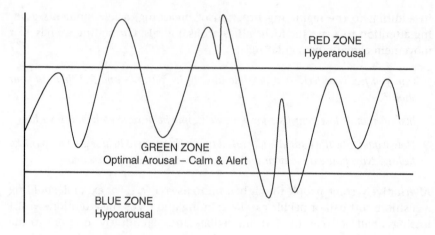

Figure 9.1 The Window of Tolerance
(Adapted from Ogden et al., 2006)

Having done a quick diagram, I might ask 'where are you most of the time?' Often people say 'here and here', indicating the areas of under and over-arousal, 'but hardly ever in the middle'. Or, 'I seem to get stuck down here', or 'I'm always up there in the red … always speeding'. This opens the field for enquiry. Note, I might call the zone of optimal arousal the 'just right space' or 'your window' or the 'calm and alert place'. I want to choose something that can become an accessible shared language. The next step might be to enquire about all the strategies people have found to lower or raise their arousal level, including activities, substances, being with people or animals or going to particular places. If some lead to unintended consequences this provides a springboard for exploring possible alternatives. The beauty of using the model in this way is that it helps reduce shame and defensiveness. Instead of giving the message that what the client is doing is wrong, we need to communicate a genuine interest in how it is trying to help and to stress our common humanity. 'We all go in and out of our window. We all have strategies to bring ourselves up or down and sadly some have negative consequences.' Here are some examples of questions we might ask:

- *What do you notice takes you up or down?*
- *Are there some days when you are more in the window of tolerance? What do you do that helps?*
- *What are the warning signs that you might be slipping into the red or the blue?*
- *What do you usually do to get back into the just right space?*
- *Before you started cutting yesterday, where were you on the diagram?*
- *When did you first discover that drinking could pull you out of feeling flat and numb? Is it always that way or do you sometimes use alcohol to calm you down?*
- *How do other people respond when you are out of your window? What would you like them to do differently?*

Once we have established a shared language it is easy to return to the model in subsequent sessions. For instance, if a client arrived one day in a state of intense distress I might say, 'would it help to slow things down and do something to bring you back into your window of tolerance? I think it'll be easier then to talk.' Or at the end of a session, if she admitted to feeling anxious about being tempted to drink later on I could ask, 'shall we think together about things that might help if you go out of your window?'

Sometimes other therapists tell me that they don't feel confident enough to use psychoeducation. My position is that if I have learned something I think might help a client it would be wrong not to share it. I also believe that trying to find ways to explain things to different people helps clarify our thinking and that, as our language grows, so too does the client's ability to articulate his or her experience. It is just one aspect of developing a shared narrative. However, we have to be sensitive to when slipping into psychoeducation is not actually helping and when it might be an escape into thinking and 'doing' which takes us from something that is hard to bear.

This brings us back full circle to the challenge with which I began the chapter – how do we integrate the *'how we are'* and the *'what we do'*? The four therapeutic 'tasks' highlighted in this chapter – creating safety, offering a different sort of relationship, sitting with despair, and alerting and enlivening – are tasks which blend 'doing' and 'being'. For me it is not either/ or. Both have their place. Some of the interventions described may feel too directive for someone who works in a client-centred, psychodynamic or relational way. But with highly traumatised clients or people who are so over or under-aroused that it takes them out of contact with themselves and with us, I agree with Alvarez that our therapeutic approach has to be modified. Directive interventions don't exclude more instinctive, relational ways of helping to regulate our clients' arousal levels – for instance, through attunement, pacing, use of our own bodies and emotional containment. Nor, and this is important, will they have impact unless we can work in an authentic, affectively immediate way. To use an analogy, some of the specific things we do to bring someone into the present moment, shift attention and invite curiosity are the scaffolding. But the 'bricks and mortar' of change come through authentic 'moments of meeting' and shared humanity. As the Boston Change Group argue, these 'moments of meeting' hold the potential for 'something new [to be] created in the relationship that alters the intersubjective environment'. It is not, they stress, that such moments correct past empathic failures or replace past deficits, but that 'past experience is re-contextualised in the present such that a person operates from within a different mental landscape, resulting in new behaviours and experience in the present and the future' (BCPSG, 2010, p. 28). And I believe that having a different mental landscape is a fundamental part of regaining hope.

In the next chapter I will continue the subject of how to work with hopelessness by discussing three interlinked processes which contribute in a more long-term way to the formation of new mental landscapes: developing the capacity to think of alternative perspectives; accessing grief; and moving from illusory thinking to creative, realistic imagining.

Notes

1. Bear in mind that 'internal clamour' also creates 'noise' and this is likely to be especially acute for anyone who has experienced trauma. To be bombarded by waves of overwhelming sensation and emotion, intrusive thoughts and images, or by the voices of different parts of self leaves little mental space for attending to anything else. For other people the internal 'noise' takes the form of obsessive thoughts, bitter rumination, self-conscious anxiety or addictive cravings. No doubt many other examples could be added to the list.
2. Continuing the analogy of a signal to noise balance, there are also times when there is too little 'signal' to work with. This might be because our clients have slipped into a flatter, numb state – sometimes because of depression, sometimes because they have numbed themselves with drugs or have needed to dissociate from aspects of their experience. In such cases our task is more about alerting our clients and reclaiming their attention than reducing the background noise.
3. This includes demonstrating that we can survive our client's anger when we fail to provide the magic cure or be the 'loyally awaited other'.
4. As Joyce and Sills point out, 'clients often come to therapy believing that they can change according to a predetermined plan, or want just to get rid of particular unpleasant feelings, thoughts or attitudes. They hope to achieve an idealised picture or idea of how they want to be different' (2010, p. 39). But according to this theory change is more likely to occur when people let go, at least for the moment, of what they would like to become and first get to know and be more fully who they are.
5. In the words of the Serenity Prayer, the important thing is having the wisdom to know the difference.
6. I am indebted to all I have learnt from the work of Ogden and Fisher and recommend their books for further information (2006, 2015).
7. Stabilisation and symptom reduction is seen as the first and in some ways most important phase of trauma therapy (van der Hart et al., 2006, pp. 215–17; Ogden et al., 2006; Wright, 2009a). But at all stages helping clients to come back into their window of tolerance and to develop skills and tools for affect-regulation is important.
8. Another way to conceptualise such interventions is that we are tying to develop our clients' capacity for mindfulness.
9. Orienting to our surroundings through our senses is another crucial, but often under or over-used, survival strategy. One reason for inviting people to mindfully notice things in the environment is that it helps shift attention when they are preoccupied with and anxious about what they perceive internally (Ogden et al., 2006, pp. 65–7; Ogden and Fisher, 2015, pp. 111–19).
10. There are many ways of adapting the model if working with children and young people, and on the premise that a couple and a family will also have its 'window of tolerance' and that when other people are out of their 'window' it can dysregulate us, it can be applied to couples and family work.

10

Finding New Perspectives

Hope ... kindled spans the horizons which then open over a closed existence.
(Moltmann, 1993, cited in O'Hara, 2013, p. 26)

A repeated theme in this book, and something I believe we need to be alert to, is the extent to which a client is in a reflective or mentalising state of mind when communicating about future hopes, wishes and fears. Time and again I have witnessed when despair takes people – myself included – into teleological or pretend mode.[1] In the former 'only action will do' and in the latter what is imagined is taken for real. The problem is that in responding to the urgent call for something to be done or investing in comforting 'if only' fantasies, little changes. The dance between hope and despair continues to its old recursive tune when what is vitally needed is something new.

I believe that finding alternative perspectives and having a sense of choice is crucial to gaining or re-gaining hope. As O'Hara eloquently puts it, 'hope is a habit of mind that embraces possibilities' (2013, p. 24). Once kindled, as the opening quotation stresses, it can indeed span the horizons and open the door to alternative futures. However, the problem for many of our desperate, hopeless clients is that they get stuck in a 'no-way-out' viewpoint and take this as the only reality (Holmes, 2010, p. 142). They discount that change is possible, for instance denying that anyone could help – an understandable script after repeated let downs – that they could change or that they might have options. They can also get stuck in an 'only-one-way-out', often illusory viewpoint which they pursue to no avail. Such rigid thinking keeps people stuck, whereas mentalising, as Jeremy Holmes argues, is 'the antithesis of stasis'. It leads to a mode of thinking that is 'always mobile, provisional, subject to visions and revisions, expressing points of view, not final versions' (2010, p. 150). Again quoting Holmes: 'a held child/patient can use mentalising to overcome despair and thus himself hold hope in mind'. 'To mentalise is to construct a reparative bridge over the chasm of loss.' It helps us to cope with and survive the separations, losses, failures, disruptions and 'potential traumata of everyday life' (2010, pp. 95–6). Holmes' meaning here is that through putting things into words and reflecting on them we can find a way out of unendurable stuckness. When we mentalise, a world of self and others is revealed to us 'that is rich, complex and ambiguous – and one in which we have the potential to revise our mental representations of external reality as our actual realities change'

(Wallin, 2007, p. 47). A way I often describe it is that if we can jump onto the bank rather than drowning in our feelings and notice rather than judging or trying to change them, we might discover that we *can* manage emotional arousal and, from this new vantage point, find new ways of thinking about and dealing with our difficulties.

The stress on helping people to notice their habitual ways of seeing things and to find alternative perspectives is trans-theoretical. For instance, interventions informed by the idea of script change and re-decisioning from Transactional Analysis, or the Systemic concept of re-storying, can help people to gain different perspectives on themselves, their relationships and their past, present and future. So too can the creative, experimental processes of Gestalt, Sensorimotor Psychotherapy, psychodrama and the arts therapies. Some therapists might adopt a Compassion Focused approach to help their clients shift out of shame and blame and see their struggles and survival strategies from a more compassionate place (Gilbert, 2005). Others use cognitive approaches and behavioural experiments to challenge old assumptions (cognitive reframing), examine and enhance pathways thinking and address whatever blocks people from achieving their goals (O'Hara, 2013, pp. 70–1). Alternative perspectives can also be discovered through experiences with others. The Boston Change Group thinks of this in terms of 'moments of meeting' which re-contextualise the past. Relational psychotherapists like Bromberg and Stern argue that through encountering and learning to tolerate internal conflicts we gain the possibility for multiple perspectives and this leads to freedom rather than the constraints of rigid single-mindedness or what Wallin calls 'embeddedness' – meaning taking whatever we sense, feel and believe at any given moment at face value (Stern, 2010, pp. 86, 102–3; Wallin, 2007, p. 135). They also stress that it is within the therapeutic relationship that inner conflicts often emerge in full force in the form of rifts, misunderstandings and enactments. These challenge both therapist and client, but can be pivotal in the process of change.

My own approach to helping people develop what I am calling an 'alternative perspectives mind' entails an integration of ideas from the Relational school, mentalisation theory and Sensorimotor Psychotherapy's unique use of phenomenological enquiry. There are several reasons why I am drawn to a relational perspective, one being the belief that developing a different relationship to oneself and therefore to one's future demands more than learning to think and act differently. It emerges primarily through relationship and this is especially true when relational failures and injuries have damaged the individual's capacity to hope. I know from experience how stumbling into and working together through misunderstandings and trauma-related enactments really can help to re-contextual the past and to envisage oneself in kinder ways. And even without edgy, difficult moments between us, the very fact of having another mind to think about you and with you – a process of shared mentalisation – can help our clients to see things in different ways and embrace new possibilities.

To be able to play with ideas in that mobile, provisional way that Holmes speaks of, our clients have to feel safe. We need, therefore, to keep in mind what might be necessary to create a secure base. In addition, we need to be pro-active in order to evoke their curiosity, or in other words, their Exploration system. My plan in what follows is to discuss some specific ways of evoking curiosity. I shall then return to the argument that learning to tolerate internal conflict can loosen the 'constraints of rigid single-mindedness' and create greater freedom of choice by discussing what we mean by inner conflict and how we might work with it. The chapter continues with two related themes – working through grief and moving from fantasy to creative imagining, both of which are also crucial for regaining hope.

Harnessing the exploration system

From a neurological perspective one reason for adopting a curious, experimental stance is that a curious mindset supports neuroplasticity. There is now substantial evidence that all areas of the brain are capable of reorganising themselves, developing new neural networks and making other areas obsolete in response to experience (Doidge, 2007, 2012). We also know that such change is fostered by interrupting and inhibiting old responses and repeating new, more adaptive ones. When we shift the spotlight of our attention and observe our experience with non-judgemental curiosity this helps to inhibit automatic responses and, particularly important, it involves different areas of the brain to those most associated with habitual survival responses. In order to help our desperate clients develop an 'alternative perspectives mind' and a more flexible attentional style, first, as I have argued, we need to provide a relational climate in which they feel safe enough to explore. Then we need to use our own curiosity to evoke their interest. Through mindful questioning we can invite them to step out of the habitual and the known. It is what Ron Kurtz called 'jumping out of the system' (1990, p. 190). We all get caught in habitual ways of doing and perceiving things. We engage in these habits or character patterns in an autopilot, mind-blind way and although they might initially have been adaptive, they can become limiting. When anyone is stuck – and the same is true of a couple or team – to 'jump out of the system' and begin to reflect is often the first step towards change.

Kurtz coined the phrase 'jumping out of the system' in response to Hofstadter's argument that 'it is an inherent property of intelligence that it can jump out of the task it is performing, and survey what it has done; it is always looking for, and often finding patterns' (1990 patterns' (1990), p. 189). I like Kurtz's down to earth way of putting what others might call using dual awareness, decentring or the observing self, and its inherent playfulness, a state of mind which helps us to explore. This sense of playfulness also captures the fact that a curious therapeutic stance needs to be an indifferent one. As soon as we invest in a particular response we fall into the trap of trying to make something happen. Remember that agendas, whoever they belong to, are part of the background 'noise'. They mask awareness and can pull the client back into old scripts rather than providing a space for something new to emerge.

During a therapy session we can help a client 'jump' out of his system (his scripts and schemas) and begin to reflect when we enquire about his present moment responses to the stories or difficulties he brings. We also 'jump' inter-subjectively each time we ask ourselves 'why am I feeling like this about this person?' or raise the question – 'what's happening between us right now?' It is the interweave of non-judgemental curiosity about what is happening inside me/you and what is going on between us that forms the crucible for change. Of course, all therapists use enquiry in various ways and are interested in how people organise and respond to their experiences, and the direction of that enquiry will be coloured by their model theories. As a Sensorimotor Psychotherapist I am informed by Kurtz's argument that 'the goal of therapy is not any particular experience: it is a change which organises all experiences differently, a change in the way of experiencing. To make that kind of change we must deal with meanings and not just experiences. We must bring out the meaning of the way we organise experience, the way we do things, the way we put our world together, perceive it and think about it' (1990, p. 139).[2] Kurtz envisaged this as finding the 'map maker'; in other words, looking for the narrative points of origin of these meanings and what I call the 'survival logic' of adopting certain beliefs and strategies. The 'map maker' is the self who built a particular world view and self-image as a result of his or her experiences in childhood and, as Kurtz argued, when you can contact and work with that child 'you have the possibility of changing those maps and the person who is now using them' (1990, p. 133).

'Bringing out the meaning' demands shifting attention away from content to process[3] ... and moving from ordinary consciousness, with its blend of thinking, associating, interpreting, judging and daydreaming, to a state of mindful curiosity. Kurtz and Ogden, who expanded and refined his work into the sensorimotor approach, developed a particular way of questioning to facilitate this (Ogden et al., 2006, pp. 193–200). Having slowed the process down, the therapist enquires about what Kurtz called the 'core organisers' or five building blocks of experience – the emotions, thoughts, body sensations, impulses to move or five sense perceptions our clients have in response to something they have just told us or reacted to (1990, p. 14). The last of these include the images which come up when we recall something, or the taste, smell or feel associated with it. Impulses to move can be very subtle, such as slightly contracting a muscle, or a big movement such as pulling back. Thoughts often included limiting beliefs or opinions, hopes and fears internalised from others.

Let me give some examples of questions involving the core organisers:

- *When you think of him ... what happens in your **body**?*
- *Do any **emotions** come up when you remember ... ?*
- *When you touch on that sadness, do any **thoughts** go with it?*
- *When you have that familiar **thought** "I should ..." do you feel more energy? Less? Is there an **emotion** that goes with it?*

- As you think of those words and notice that churning in your stomach does an **image or memory** come up?
- Check inside – what happens when I repeat those words ... Do you notice any **sensations?** Do you feel an **impulse to move** in any way?

Inviting people to notice specific core organisers helps bring them into the present and 'lowers the noise' because it reduces what is being attended to. Both are important when working with highly traumatised people who are easily triggered and get flooded by dysregulating waves of affect and sensation. When we consider a question that involves self-referencing, it engages a different part of the brain to the emotionally reactive survival brain (Ogden et al., 2006, pp. 169, 194).[4] If this occurs in the presence of someone calm and non-judgemental this also helps to dampen the familiar responses of the survival brain and can open the door to something transformative. As Alan Schore argued, to re-experience 'dysregulating affects in affectively tolerable doses in the context of a safe environment' is a way of slowly 'regulating and integrating overwhelming traumatic feelings into the patient's emotional life' (in Bromberg, 2011, p. xxxiii). This in itself may be sufficient for change. But a Sensorimotor therapist also uses this type of enquiry as an access route to memories or aspects of our somatic, emotional or cognitive experience that we are unaware of.[5] This can facilitate working more directly with the body, for instance, to develop resources and to gain a sense of physical mastery and vitality[6], or with child states – in other words, with state-dependent memory, or to highlight and explore internal conflicts (Kurtz, 1990, pp. 115–24; Ogden et al., 2006, pp. 244–61).

To illustrate how I use this approach, here is an excerpt from a session with Bill with explanatory comments.[7] If you recall from the examples in Chapter 3, re-kindling Bill's curiosity had helped to shift him out of hypoarousal and hopelessness so that he could think more creatively about options and alternatives. It also served to reconnect him with disconfirmed aspects of himself which he had needed to override as a child in order to prioritise safety.

S: Did anyone else in your family suffer from depression?

B: I'm not sure ... maybe my Uncle Bob. I remember Mum saying he's taken to his bed again and that he'd stay there for days. I don't think anyone called it depression, but he seemed kind of grey and not interested in anything.

S: How did other people respond when he was like that?

B: Mum worried about him. But Dad just got impatient. He'd say things like 'Bob's bone idle. He needs to get off his backside and get on with it. What sort of man goes to bed in the middle of the day?'

Seeing that Bill's face had flushed and he was drumming his fingers against his thighs I asked if he could pause a moment and notice his body. I then began to ask questions based on the core organisers.

S: *What's happening right now?*

B: *I've tightened up.*

S: *And your breathing?*

B: *I'm not. (He took a deeper breath and made eye contact again.)*

S: *What emotion goes with that tensing?*

B: *I'm anxious ... a bit embarrassed ... well ashamed I guess.*

S: *Is there a thought that goes with those feelings?*

B: *I was thinking, if Dad was alive he'd be saying the same about me. He'd say, 'just get on with it! Pull yourself together!'*

Noticing that Bill's agitation had returned in response to this thought, I paused him again by saying 'for a moment, just look around this room. Remind yourself that you're here'. Once he was back in the window of tolerance we could go deeper and my enquiry shifted to asking about conflicting parts of self.[8] What I observed was that I evoked Bill's curiosity and he became more socially engaged. I could then risk a more challenging question.

S: *I wonder, is there a part of you that says things like that? A 'critical Dad' part?*

B: *(smiling) I guess so!*

S: *And when that critical self is around how does the part of you that feels depressed and hopeless feel then?*

B: *Worse ... useless ... like giving up.*

S: *So I'm curious. You're a kind person. I don't suppose you'd be so scornful to a friend who was struggling.*

B: *No, of course not.*

S: *So how is that critical part trying to help?*

Now that Bill seemed interested and very involved in the process my aim was to invite him to consider the 'survival logic' for his habitual self-attack. He realised that telling himself off had two functions. It 'got it in' before anyone could criticise him and it was part of his vain attempt to be like his Dad. But in endlessly comparing how he was with this 'ideal self', the more he undermined his sense of worth. When combined with the squashing of his true self, no wonder he felt so hopeless and depressed. This formed part of an ongoing process in which Bill was slowly able to step back and reflect on the conflicting inner voices which had trapped him in a stuck, hopeless place and which helped him to see the 'shameful' depression and himself in a new light.

Although I said that the process of noticing and naming specific core organisers is inherently regulating, it is important to keep tracking the client's arousal levels and intervene if necessary. In this example notice, for instance, that point when I said – 'for a moment, look around this room. Remind your-self that you're here'. I had observed how Bill had suddenly tensed and his feet were jigging and knew we had to pause before continuing. The other impor-tant thing to remember when using this type of phenomenological enquiry is to keep what we say very simple (not easy for a wordy person like myself!) and avoid 'what do you think?' questions.

A key aspect of Sensorimotor Psychotherapy is its attention to body process and the way the therapist uses present moment noticing or 'applied mindful-ness' to help people discover alternative perspectives and different ways of doing things.[9] By contrast, in Mentalisation Based approaches, which also use curiosity in a systematic way, the invitation is to wonder about the mind and its contents. It is an invitation to 'jump out' of assumptions and reactions and be curious about the mental states which might underlie behaviour. Allen described men-talising as 'mindfulness of the mind' (2006, p. 16). However, whereas mind-fulness is inherently present-centred and in Sensorimotor Psychotherapy the invitation is to study present moment responses, it is possible to mentalise about the past or the future (Allen, 2006, pp. 15–16). For example, compare the list of core organiser questions with the following mentalising questions:

> 'What do you suppose was in her mind when ... ?'
>
> 'What feelings were around when you did that?'
>
> 'What is it that I said or did that left you thinking that ... ?'
>
> 'How do you imagine I might respond if you did tell me?'

In my own work there are times when I use core organiser questions and wonder about the client's here and now responses to the events they are describing. At other times I adopt a style of questioning which would be familiar to someone trained in Mentalisation Based Therapy. Whilst arguably less experience-near, this can further the exploration of relational dynamics. The use of circular questioning, an approach developed by Systemic thera-pists, offers further tools to help people jump out of what they know and to discover new ways of viewing their problems. The approach is based on the premise that information comes from difference and that 'a difference makes a difference'. Whilst designed for family work, circular questions which draw out differences can be applied to individual therapy. For instance, the therapist might ask questions which highlight differences between people, between parts of self, over time or in different situations.[10] They might also draw out behavioural or relational sequences. I shall give an example from each category:

> 'In your family who was the one who worried most about things being perfect? And who next?'
>
> 'When nothing seems to be working, which part of you is more likely to take over: your critical self or your give-up self?'

'When is the problem most difficult? Least evident?'

'Do you feel more in control at home or at work?'

'When you're depressed how does he respond? Then what do you usually do?'

Curiosity, whatever inspires it, can alert and enliven someone in a hopeless, hypoaroused state of mind and calm someone who is agitated and hyper-aroused. It enhances the individual's 'contact' with himself, with us and with his environment. It helps shift the spotlight of attention from trauma-related cues and widens the field of what is being attended to. But although I am emphasising the importance of curiosity, it is curiosity *plus* reflecting on experience that really makes the difference. We could spend our time asking curious questions, but in a mechanical way that goes nowhere. The art is in being able to ask questions that are sufficiently attuned to the client's experience to open up a new kind of meaning making and experiencing, which is what I think Kurtz was getting at when he said 'we must bring out the meaning of the way we organise experience, the way we do things, the way we put our world together, perceive it and think about it'. David Wallin says something important here: 'We must be able to find our way to an intuitive grasp of the mental states that underlie our patients' present experience. This is *implicit* mentalizing and it allows us to reach, resonate with, and respond in an attuned fashion to experience in the here and now for which our patients may as yet have no words. Then having accessed this unspoken experience that has been dissociated or disowned, we must be able to reflect on it with the patient in order to further its integration. This requires ex*plicit* mentalizing, which enlists language to help patients make sense of their experience by situating it in the context of the lived past and anticipated future as well as the present moment.' Wallin concludes, 'mentalising implicitly and explicitly, we gradually enable our patients to do the same' (2007, p. 134).

Tolerating internal conflict and moving from single-mindedness to the freedom of multiple perspectives

As therapists our use of both implicit and explicit mentalising is especially important when working with people who are stuck because of internal conflicts. In various ways we will get an intuitive sense of incoherence and ambiguity through what we observe in the body, through our countertrans-ference and through the sometimes contradictory ways such clients make use of us. We have in effect to attune to not just one but several selves and to help the individual to become an impartial and compassionate observer of these different parts of self. The rationale behind this is that as he learns to tolerate and reflect on internal conflict he will gain the possibility for multiple perspectives and, hence, greater freedom of choice.

Before going further I want to look briefly at how different schools of therapy explain and work with inner conflict. A traditional Freudian would argue that we are all troubled by conflicts between the ego and the id and utilise a range of 'defences' including repression in order to avoid recognising what we don't want to know. This 'resistance', it is argued, is dissolved through interpretation and insight. A Kleinian analyst would use the language of splitting and projection, but again emphasise the importance of interpretation to resolve unconscious conflicts. For relational, intersubjective therapists however, the emphasis has changed from this rationalist, cause and effect, one-person psychology. First, they have a very different view of the mind, arguing not for repression, what we don't want to know getting pushed into another layer of the mind, but for dissociation and an ever-shifting, dissociative relationship between self-states. As Bromberg argues, these self-states can be either separate but collaborative, or adversarial and sequestered from one another as 'islands of truth'. In the latter case each functions as 'an insulated version of reality that protectively defines what is "me" at a given moment' and forces other self-states that are 'inharmonious with its truth to become "not-me" and unavailable to participate in the complex negotiation we call internal conflict' (2011, p. 69).

Another major difference lies in the account of what contributes to internal conflict. Classic Freudians emphasise repressed emotions, thoughts and infantile impulses and fantasies, often relating to Oedipal struggles. A Kleinian therapist would think of a conflict between the urge to love and to destroy, with a need to split off envy and hatred in order to preserve what is good, and between life and death instincts (Gomez, 1997, p. 35). But contemporary theory places far more emphasis on real trauma rather than primitive fantasies. In earlier chapters I talked about how certain experiences have to become "not-me" as a result of severe trauma. I also mentioned what Bromberg describes as a more 'subtly protective dissociation' caused by the trauma of disconfirmation when aspects of the child's personality and certain interests and talents are ignored or scorned by his parents. These disavowed attributes may become dissociated from the self as the child learns to adapt to who the parents want him or her to be (2011, pp. 69, 57).

Another trauma-based perspective takes us back to our evolutionary heritage and sees inner conflict as a manifestation of competing survival responses.[11] For instance, our traumatised clients may simultaneously seek attachment, whilst feeling an impulse to flee and push people away. They may struggle with legitimate anger (a fight response), but out of fear respond to others in submissive ways. And for many the need to get on with normal life (remember the action systems of daily life) is compromised by defensive survival responses such as hypervigilance, immobilisation or flight. The pushes and pulls of contradictory somatic impulses and warring inner voices keep people stuck, and in my opinion this is often one of the main causes of despair. Until the inner conflicts can be noticed, named and worked through, thus transforming procedural memory into explicit memory, the trauma stays unresolved. They can emerge via interpersonal enactments but they also emerge in the body, and this is where a sensorimotor approach offers something unique, namely an invitation to people to witness their emotional and somatic experience in a curious, non-judgemental way and use this as a route to deeper enquiry.

As therapists we need to look out for signs of competing survival responses. At the same time we need to consider the questions: 'Which survival responses are not available to my client and how might they be developed?' 'Which are overused and get in the way of daily life?' All of us need to be able to turn to a range of strategies – to be able to reach out to others (attachment); to take a stand and set boundaries (fight); to avoid or run from things that might harm us (flight); to minimise harm when it is unsafe or impossible to use fight or flight and, *in extremis*, to be able to shut down. To describe ways of working with this is beyond the scope of this book.[12] But I want to stress that when people learn to safely and flexibly utilise different survival responses and, significantly, to step out of them when pulled into an 'autopilot' response, this itself opens up alternative ways of living and construing one's world. As examples I am thinking of Anna, who learned to recognise and come to terms with acute hypervigilance; Megan, who gradually found ways to avoid dissociating and hence become more present to daily life and Bill, who came to appreciate the logic of shutting down as a way to survive when younger rather than something shameful.

'The creation of internal conflict', writes Stern, 'is also the creation of a sense of initiative. Desire in the absence of a conflicting alternative is nothing more than compulsion, and compulsion negates the feeling that one is choosing one's own life' (2010, p. 102). This eloquently captures the struggle our troubled and traumatised clients face when they are repeatedly hijacked by competing animal defences. It also captures the struggle of someone whose childhood entailed an adaptive disavowal of aspects of him or herself. The adaptations the child and teenager had to make to live in a world where adults were threatening or love was conditional meant that the choices they made – and still make – were not really choices at all. And somehow, in therapy, we have to get close enough to the conflicts – to be 'in them' – for someone to move from the constraints of single-mindedness and experience a more flexible 'being in two minds' about something. It could be argued that once people can reflect on inner conflicts they gain a stronger sense of knowing their own mind and with this the freedom to make authentic choices.

So how does this occur? What in Stern's words leads to the 'creation of internal conflict'? For relational therapists the 'action' takes place in the intersubjective domain. However, I believe that talking about what goes on between us – a relational approach – may not be possible with some people or certainly not for a long time, and even then, not on all occasions. It might be because they are so prone to becoming dysregulated (going out of their window of tolerance) or slipping into acute shame that our focus may need to be more distanced. I will still own when I think I might have got something wrong, or observe that my client seems suddenly scared of or angry with me. But this does not necessarily mean spending a long time exploring the nuances of whatever created a rift. I also believe that as well as being curious about what goes on between us alternative perspectives can be found when we focus on the body, where there may be struggles between competing action tendencies, or on internal dynamics using the language of 'parts of self'.[13] This language has particular relevance to people who had to develop dissociative strategies as a result of trauma or attachment failures. But given how we all shift self-states it is applicable to us all. For instance, if I were to question my responses to a current situation or memory it is quite likely that I might reply: 'Part of me feels sad and another part feels angry' or 'my first thought was ... but then another part of me thought ... ' or 'I notice in my body that I want to reach out, but it also feels like something is holding me back'. Experiencing mixed feelings is part of being human.

Using this mode of enquiry we can be curious about the contradictory views of different parts of self; about how they might be trying to help (their 'survival logic'); and about what it's like to be hijacked by other parts of self or stuck in the grip of competing responses. At the same time we can endeavour to encourage internal dialogue.[14] Alternatively, we can use this language when exploring what is going on between us: for example, 'I keep noticing that one part of you seems to be pushing me away, but another part hates it when I am quiet', or 'It seems as if part of you is sceptical that I can help and that a "younger self" keeps hoping that I'll step in and rescue you. What do you think the sceptical part is most worried about?'

As an example, my conversation with Bill about depression enabled us to access a familiar internal conflict between what I called his 'critical self' and a more hopeless, giving-up part of self who had learnt to be compliant and minimise his expectations. As discussed in Chapter 4, on another occasion we 'discovered' that there was also a 'stroppy teenager' inside who wanted to rebel against the constraints of his play-it-safe existence and be free to be creative and explore. That self could be headstrong, sometimes getting him into trouble. But Bill learned to listen to its voice so that he did not have to keep disconfirming his creativity and liveliness. These characteristics could be integrated into a richer, more textured self who was freer to live life according to his own dictates. One day when I asked Bill for an image that captured being creative and free he said a buzzard soaring above the earth. He returned to that image on many occasions, drawing inspiration from the buzzard when he encountered setbacks and dips in mood.

The more I work, the more it makes sense to hold a trauma-informed perspective about internal conflict. Some of the people mentioned in this book were stuck in a conflict between yearning for attachment but terrified about allowing themselves to become close to anyone because of childhood trauma. For others the struggle was between parts of self that held vulnerability and tougher 'fight' parts that hated and wanted to get rid of the vulnerable self. Some, like Bill, learned to hide a more alive and assertive self under a depressed, being good and not hoping for much self. And from a trauma perspective it is important that we can welcome those different selves into the dialogue and listen for their messages about what's safe and not safe. But starting to recognise and integrate conflicting parts of self is not the whole story. As our traumatised and desperate clients develop more of an 'alternative perspectives mind', grieving is often not far behind.

The need to grieve

Finding true hope often entails letting go and grieving things that were lost or could not happen in the past – one's childhood, former dreams, significant people – and in some cases the inability to mourn lies behind states of depression and despair. There are many reasons why grieving gets blocked. Sometimes external circumstances prevent closure. For instance, when listening to an interview with the relatives of people on a missing plane I was struck by one man's words. He said 'when you don't know and are hanging onto hope it's impossible to grieve'.[15] It reminded me of people I have worked with who have hoped against hope that one day their abusive or neglectful parents would give them the love and affirmation that they needed and deserved as children. But such loyal waiting, like other forms of illusory hoping, means never facing the loss. The pervasive grip of traumatic memories and the legacy of an out-of-kilter nervous system can also interfere with mourning.

Returning to the theme of inner conflict, sometimes the grief process is impeded by an inability to face conflicting feelings and impulses. It has been a long-standing tenet of psychodynamic thinking that there is a link between unresolved conflicts, blocked grief and depression. Whilst I think it is more complicated than this, it is a position which offers further variations on the theme of hope and despair.[16] For instance, David Malan argued that one of the roots of depression is 'grief that has in some way miscarried and has never been worked through' (2001, p. 139).[17] The grieving process has become complicated by the need to repress or dissociate irreconcilable feelings and impulses such as anger, rage and contempt, and this is especially true if the target of these feelings and impulses is someone one needs, loves or thinks one should love. 'The mixture of love and hate for the same person', he argued, 'is one of the deepest and most painful conflicts that human beings suffer from, and depressive patients will do everything in their power to avoid it.' Sometimes the avoidance entails giving up one's vitality and aliveness. It is a turning away from life and a failure to commit oneself to relationships, a suspension of feelings and settling for a constricted, unimaginative life. *In extremis* some people come to believe that the only way out of the conflict is suicide (2001, pp. 147, 152).

Malan believed it is this conflict that has to be reached when working with the most deeply depressed people and 'when it is reached it can afford the most profound relief – with the result that the despair and utter deadness of depression become converted into hope and life' (2001, p. 144). If hatred and anger can be acknowledged along with any ensuing guilt, then there is space for the sadness to be heard and for healing rather than depressive tears. Like ruminative thoughts, depressive tears feel stale and inspire little empathy. They are not in touch with their origin. By contrast, healing tears feel more real. They move us and move things along. In Malan's words they 'are the conversion of depression, which leads nowhere, into grief, which leads to hope and the possibility of a new life in the future' (2001, pp. 145–6).

Although I have observed how once it has become safe to acknowledge anger, sadness often emerges and, if it is possible to stay with this, it is followed by relief and more energy and vitality, I think we need to take a much broader view on the causes of blocked grief. This is especially important when trauma lies in the background. Indeed, it is widely acknowledged that grieving occupies a central place in the recovery process. For instance, Judith Herman identifies remembrance and mourning as the central task in the second stage of trauma therapy and writes, 'survivors of chronic childhood trauma face the task of grieving not only for what was lost, but also for what was never theirs to lose. The childhood that was stolen from them is irreplaceable. They must mourn the loss of the foundation of basic trust, the belief in a good parent. As they come to recognise that they were not responsible for their fate, they confront the existential despair that they could not face in childhood' (1994, pp. 155, 193). Moreover, it is often not just the loss of a normal childhood that has to be faced but, because of the pervasive after effects of trauma, the loss of a normal adulthood and the loss of a hoped-for future (Allen, 2001, p. 115).

What keeps our traumatised clients stuck in despair rather than being able to move through a natural grieving process is much more complex than an inability to tolerate the conflict between love and hate. As pointed out in Chapter 7 any emotions that might pose a threat if expressed need to be banished from awareness. For anyone brought up in an environment where expressing anger was unsafe then it makes sense to do all you can to avoid expressing anger or provoking it in others.[18] If tears were met with ridicule or, worse, physical cruelty, then sadness has to be disavowed. If you were goaded when you betrayed that you felt scared or ashamed, then hiding vulnerability is imperative. 'You feel what you must feel in order to be convincing in the role that will save you' (Frankel, 2002, p. 109). But when memories, emotions, pain, wishes and hopes are consistently dissociated, and when feelings about cumulative losses and injuries cannot be processed, then the child and later adult becomes trapped in a state of depression or prone to angry outbursts with self or others, or endlessly troubled by a range of somatic problems.

Healthy mourning is an ebbing and flowing process. It cannot be rushed and, as Bowlby was one of the first to appreciate, entails moving through specific stages in order to come to terms with the reality of all that has been suffered and lost. But it could be argued that some people get stuck at certain stages in the mourning process. For instance, let us take Bowlby's four stage model of numbness, yearning and searching (which includes outbursts of angry protest), disorganisation and despair, and lastly reorganisation (1989, pp. 82–9). Someone stuck in numbness may have had to shut off all emotions. Someone stuck in protest may be using anger to mask other emotions such as sadness and fear. This is the person who is either cynical about hope – 'it's adaptive not to hope' – or who clings to fantasies of compensation or revenge and blames and shames rather than facing his or her vulnerability – the position of trying to turn passive into active. Other people who invest in magical solutions might be stuck at yearning and searching, whilst our most hopeless, despairing clients could be stuck in the third stage of the cycle. This is a simplistic interpretation because different parts of self may get stuck at different stages or the individual may keep shifting between two stages without ever reaching that final stage of acceptance and moving on.

Once people have been able to face hitherto discounted or dissociated emotions, to rage against wrongs and grieve for all that was missing, the past can become something that happened and is over rather than being constantly relived and with this, as Herman suggests, comes 'renewed hope and energy for engagement with life'.[19] However, she cautions that the descent into mourning can itself feel endless and when people ask how long the painful process of working on traumatic memories and grieving will last, she explains that it cannot be bypassed or hurried. 'It will almost surely go on longer than the patient wishes, but it will not go on forever' (1994, p. 195). This is useful to remember when we or our clients succumb to hopelessness because of the snakes and ladders process that typifies working with complex trauma. It is also important to remind ourselves of the healing potential of the relationship we offer. Again quoting Herman: 'what sustains the patient through this descent into despair is the smallest evidence of an ability to form loving connections' (1994, p. 194). She had in mind a positive memory of someone caring or a connection to animals or children. But our holding presence and 'alongsideness' can also be a lifeline and, in time, form a new memory to draw upon.

In this sense grieving serves as a bridge between self and others and between past, present and future (van der Hart et al., 2006). As DeYoung says, 'it brings past and present together into coherent meanings, dense and rich with feeling'.[20] But more than that – it bridges or helps to integrate different self-states. For anyone who has needed to shut away certain experiences and make them 'not-me' in order to survive, the work of remembrance and mourning in the presence of someone willing to listen and to hold the pain enables a 'once-fragmented self to emerge as a self of integrity' (DeYoung, 2003, p. 115). This is where some of the earlier work inviting curiosity about different parts of self and self-with-other patterns bears fruit. So often, as discussed in Chapter 7, people who have been badly hurt don't want to know their more vulnerable selves – the parts that hold the knowledge of being little and helpless along with sadness, terror and shame – and why should they when significant others have repeatedly not wanted to know? They learn to scorn tears as 'weakness' and want to get rid of the vulnerable self. In many cases anger and rage have to be heard and integrated before grief can be felt. This often begins by gently challenging self-directed anger. Our gentle curiosity and capacity to dance with the resistance – 'how does/did attacking yourself help?' – plus repeatedly saying 'that's not how I see you' when people deride themselves, will slowly make a difference. In time, the sadness will have a space and they can start to see themselves in a more compassionate light. We could say that of all 'alternative perspectives' this is the most important.

Megan was one person who had shut away both sadness and anger in order to survive as a child and who, in the later stages of our work, began little by little to mourn the loss of a normal childhood. We had been working on helping Megan to manage the panic she felt coming home at the end of the day, and on one occasion I asked her to describe walking back from school. She immediately tensed and said she felt scared. 'I don't want to go home', she said in a childlike voice. Instinctively, I responded: 'that's not right that a child should feel frightened about going home'. Her expression altered. 'What are you noticing?' I asked. Megan said she suddenly realised that it wasn't normal and had then felt sad. I repeated, 'no it's not normal'. She sobbed quietly then said, 'I'm thinking, what a waste, those years ... the things I missed.' I agreed. 'So sad, the awful things that happened and the things that could not happen. That's something to grieve.'

We talked about what Megan missed in particular and in a choked voice she said, 'no one welcoming me when I got back or being interested in my day'. Again I reflected how sad that was, and then asked what she did with her sadness? 'Push it away like I do now', she replied. 'I tell myself it's stupid to cry.' She laughed when I observed that she was not doing that now. We talked about how we need someone to take our feelings seriously when we are upset or scared – not to 'busy' them away or tell us we're silly. Then we discussed how Megan could respond when a younger, sad part of her pops up. 'What would you say or do', I asked, 'if you could join that young girl walking home?' 'I'd hug her and tell her she's not alone.' When we next met Megan told me she had gone home and found a soft toy to hug. 'I wanted to find a way not to forget her', she said. 'If I do this everyday maybe she won't feel so scared about going home.'

This moving example illustrates De Young's point that grieving helps in the process of integrating different self-states, and in particular parts of self that 'hold' attachment needs but have repeatedly been scorned and criticised by protector/persecutor parts. In some therapies there are certain pivotal and transformational moments which unleash deep grief. Enabled by our presence to 'ride the rapids' of intense emotion (Kurtz, 1990, pp. 125–30), the client moves through a sequence of feelings which often includes despair, anger and sadness followed by relief and calm. In others there are many smaller, less emotionally charged moments when sadness is touched on and each time it is shared and taken seriously it can be woven into the fabric of the individual's affective life. This was true for Megan. It was also true for Bill. For example, as Bill grappled with the conflict between his wish to be free like the buzzard and his anxiety about not matching up to other people's expectations, he often touched on sadness. 'I'm sad when I think of the waste', he explained. 'Over 30 years trying to be the man my father wanted me to be. But I'm not him. I can't be!' Catching the tears in his eyes I said, 'It's OK to cry … even though I guess your father would have said "grown men don't cry"'. 'Too right!' Bill exclaimed. 'But that's balls. I think I've been crying for a long time. It was just hidden inside.' Without it needing to be said, I think Bill was beginning to understand how depression had masked his grief as well as 'keeping him below the radar' in order to avoid his father's anger.

On another occasion Bill's grief seemed more impassioned. He had mentioned watching a documentary about suicide. 'I can understand why people do it', he said. 'You've been there', I reflected noticing tears in his eyes. 'Yes. When I can't see a light at the end of the tunnel.' 'How do you think having thoughts about killing yourself might be trying to help?' I asked, adding when Bill looked puzzled, 'because I guess they are thoughts about ending something'. He responded with more energy. 'Yes. I don't want to end my life – just this endless struggle! I want to study, to travel. I want to make something of my life.' The passion in his voice made me appreciate that there is a difference between the despair of someone who cannot envisage anything else and of someone like Bill who sees alternative futures but is blocked from getting there. Bill did cry that session, then spoke of feeling determined not to let old fears keep holding him back. 'It makes me think of a log jam', I said, 'all the logs floating downstream getting jammed because one or two drift out of line. And our job is to free them.' Bill liked the idea. 'We are loggers. But first we have to spot the jams.'

Grieving demands being able to access the full range of our emotions and parts of ourselves that have had to stay hidden. It also demands coming to terms with the reality of what happened and accepting how things are now in order to move on.

But whilst people stay wedded to illusory hopes neither grieving nor acceptance are possible. This takes me to the third theme of this chapter – the need to move from illusory, fantasy-based hoping to a form of imagining that is flexible and creative whilst also grounded in an acceptance of reality.

From illusory hopes and fantasies to creative imagination

Hope, as O'Hara says, 'enables us to imagine new ways of being in the world', and the reverse is also true (2013, pp. 24, 57). We cannot hope unless we can imagine. But there is a difference between fantasy and creative imagination. As Winnicott discussed in *Playing and Reality*, in the former external reality is shut out and in the mind anything is possible. It is one-dimensional. Nothing happens or is likely to happen because in this dissociated state so much is happening (1990, p. 27). It creates a dead end which enables the individual to retain omnipotence because limitations don't have to be faced, nor do feelings of hopelessness and despair or anger, fear or shame. Indeed Winnicott argued – and this fits well with what we know now about dissociation – that whilst 'fantasying', his term for what mentalisation theorists would call pretend mode, the individual does not exist. It paralyses action and the kind of dreaming and playing within a transitional space which opens up new possibilities (1990, pp. 27, 33).

In describing 'fantasying' Winnicott drew on his work with a woman who had retreated into fantasy for most of her life. He compared her doing something in her fantasy such as walking on pink clouds with someone imaginatively thinking about the future, such as creating a garden or planning a holiday. Winnicott defined this as a fantasy about something real and hence two-dimensional. It is a looking-forward-to action, unlike fantasying which occurs in a different time sphere. 'What happens happens immediately, except that it does not happen at all' (1990, pp. 26–37). He also differentiated fantasying from dreaming, which can hold layer upon layer of symbolic meaning.

The capacity to imagine creatively, in Winnicott's view, depends on being able to access a transitional or potential space between inner and outer worlds, the area of illusion and play which he argued lay at the heart of all creative living[21] – and it is a capacity which can be severely compromised by trauma (1990, pp. 1–14; Turner, 2002). As Kalsched points out, Winnicott has helped us understand that when something 'unthinkable' occurs, then something dreadful happens to the transitional space – that intermediate area to which both inner reality and external life contribute. Repeated exposure to traumatic anxiety stifles the capacity to think from alternative perspectives, which as discussed earlier is a pre-requisite for hope, and it 'forecloses transitional space, kills off symbolic activity of creative imagination' and replaces it with 'a dissociated state which is neither imagination nor living in external reality, but a kind of melancholic self-soothing compromise which goes on forever, a defensive use of the imagination in the service of anxiety avoidance' (Kalsched, 1996, p. 35). With the benefit of a greater understanding of dissociation, Kalsched could appreciate this protective aspect of fantasying. 'The psyche's capacity to invent fantasies', he argued, 'keeps the traumatised individual alive by telling herself stories – stories that give her a meaningful place in life and therefore hope. By altering her state of consciousness she takes care of herself in fantasy' (1996, p. 49).

Whilst fantasying or pretend mode holds the lure of seemingly endless possibilities, Kalsched emphasised that to live in and accept reality means making choices and tolerating limitations. The aim of therapy should therefore be to help people 'to reach a place where reality is not denied and fantasy retains its vitality' (1996, pp. 173–4, 204). In other words, for change to occur people may need to let go of old hopes and develop a capacity to

play with different alternatives then step back from this private imaginative sphere – Winnicott's transitional space, to sift through options, make
choices and think how to translate dreams into action. It is a process in
which 'groundedness' and imagination are synthesised and where we can
hold both external and internal reality (our hopes, desires, beliefs and feelings) in mind when we respond to events (Wallin, 2007, p. 143). But before
we can creatively imagine new ways of being in the world we must also learn
to accept and let go.

What do we mean by acceptance? Acceptance entails acknowledging this
is how my life had been and how I am at the moment without slipping into
resignation, stagnation or self-criticism, and having the courage day by day to
take small steps towards trying something different. It can include accepting
having felt powerless and helpless without labelling this as being weak or bad,
and accepting mistakes and failures without interpreting this as meaning 'I'm
a failure'. We are all fallible, make mistakes and can be disabled by circumstances. But a lifelong task is to view ourselves with compassion and, to adapt
a quotation from Khan, 'not be devalued in our eyes' by our failures (Willock,
2014, p. 241). I recall Pema Chodron's belief that hopelessness is the beginning of the beginning. As she argued, 'without giving up hope – that there's
somewhere better to be, that there's someone better to be, we will never relax
with where we are or who we are' (1997, p. 38). This is the stance behind
radical acceptance and the concept of paradoxical change. If we can make the
conscious choice to experience our sensations, feelings and thoughts 'just as
they *are* moment to moment' and accept ourselves as we are right now, paradoxically change will occur (Germer, 2009, p. 32).

The journey towards acceptance is a theme encountered in many myths
and stories. For instance, in a fascinating study Allan Chinen traces how,
across cultures, fairy tales in which the protagonists are older people highlight a task of being able to let go the dichotomous thinking of youth (good/
bad, black/white) in order to 'think of shades of grey, accept compromises,
ambiguity and uncertainty and to surrender, however painfully, youthful
dreams of perfection' (1994, p. 29). He cites 'elder tales' in which youthful
ideals are transformed into mature pragmatism (1994, p. 35). Of course, there
is a difference between the heady idealism of adolescents and young adults
who can explore the world from a securely attached base and the desperate
hope-against-hope dreams of people like Mae and Pam for whom experiences
of love and safety were at best fleeting. But for both groups the letting go of
dreams can entail painful soul searching and grieving. As Chinen points out,
'extraordinary events are sometimes necessary to force self-confrontation
and growth, and sometimes only tragedy – the death of a child, a traumatic
divorce, or failing in a job works' (1994, p. 28). And as many of the elder
tales illustrate, this requires hard work. Through experiences where they
had to confront themselves, the 'heroes' of these tales find ways to let go
of magical illusions and reach the position of wisdom and integrity which
Erikson identified as the challenge of later life. But interestingly, in the tales

this achievement generally occurs **in** relationship – even if the 'other' is an animal or faerie-being. For example, sometimes it is after an out-of-luck, desperate old man or woman shows compassion to another being that they are bestowed a magical gift and so 'live in comfort and honour for the rest of their days'.

From a very different perspective John Wilson's research into the characteristics of self-transformation after trauma identified that they include accepting the loss of invulnerability and that much of life is illusory, accepting one's smallness in the face of horrific experiences and the vastness of the universe, and accepting the continuity and discontinuity of life – in other words, change, loss and death (2006, pp. 406–8). These are things that someone stuck in hopelessness or a dependency on idealised others (loyal waiting) or reliant on their own self-care system can find so hard to accept. However, one of the privileges of working with people in a long-term therapy is being able to witness the transformation that occurs when they are able, after a snakes and ladders journey through pain and despair, to grieve and find acceptance. For some people like Sonia and Megan it entails facing and accepting the painful truth of parents who hurt or failed to protect or cherish them; for others the reality of childlessness or disability or, like Bill, the wasted years spent trying to please others. This process entails letting go the magical 'if only' hopes that have kept them going for so long and the development of what Mitchell calls 'a more mature, authentic version of hope generated through the capacity to sustain an integrated, textured experience of self and others despite loss and vulnerability' (1993, pp. 204–7, 261). It is a version of hope that enables people to find a new beginning rather than trying repeatedly to make a better past.

To illustrate this process let me return to Pippa, whom I introduced in Chapters 6 and 7. It was moving to see the changes in Pippa as she grappled with the loss of what she called her 'ridiculous hope' and as she slowly began to own and accept those parts of her that felt terrified or hopeless and helpless. During this phase of therapy Pippa wrote me a moving letter about hope. I am grateful to her for allowing me to use her words here as they convey so movingly the points I have been trying to make. Pippa explained how hope got her through the most awful years of her childhood. Through all the worst days 'this incredibly brave and somewhat magical tyke that lives within me continued to urge me to keep skipping forward with the certainty that I could do anything I set my mind to. It was like a force within me that no one could break; nothing could stop me, nothing could beat me, nothing would hold me back from achieving my goals.' Then came the devastating day when the hopeful part of her 'vanished' after that difficult meeting with her manager (see Chapter 6). 'It felt as if hope died inside me that day. She took it away and Tyke hasn't skipped since. Now instead he wonders if there is a future and maybe dreams don't come true? Maybe we can't achieve all of those things that we'd imagined; maybe we have to finally admit defeat. I tell Tyke this is a much more realistic view of life, that maybe it's about time he grew up and stopped believing that anything is possible. He laughs in my face!'

Even now, as I re-read Pippa's words, I feel a mix of sadness and admiration for that child self and a sense of energy and – is it triumph? – to hear that Tyke's determined, 'I'll do it my way!' spirit lives on. I also recall the emergence of a quieter, steadier form of hope as Pippa slowly worked on early memories and began to let go of some of her ambitious striving, do less for others and, now and then, accept help. And with this increasing integration and self-awareness hope re-emerged. I caught Pippa's excitement some weeks after she sent that letter when she arrived, saying with delight, 'I've found my hopeful part again!' She explained that a few days after our last session she had bought a new diary and on turning the blank pages realised that from now on she could choose what she wanted to do. There were no 'shoulds and oughts'. There were lots of places she wanted to visit and new things to learn. Pippa added that she knew this was different. It sounded more like hope grounded in reality and my sense of her in that moment was of a more centred, very present woman.[22] I acknowledged that when Pippa had lost the hopeful part of her it had been very scary, but commented that this seemed to be coming from a wiser self rather than that tough child who believed she could do anything. Pippa laughed and said 'yes, but Tyke saved me many times and I don't want to forget that'. As we talked the image emerged of this new hopefulness being like a tiny pearl hidden away, perhaps never lost even in the most frightening times, but now getting bigger and bigger.

Was this a 'new' form of hope – the evidence of a more integrated, insightful and resourced woman? Or something that had always been there – a wiser self, an innate aspect of her personality that transcended the structurally dissociated selves which had emerged out of necessity in order to help Pippa survive emotionally during some horrific experiences? Probably both. However we might conceptualise that 'wiser self', in addition to her 'ridiculous hope', Pippa seemed to have a quiet faith that things would get better and, in addition to Tyke's defiant optimism, this quiet faith appears to have sustained her at intervals throughout her life. For instance, she described how on one occasion she had been very ill and spent many months in hospital, but had told herself every day that she would get better. In the bleakest days during the therapy she said that it felt like that too. She knew that what she was going through as horrific memories emerged would be worth it. Things would get better. This helped Pippa persevere despite periods when she was hijacked by the terrified child or flight parts that argued for 'upping sticks' and going to live a different life somewhere else or, on the blackest days, for suicide.

For many people, and Pippa was no exception, acceptance comes and goes, intermingled with outbursts of anger and grief, renewed attacks on the self and descents into despair and that is because transformation in real life is a far more complex and painstaking process than in fairy tales. It often demands revisiting the traumas and 'failure situation' many times (Winnicott, 1955, p. 20 cited in Orange, 2011, p. 153), and for anyone who had to become what others needed him or her to be in order to preserve attachment bonds, it means learning compassion for the child who did not fail but heroically found the best ways he or she could to survive and a frightening process of daring to be oneself (Frankel, 2002; Orange, 2011, pp. 201–5). As the ones who witness their story our attitude of acceptance, whether we think of this as unconditional positive regard or adopting a mindful stance of non-defensive receptivity to whatever our clients say or feel and however they are in relation to us, is probably far more important than we could ever appreciate. I recall how one day a woman to whom I had repeatedly voiced my belief that she was not bad and that what happened to her was not her fault, said 'don't ever stop saying that will you, even though I can't believe it'. 'Can I really be me and still be welcomed and accepted here?' is a refrain our most traumatised and troubled clients communicate both overtly and in numerous subtle ways, and we can hold the belief and hope that our willingness to hear their truth – sometimes for the first time – and our acceptance of them may ultimately be contagious.

Acceptance is not the letting go of infantile hopes and dreads to establish a 'rational normality' of the Freudian project. Nor is it a passport to happiness and everything feeling miraculously better. It is a coming to terms with the losses and hurts of real trauma and the failures of others, including wider society, to see and stop the trauma happening. When someone asks me in an anguished voice, 'why didn't anyone notice?' 'Why didn't anyone do something?' I have to say 'I don't know. But what I do know is that help and care was what you most needed and deserved.' 'Deserved? Do I?' What our most traumatised clients hope for is often coloured by notions of deserving. Years of shame and blame set up a 'negative deserving system'. 'I don't deserve!' 'I deserve to be punished!' The new version of hope, when it emerges, goes hand in hand with a more positive sense of deserving and this only comes when people are able to really hear the message that they were not bad and unlovable as children and are not bad and unworthy of love and good things now – just human beings who have suffered and found the best ways they could to survive in a dangerous and inhospitable world.

Thinking about the many people whose stories have moved me I realise that I could have written about many small and big moments when something a client says highlights a shift into acceptance of what was and what is, and I mused why I chose to mention Pippa. Perhaps it was because of the power and eloquence of her words, more poignant because, when caught in a frozen, dissociated state all words vanished and she became acutely distressed by this loss of a capacity to communicate. Perhaps too because the defiant courage of little Tyke speaks to me of something resolutely determined in all of us to fight for life – of the hope that lies behind despair. Believing that that spirit is there, somewhere deeply hidden like Pippa's pearl, gives me hope for my desperate clients.

Notes

1. See Chapter 2 for definitions of these terms.
2. Kurtz was influenced by the work of Perls, and so the idea of using phenomenological enquiry to illuminate how people organise their experiences will resonate with Gestalt therapists.
3. Bromberg argued that this is one of three clinical shifts that represent a paradigm change in current analytic thinking (2011, pp. xxxvi, 126).
4. Brain scans show how the Medial Prefrontal Cortex lights up, and significantly this area of the brain has a direct connection to the amygdala, the body's early warning system.
5. See Ogden (2006, 2015) for more detail about these Sensorimotor approaches.
6. This, as I will discuss in the next chapter, can be very important for people who are stuck in depression and hypoarousal.
7. For confidentially this excerpt is fictitious, but true to the spirit of my work with Bill and other clients.
8. Another option might have been to ask a mentalising question about his father, such as 'what do you imagine from your Dad's life might have made him impatient if anyone was depressed or unwell?', and we explored this in subsequent sessions.
9. To learn more about 'applied' or 'embodied relational mindfulness' I recommend Ogden et al. (2006) and Ogden and Fisher (2015, pp. 41–3, 132–43).
10. See Brown (1997) for examples of different types of circular questioning and a discussion about their use.
11. My thanks to Janina Fisher for all she has taught me about conflicting 'parts' of self.
12. For further information see Ogden and Fisher (2015, chapter 25).
13. The two are closely interconnected because in different states of mind we often have very different somatic responses.
14. This is an important strand in Sensorimotor Psychotherapy, but is by no means unique to that approach.
15. Another interviewee said 'where there's no news, there is hope. People have to hang onto tiny threads of hope'. As I thought about the families of missing persons I could appreciate this need to cling to anything that kept hope alive. Indeed, all the positions on the Hope Scale are probably visited – perhaps initially on a daily basis, and later, under the protective shield of detachment, less frequently until something brings the loved one back to mind. These relatives are stuck in limbo, unable to grieve and move on.
16. The psychodynamic view is rooted in Freud's writing on melancholia and Klein's on the depressive position.
17. Malan emphasised the fact that depression can have endogenous as well as emotional causes. Also important to bear in mind is the function of shutting down as an evolutionary based survival strategy.
18. Anger being unsafe is a reality for the survivor of childhood trauma and not simply, as in Kleinian theory, a fantasy that the object of one's hate will either be destroyed or become destructive.
19. This is what van der Hart et al. call achieving 'personification' – 'it happened to me' – and 'presentification' – 'it happened back then' (2006, chapter 8).
20. I also like Mary Welford's point that grief is important but needs to be paired with hope – the hope that we **can** change (personal communication, 2014).
21. See Chapter 2.
22. Returning to the language of biological action systems, what added to my hopefulness was the increasing evidence, both when I was with Pippa and from the new things that she was embarking on in her life, that she was slowly shifting out of defence system dominance into the Play and Exploration systems.

11

Moving into Hope: New Meanings and New Experiences

Isn't it the moment of most profound doubt that gives birth to new certainties?
Perhaps hopelessness is the very soil that nourishes human hope; perhaps one
could never find sense in life without first experiencing absurdity.

(Havel, 1993)

The dimensions of hope

Working on this book has challenged me, and I hope will challenge those
who read it, to keep questioning how I work with people who are stuck in the
dance of hope and despair and how I approach the dilemma between offering
something hopeful and reassuring and staying with unspeakable pain. It has
also stimulated many questions about change and transformation and, to use
Havel's words, about what nourishes us in the face of life's absurdities. They
are questions which I often grapple with as I encounter new clients, struggle
through moments of impasse and read what others say about the significance
of the therapeutic encounter. As clinicians we are continually updating our
position. We have to go through periods of profound doubt and let go or modify old certainties in order to grow and what I have written here will certainly
not be my final answer. However, for now I want to draw together some of the
strands which have emerged in earlier chapters and then to consider the place
of hope as we end therapy.

In Chapter 1 I outlined what I have called the dimensions of hope, a heuristic for considering the factors which foster and sustain hope. To remind you,
the list includes:

- *A sense of mastery and strategies to feel in control of ourselves, our emotions and our world*
- *Something that gives meaning to our experiences*
- *Discovering a purpose to our lives*
- *A sense of a future with good things to look forward to*
- *Trust in others and the capacity for meaningful relationships*
- *Faith in something larger than the self*

Here I shall explain why I believe each dimension is important, what supports its development and how they are linked. The quotations heading each section capture something of the essence of that dimension. Although I devote more time to the first, it is no more important than any of the others. But it builds on the discussions in the last two chapters and connects with the developmental theme that emerges throughout the book.

Mastery and agency

If I accept you as you are, I will make you worse. If I treat you as though you already are what you are capable of, I will help you become that.

(Goethe)

Anna Alvarez comments, 'there is a difference between a feeling that I want something and a feeling that indicates that I can also reach out and get it, or at least try' (2012, p. 183). This is important to bear in mind when working with people who are stuck in hopelessness and despair and who may have lost, or perhaps never developed, a sense of agency or, in Goethe's words, what they are capable of. We can get an impression of where someone is on the Hope Scale by observing the extent to which he or she is willing or able to reach out for something. Has our client given up trying – the individual who is stuck in chronic hopelessness or despair? Is he cynical about anything working because long ago he learned that it is better not to hope? Does he keep trying against all odds or turn to more and more people or therapies in the hope that this time he will find what he yearns for? Often we drive ourselves forwards in the belief that we will feel better if we, or someone else, can only **do** something about the problems we face (Orange, 2011, p. 66). But is this fuelled by illusory hopes and an avoidance of what needs to be grieved, or is it a determined and realistic taking charge of our lives which needs to be supported?

From birth onwards we have a need to make things happen and to be seen as intentional beings and it is within the matrix of our earliest attachment relationships that a sense of mastery or agency is born. It includes a baby's delight in discovering that he can have an impact on his world – whether this is to elicit a smile on Mum's face or make a toy move. It evolves as he masters gravity and space during repeated attempts to roll, crawl, come to all fours and stand. It is then strengthened as a result of successful excursions from the secure base as the toddling child enjoys the triumph of 'I can' moments. Meanwhile, mastering what happens inside the self – all the feelings and sensations which pattern and at times disturb the young child's life – develops as a result of repeated interactions with others who contain and reflect back his experiences in an attuned way.

As the stories in this book illustrate, many of the people I have been privileged to work with no longer feel that they are the authors of their lives or that they are in charge of their bodies and their emotions. Trauma has robbed them of a sense of agency and each subsequent knock in life has eroded their confidence and sense of the possible. With this in mind our question should be – 'how can psychotherapy help people, and especially anyone who has endured severe trauma and been objectified in some way, to develop a greater sense of agency?' Sometimes, if I get caught in despair about what I can offer, I remind myself that if we do nothing else we can behave differently to the people who hurt, shamed or neglected our clients in the past and, crucially, that the past can be re-contextualised in the present as a result of 'moments of meeting' between therapist and client (BCPSG, 2010, p. 28). I also remind myself that the past can be re-contextualised as a result of new somatic experiences. Of particular importance are experiences which provide a greater sense of safety in the present and of empowerment as people develop new strategies to manage being triggered. This includes learning that it is possible to talk about what happened without going out of their window of tolerance, and that intense emotions can be managed. We could describe this as finding alternative somatic perspectives. All the work we do to regulate arousal levels is crucial here. People need strategies to flexibly shift their attention and orient to the present and resources to calm their bodies. We can teach them to 'put the brakes on'; to shift between talking about a distressing memory and a here-and-now focus; to use 'safe place' imagery[1] and to focus on breathing or grounding. We can also help our traumatised clients to recognise and anticipate triggers and to access more mobilised defences rather than habitually going into states of freeze or shut down.

Janet, a contemporary of Freud, was one of the first to observe that traumatised patients have been unable to execute empowering actions or what he called 'acts of triumph' (Ogden et al., 2006, p. 21). If we go back to the defensive systems listed in Table 3.1, flight, flight and attach for survival are all mobilising responses. They entail dramatic action and if successful lead to feelings of triumph and relief. But as Janet realised, for many trauma survivors who are stuck in depression, hypoarousal and hopelessness, it was not possible to fight or to run at the time of the trauma. Indeed had they tried, it would often have made things much worse. Nor, and this is especially true if the people they would normally turn to were the ones who were hurting them, could they call or reach out to others for support. In consequence, they had to resort to freeze or shut down and to adopt behaviours that would minimise harm.

What we now appreciate thanks to the pioneering work of therapists like Pat Ogden and Peter Levine is that 'fight or flight impulses that were inhibited during the original traumatic events, remain as urges and impulses concealed within the body' and that we can help people to rediscover and complete these failed or 'truncated' defences (Ogden et al., 2006, p. 21; 2015; Levine, 1997). In Sensorimotor Psychotherapy this is achieved by using mindful enquiry to draw people's attention to dissociated impulses. They are often very subtle – a clenching of the fists or tightening of the jaw; a hint of movement in the legs or the head turning away. Then we can use somatic experiments to transform habitual, trauma-related patterns of response based on what we notice is happening already, albeit minimally, or observe is missing from someone's repertoire (Fisher and Ogden, 2009, p. 326). For instance, we can invite people to try out a movement, exaggerate a pattern or observe the tension between conflicting impulses. We can join them in making a boundary gesture – sometimes simultaneously saying 'no', 'stop' or 'leave me alone' – or in seeing what it feels like to push something away.[2] Such experimental processing needs to be collaborative and mindful.

Sometimes I make use of visualisations, for instance imaginary running[3] or envisaging an animal or tree that represents strength, then studying what it feels like to stand or move like this. For someone with difficulties with social engagement we can experiment with proximity and reaching out. We can also encourage people to simply follow how sensation sequences through the body. Sometimes this facilitates the natural process of discharge after a state of freeze (Levine, 1997; Scaer, 2007). Sometimes sequencing moves organically into an active defence. Remember what Kurtz said: 'every client is an experience that wants to happen not a problem to be solved' (1989, p. 139). When something transformative emerges the experience needs to be integrated, perhaps by deepening into it and observing any accompanying feelings, body sensations and thoughts; by exploring how the new experience could be used to deal with a current problem or by practising movements, postures or words that support the change (Ogden et al., 2006, pp. 232–3; 2015). As Ogden says, once people have found ways to execute new, empowering physical actions their window of tolerance expands (2007). They feel a greater sense of control and what they have discovered often opens up alternative ways of thinking about themselves and their experiences.

Anna was one woman whose life changed significantly as a result of all the work we did on regulating arousal and small collaborative experiments. One week she arrived in distress because of a traumatic memory which had emerged during the week. Simply noticing and tracking her body as she thought about it enabled Anna to manage the intense arousal which the memory had evoked. As she calmed down Anna used the words 'I can' and repeated them as if testing them out. It felt good to be able to say those words and I repeated them back to her. Her first response was to say, 'but I don't believe it', so I modified my statement: 'most of the time you can do things'. That led to a visible shift. It was bite-sized enough for Anna to take in and her body relaxed. It reminded her of past achievements and more recently of a successful campaign she and friends had run to save their local shop. We stayed with the memory of working with others, noticing how she sat and how she might move with a sense of mastery. I invited Anna to practice sitting in this confident way and to keep remembering small achievements as a reminder of 'I can'.

Reflecting later on those words 'I can', I realised that they spoke both about the importance for the hope-deprived of experiences of mastery and shared activity. But they also held the implicit meaning 'I can bear the part of me that suffered and was so hopeless'. This was what lay at the heart of our work – not 'fixing' Anna's problems as I discussed in Chapter 9, but building up tolerance of the memories. It was not that we needed to talk about them – and I never discovered exactly what had happened to Anna – nor to process them in depth. More important was to deal with Anna's phobia of the memories and the emotions and sensations that went with them so that she could tolerate remembering without such overwhelming fear. In our final session Anna said that what she had most appreciated was that therapy had provided her with a safety net in which to explore. She shared how previously it felt as if she had been left out on a hill to die, feeling very lonely and scared. Now she realised that safety nets did exist which could hold her through the worst moments and with this knowledge it was easier to enjoy daily life. 'I am not scared any more', she announced. 'I'm not powerless. I can do things I want and I know that it's OK to take time for myself.' These were amazing changes for someone so deeply traumatised and dependent on old ways of surviving.

Anna's words remind me how important relational 'safety nets' can be in the healing process. They also play an important part in restoring or promoting a sense of potency. It is not just that we have a need from infancy to act on the world and make things happen. A baby also needs others to respond sensitively to what he or she does. The caregiver's thoughtful interest or even delight spurs the baby on to continue exploring, try again or try something in a different way. Equally important is the experience of having an impact on others. The baby elicits a smile or look of concern from Mum and, as Alvarez says, 'if I cause things in her then "I begin to feel that I am, and I also begin to feel that she is" and that she can keep me in mind' (2012, p. 31). Through repeated experiences of attuned and contingent responsiveness we develop a core sense of self – of an 'I can' self – and this process can be replicated in therapy.

A powerful example of our need to have an impact on others emerged in my work with Rees, a man mentioned in Chapter 6, at a point when his mood and hopes had plummeted. His eye sight was getting worse and he had been hoping to move into a flat that would be easier to manage. But he was suddenly told that pets were not allowed. He didn't want to go without his dog and felt as if all choice had been taken away. Rees was also having problems with his welfare benefits. Underneath his defeated mood, however, there was fury which, once he realised it was safe to express, led to vehement complaints about being 'treated like an object by a patronising, uncaring system'. I asked, 'what would you need to feel more like a subject?' He replied, 'for people to know that I am opinionated and piss-offable!' I echoed his energy saying 'yes, for others to recognise that you have opinions and that things have an emotional impact. Of course you feel pissed off!' Seeing the energy in his body and hearing that he felt like hitting something I asked if he'd like to experiment with using a drum. Rees's eyes lit up and after some tentative taps he began to hit the drum ferociously. 'It feels good', he said. 'I feel alive. I'm telling everyone exactly what I think!' Later we worked on translating the voice of the drum into statements that he wanted to say to people who had let him down. We practised drumming the words, then standing tall and saying them out loud. After that work Rees's mood lifted significantly and he felt more motivated to keep looking for a flat and to persevere with his benefit claims.

Not only was this an example of how Rees repeatedly suppressed potentially socially unwelcome emotions and how liberated he felt when he could express his feelings creatively, but the session spoke to me of his need to be viewed as an intentional being who could be both impacted by the world and have an impact on it. Someone 'piss-offable' who needed others to know that things mattered to him and for this to be validated. It made me think how as a teenager Rees could not allow himself to be pissed off with his parents, to let them know and through the rifts and repairs negotiate his own identity. It also made me think of Bowlby's phases of protest, despair and detachment. Angry protest holds the hope of change, of a different response or outcome. It is when the hope fades that children and adults sink into despair and then, if prolonged, into detachment.

The other relational element that contributes to mastery and agency, which I mentioned in Chapter 4, is for someone to act as 'a container for the child's aspirations' and carry for him 'a sense of the man or woman that he will become, and *is* becoming' (Alvarez, 1991, p. 183). We all need experiences of others believing in us and in Goethe's words treating us as though we are already what we are capable of. I can certainly recall how centred and energised I felt when someone said to me, not so long ago, 'I trust you. I know you can do it.' And for those people who could not see their growth potential in the eyes of a parent and were never treated as more than they were, then our therapeutic task as 'the holder of the patient's developmental potential' becomes even more important (Bromberg, 2011, p. 93).

Something that gives meaning to our experiences

Man is ready and willing to shoulder any suffering as soon and as long as he can see a meaning in it. (Frankl, 2004, p. 117)

The second dimension concerns what Frankl learned at Auschwitz: our need to make sense of our experiences and in particular to find meaning in suffering. Why should this be so important? Developmentally, it links with what Daniel Stern wrote about the formation of a 'verbal self', his argument being that the emergence of language 'permits two people to create mutual experiences of meaning that had been unknown before and could never have existed until fashioned by words. It also finally permits the child to begin to construct a narrative of his own life' (1985, p. 162). My work with Margie highlighted how important this is. During recurrent periods of illness she complained that 'nothing speaks to me', 'there is no input' and she was unable to focus or to make sense of things. Everything was a void. Slowly, we began to understand how this repeated something from infancy when her acutely depressed mother was unable to provide a lively, attuned feedback to help her make sense of her experiences. The origins of the void could also be traced to her later childhood when neither parent offered encouraging, validating responses to her achievements. There was simply no feedback. During this long-term therapy I was struck how our interactions shifted from a nonverbal focus, with repeated mirroring through facial expression and gestures, to feeding back verbally through conversations, letters and emails (Wright, 2009b). It gave Margie that missing experience of creating mutual experiences of meaning and in time this enabled her to become more fully the author and witness of her life.

In order to explore the importance of constructing a narrative and how this is connected with our capacity to hope let me give two examples – the first fictitious, the second a true story. In describing the main character in a film called the Shrinking Man, Donnell Stern was curious how writing a diary when deprived of any form of real communication with others helped the protagonist. He writes:

> When life feels arbitrary, senselessly cruel, or meaningless, as it did for the Shrinking Man before he began his diary, one is liable to be aware of no story at all. Events seem arbitrary and do not fall into narrative order. Affect is flattened or diminished; one may consciously feel only a kind of numbness or deadness. The living, hurt places in one's mind – actually, the injured parts of self, the parts we most need to protect – despite their influence on day-to-day life, go undiscovered *until something happens in ongoing relatedness* that allows us to see that someone else recognises the pain we ourselves have been unable to know and feel. Our grasp of our previously dissociated experience through what we imagine to be the eyes and ears of the other is synonymous with the creation of new meaning. (2010, p. 114)

I suspect that if Margie could read this she would agree that it eloquently describes her experiences during her long years lost in a dissociated state.

The second example is of the 'man with the shattered world', a Russian soldier who suffered severe brain damage following a bullet wound.[4] Zasetsky was left with profound amnesia and lost the ability to combine sensory impressions into a coherent whole, grasp spatial relationships and use language in a fluid way. His world became one of fragments. The meaning of common words and the relationships between them eluded him. He could not follow a conversation or what he read in a book. For years, in a heroic attempt to regain memory and language, Zasetsky worked on a journal (Luria, 1987). To add to the tragedy, because his frontal lobes were intact he was aware of his situation and of what it means to be human – hence his determination and very human clinging to hope.

I cite these examples because they illustrate several important points. First, Stern's description of an arbitrary, meaningless life could apply to anyone who has experienced traumatic events and tragic losses. Such events call into question all that previously gave meaning and purpose to life and can leave people without 'psychological or spiritual meaning structures that offer safety, hope, control, trust and esteem' (van der Hart et al., 1993, p. 23). No wonder that daily events can feel pointless and the future bleak. The second point, and a theme throughout this book, is the importance of intersubjective experiences to create meaning. In the words of Levinas, 'suffering is ungraspable; we cannot dominate it. It breaks down meaning, at least until another responds' (Orange, 2011, p. 69). From the micro-traumas and disturbances of daily life, to the tragic and frightening, we instinctively turn to others to tell the tale, and through their eyes and ears, and through thinking about it from different perspectives the event begins to take on emotional and cognitive meaning. Neither of the two journal writers could do this – Zasetsky, for instance, could not grasp the point of a simple conversation. Nonetheless, I suspect that they wrote with an audience in mind and that in a relational sense, their diaries *were* their witnesses. The third point is to highlight the connection between the process of finding meaning and grieving. As Stern says, 'as a coherent narrative of the experience falls into place, there is an awakening including an awakening of pain' (2010, p. 114).

In the therapeutic context a significant part of our role is to help people to construct a narrative and find a rationale within which their difficulties can be located. It is what Kurtz described as bringing out the meaning of 'the way we organise experience, the way we do things, the way we put our world together, perceive it and think about it' (1990, p. 139). This might be through learning that after trauma the survival brain keeps responding as if danger was around every corner, or in discovering the survival logic behind longstanding coping strategies. I can certainly think of many examples when finding meaning brought relief to someone who believed she was mad or bad and felt hopeless about the possibility of change. For example, in Anna's case, although therapy did not eliminate her hypervigilance and anxiety, it enabled her to appreciate how since the assault she – or rather her survival brain – had organised experiences around the premise that it might happen again and that nowhere was safe. Once Anna realised this things felt less random and chaotic. She began to regain confidence in her own judgement, to accept having needs and allow herself to do things she wanted to without slipping into guilt. For another client change came when he realised how he had always organised experiences from an Asperger mindset. Being diagnosed with Asperger Syndrome enabled him to stop blaming himself for being 'anti-social' or 'selfish', and for the first time he started to like himself.[5] Meanwhile, Bill discovered how depression and self-criticism had effectively kept him 'below the radar' and how not risking potential disapproval meant he kept overriding his authentic self and confined him when he wanted to 'fly like the buzzard'.

It is the relational element as much as putting things into words and finding meaning that makes a difference. As Jeremy Holmes argued, 'meaning in itself is not mutative, it is the mutuality of meaning-making that matters' (1996, pp. 17–18; 2010, p. 53). Our role of what Holmes calls 'assistant autobiographers' is especially important after traumas that were too overwhelming or crazy to be assimilated within a chronological life-story or after the individual's truth has been repeatedly disconfirmed. We are 'assistants' – supporting, encouraging, offering alternative perspectives. But more than that, we must be prepared to act as witnesses who can be impacted. As Donna Orange argues, if we can allow ourselves to fully engage with the suffering of others, then there is 'the possibility of finding meaning in the bleakest moments of work with the most tortured souls who entrust themselves to [our] care when [we] too feel nearly overwhelmed by their "useless suffering"' (2011, pp. 69, 70). It is that place of sitting with despair that I spoke about in Chapter 9; of having nothing more to offer than our receptivity and our willingness to stand alongside our clients, to look horror in the face and hear their deepest, most shameful secrets with compassion. It is this which enables what had to be dissociated to become 'relationable' and experiences of horror, sadness, shame or guilt to be converted into expressions of a joint humanity (BCPSG, 2010, p. 209).

Zasetsky and the Shrinking Man had lost a sense of joint humanity, and herein lies another reason why finding meaning is so important. As Donnell Stern pointed out, before putting his story into words the Shrinking Man 'has become an object in his own life, a figure suffering chaotic, incomprehensible events for no apparent reason and with little feeling. The emergence of meaning from what has felt to him like senselessness, helplessness and despair confers agency and therefore dignity. He is once again a subject' (Stern, 2010, p. 109). Oliver Sachs said something similar about Zasetsky. 'Through constructing his own narrative, he managed to recapture, and re-appropriate, the sense of a life-world, a lived life, the sense (in every sense) of his own life.' Sachs continued by musing on something universal in this example. Perhaps a life 'is not a life until it is examined ... until it is truly remembered and appropriated, and this remembrance is not something passive, but active, the active and creative construction of one's life, the finding and the telling of the true story of one's life' (Luria, 1987, p. xvii). Again this resonates with my experience of the deepest work of long-term psychotherapy.

Victor Frankl also spoke of the dignity of being a subject and the risk of losing personal values in 'a world which no longer recognized the value of human life and human dignity, which had robbed man of his will and had made him an object to be exterminated'. He argued that 'if the man in the concentration camp did not struggle against this in a last effort to save his self-respect, he lost the feeling of being an individual, a being with a mind, with inner freedom and personal value' (2004, p. 66). I don't think anyone could read Frankl's book without feeling deep respect for people like him who manage to retain their dignity and integrity in the face of unimaginable horrors, as well as compassion and sadness for those whose spirits break as they lose all hope of redemption. His words and those of Stern remind me of many people I have worked with who have felt objectified in dangerous, crazy or bureaucratic worlds – the trauma survivor or the person with long-term mental or physical health problems – men and women who feel deprived of real choice and not understood or welcomed by others. It reminds me too of the importance of unconditional positive regard and compassion and of keeping in mind Mitchell's argument that our goal as psychotherapists should not be the 'establishment of a rational normality' – which risks objectifying people once more[6] – 'but the capacity to generate a sense of self and relationships felt as important, *meaningful and deeply one's own*' (1993, p. 37, my italics). In staying alongside our clients as witnesses, especially during the bleakest moments of despair and grief, and giving them space to 'pursue an authentic personal experience' (Mitchell, 1993, p. 39), the hopelessness which follows being objectified starts to shift to renewed hope – the hope of discovering something meaningful to live for as worthy subjects in their own lives.

Discovering a purpose to our lives

> *The notion of a meaningful life that transcends the self is not merely an existential appendage that becomes relevant only after our basic needs are met and biological survival is secured ... Living for something or someone other than oneself is fundamental to being human.* (Shabad, 2001, p. 38)

Finding meaning can be conceptualised as both 'sense-making' and identifying a purpose in life or what I call an 'ethic of meaning'. As Shabad argued, this is another fundamental human need. We can all adapt and survive through any number of terrible experiences, 'but those adaptations take their toll, because to be a mere survivor of trauma may distort what it means to be a person' (2001, pp. 38–9). This ethic of meaning was what enabled Frankl to survive the unspeakable horrors of the concentration camps. He was keenly aware of the dire consequences for anyone who lost meaning and purpose and argued that, 'we needed to stop asking the meaning of life, and instead to think of ourselves as those who were being questioned by life – daily and hourly. Our answer must consist, not in talk and meditation, but in right action and in right conduct. Life ultimately means taking the responsibility to find the right answer to its questions and to fulfil the tasks which it constantly sets for each individual' (2004, p. 85). Frankl continued: 'Once the meaning of suffering had been revealed to us, we refused to minimize or alleviate the camp's tortures by ignoring them or harbouring false illusions and entertaining artificial optimism. Suffering had become a task on which we did not want to turn our backs' (2004, p. 86).

Zasetsky's writing suggests that he also understood the vital importance of leading a meaningful life. He wanted to tell people about his illness in the hope that this might be beneficial to others and side by side with hopelessness and despair he had a 'fierce and indomitable will to improve, to do everything to recover, to make *sense* of his life' (Sachs in Luria, 1987, p. xvi). Writing his diary gave the man with the shattered world a reason to live. As Luria said, 'it was essential in that it was his one hope of recovering and becoming the man he had been. Perhaps if he developed his ability to think, he could still be useful, make something of his life. Reviving the past was thus his way of trying to ensure a future. That is why he undertook this exhausting labor, spending hours, days, years, searching for lost memories' (1987, p. 84).

I feel awed by this man's perseverance.[7] I am equally inspired by other people I have worked with or read about who find things to live for 'beyond the bare bones of existence'. There are many ways that people gain a sense of purpose. For some a loved one keeps them going – 'I need to be there for the children'. For others it is a new challenge – perhaps literally climbing a mountain, running a marathon, learning a new skill, supporting a charity, training to be a therapist or a creative project. Equally, we might find our personal refuge in nature or in music, books or art. Sometimes these 'refuges' or 'resources' – and we can use different terms to describe them – are enduring ones. Sometimes we adopt a purpose for a period of time – for instance, I know that having projects and goals to aim for has given me a sense of meaning and helped me get through difficult times – and then we move onto another. It does not matter what it is that inspires us, but as Frankl knew so well, it matters that it is there.

The example of people like Frankl and Zasetsky gives me hope. So too does remembering the diverse ways my clients kept hope alive as children and how, after courageously working through traumatic memories, many have eventually found something meaningful to live for. They include people like Pippa whose experiences led to a determination to help others 'so that at least some good can come from what I went through'; or Sonia who, despite debilitating social anxiety, hoped that 'maybe one day I'll talk to children who have been abused and tell them "you will get through it"'. They also include people like Bill, Mae and Anna who discovered a renewed sense of purpose once they stopped worrying about what others thought and let go of the 'shoulds' and 'oughts' surrounding the idea of returning to work. Bill found new meaning as he began to follow his creative instincts and through voluntary work. In Mae's case helping to care for her grandchildren, a role she knew her children greatly appreciated, gave her a happiness she had not known before. Meanwhile, after grieving the loss of her former career, Anna allowed herself to enjoy a slower paced life in which she could garden, read and fulfil a long-standing ambition to learn to weave. For all my clients, these things provided a reason to get up in the morning and, crucially, to stay alive.

Throughout history people have questioned the meaning of existence and debated the right way to live, and I believe that as we get older grappling with the ethic of meaning preoccupies us more. This ethic is the theme of Erikson's last two ages of man – generativity versus stagnation and integrity versus despair – and it is the lack of a sense of purpose that draws many people into therapy. 'Mature man needs to be needed' wrote Erikson, and he believed that this is manifest primarily in our concern with establishing and guiding the next generation (1965, pp. 258–9).[8] Stagnation occurs when the urge for generativity is not met, and if the individual cannot come to terms with failures and disappointments, then the last stage of life is marked by existential despair. At this stage Erikson believed that the task is to find integrity and reconcile ourselves with the finite limits of our life and 'the tragic limitations of the human condition, and to accept these realities without despair' (1965, pp. 259–61; Herman, 1994, p. 154). Life keeps posing questions about the possible and the finite. Without a sense of something more – a horizon to aim for – we would indeed sink into despair. As people find things that give them purpose and as they experience more agency the future opens up. But, as I have argued, we have to face the reality that some of our hopes may never be realised. This takes me to the fourth dimension – a sense of a future with good things to look forward to.

A sense of future possibilities

> *With this faith we will be able to hew out of the mountain of despair a stone of hope.*
>
> (Luther King in Sebag Montefiore, 2005, p. 152)

Not long after the session mentioned in Chapter 10 when Megan allowed herself to be sad she painted a picture of the sadness. It was predominantly black, but in the middle was a circle of light. Megan wanted to run towards that light and dance in it. Maybe, I thought, a time will come when there will be 'dancing' pictures, when Megan can exist in the light and be the person she truly is. It seemed such a powerful symbol of hope – something aspirational which could anchor her during the bleakest moments. By contrast, I remember another woman who had recently been diagnosed with a debilitating chronic illness telling me that she did not want to live any more. She too was a survivor of childhood abuse who felt that after years of therapy she could now deal with flashbacks and manage emotional pain. 'I've got lots of strategies now to deal with this. But I can't control the physical pain. It gets in the way of everything. I don't want a life when I can't even walk for ten minutes without feeling wiped out. I can't see a light at the end of the tunnel.' I could understand this woman's despair and why the thought of suicide offered comfort. I also knew that I needed to hold the hope that there *was* a light and that this new indignity could also be managed.

Knowing that there is a light at the end of the tunnel and that our suffering won't last forever helps us all when we are stuck in something overwhelming. Remember what Mae said: 'I can cope if I know what's at the end of the wait and if I can understand what is going on.' But despair has an endless quality and trauma distorts time leaving people stuck in an unendurable present with no vision of a better future. They cannot believe, as Luther King did, that 'out of the mountain of despair' something new and hopeful could be hewn. This is why the work we do to help our clients find alternative perspectives and to grieve and let go of unrealistic hopes and fantasies is so important. It helps them to establish a new relationship to time and to envisage something different. As argued in Chapter 10, unless we can grieve we are not only cut off from a part of ourselves, but we also get stuck in frozen time. For the survivors of severe trauma grieving means facing all that was lost as well as the painful truth of the awful things that happened, the things they needed and longed for which never came and the emotional scars and bruises which still hurt. They need to let go of shame that does not belong to them, but also to face with compassion their regrets about what they might have contributed to relational difficulties or about the cost of the strategies they have used in order to survive. There is also a need, in van der Kolk's words, to 'complete the unfinished past' (Fisher and Ogden, 2009, p. 327). This entails processing traumatic memories, by which I mean working through and integrating both explicit and implicit memories; feeling emotions that have been dissociated or minimised, as well as accessing and completing truncated survival responses. This detailed work means that it is possible to achieve what van der Hart et al. (1993, 2006) call 'presentification', namely being able to acknowledge that certain events happened and, whilst awful, they are over.

Our traumatised clients, stresses Pat Ogden, need not just a cognitive understanding that the past is over, but also an experience at a deep somatic level that they are safe now and, I would add, that they are welcomed and accepted (Fisher and Ogden, 2009, p. 327). The original traumas can then be put back into the past, rather than constantly relived, and time can start to move again. Anna's feedback indicated that she really got this after a session in which we experimented with alternately glancing at a list of words that captured an aspect of the trauma, then throwing a ball between us – a technique used in EMDR to pace working on overwhelming memories. 'To realise that by putting bits of it into the present rather than it ripping me into the past', she said, 'it'll just be words on paper. I might have feelings about it, but it won't have such impact.' Having been able to keep one foot in the past and one firmly in the present Anna said this felt empowering and gave her hope after many months battling disturbing flashbacks.

Trust in others and the capacity for meaningful relationships

The only time I felt hope was when you told me you could see no hope, and you continued with the analysis. (Winnicott citing a patient, 1965, p. 152)

I don't think I would have got through the last few months if you hadn't been there. (Magda)

The fifth dimension concerns our ability to trust and connect in meaningful ways with others. One of the central premises of this book is that hope is fundamentally a relational phenomenon and, as the stories of my clients illustrate, it can be both destroyed and fostered within relationships. If we look back to Chapter 5 where I discussed the impact of trauma across the lifecycle, I mentioned how trauma and neglect during infancy inhibit the formation of basic trust and hope and can set up a 'loss circuit' which is quickly evoked by any hint of abandonment or threat to survival. In early childhood trauma can lead to shame proneness and a tendency for submissive, accommodating responses. The child begins to hide under the mask of a false self. The traumatised adolescent is likely to mistrust dependency and being close to others. Trauma in early adulthood often leads to detachment and inhibits exploration and choice making. In middle age a traumatic event or situation that evokes memories of earlier traumas, and especially when this contributes to depression or other mental health problems, can lead to a progressive withdrawal from relationships because of fear and shame. Finally, in later life an atrophying of social networks can be compounded by difficulties in working through traumatic experiences and losses, leaving the individual at risk of slipping deeper into loneliness and despair.

It is not just the traumatic event itself that severs connections with others. 'What is truly damaging', stresses Richard Erskine, 'is the absence of a healthy relationship following such an experience' (1999, p. 6). If the natural soothing cycle mentioned in Chapter 6 is absent and if fear and shame prevent people from talking about their experiences, the event cannot be converted into an expression of a joint humanity, something truly remembered and integrated into the fabric of one's life. There is no one to help you make sense of what happened or the after effects, no responsive other to understand and bear it with you. My clients have often asked: 'How can I tell my family that every day I am just hanging on? That even when I'm with them I feel so anxious? That I hurt myself? That I want to die?' 'How can I explain to my doctor that I keep switching off? That sometimes I don't feel like an adult? That I keep seeing things that make me feel crazy?' In the context of such struggles it is not surprising that despair and helplessness are typified by a withdrawal from social engagement.

This is where I believe we can play a crucial role, for it is within the therapeutic relationship that people start to tentatively reconnect with others or, in the language of attachment theory, to develop more secure attachments. It is within this transitional space that the person who lacked a secure base as a child and who was repeatedly let down by others can test out if it is possible, eventually, to trust. It is here that the traumatised client who simultaneously yearns and fears closeness can experiment with being together and alone, with reaching out and withdrawing, with sharing and with setting boundaries. Trust after trauma does not come easily. It has to be earned – and it is often through our mistakes, mis-attunements and dissociative lapses that we discover with each person what needs to happen between us to earn trust. When I showed a colleague the quotation from Winnicott that opens this section she questioned how sharing our hopelessness with a client could help. I thought hard about this. Was she right that being open when we slip into despair might make things worse? Sometimes yes, and we have to keep reflecting on our personal process. But I have learned that there are times when being open about what we are experiencing is just what is needed to develop trust. In sharing how something impacts us our clients may at last discover that we really understand how they feel. Our openness can also provide a developmentally needed experience – for instance, if a client could never make sense of his abusive parents' minds. When we can connect honestly with our experience rather than hiding behind a professional mask, and risk connecting with the pain and despair of our traumatised clients, we are providing an experience which builds trust and helps people to slowly reconnect with themselves.

Reconnect? Or find? Remember, trauma severs connections with oneself as well as with others, and the child's need to split off or silence aspects of self to avoid feeling overwhelmed and to preserve attachment bonds makes it incredibly hard to answer the question 'who am I?' Our professional literature is full of references to helping people to access their 'true self', to individuate, to self-actualise. However, I think Molnos makes a critical point – that 'no significant step in a process of "personal growth" ... can be achieved outside interpersonal relationships'. She writes: 'psychic "improvement" means an increased ability to be oneself, to fulfil one's essence, one's potential, while relating constructively to other human beings' (1995, pp. 91–2). For me a meta-goal of psychotherapy is in helping our clients to be fully themselves and **not** to have to diminish or jump over themselves to be in relationship. It is about the capacity to be alone and together, 'distinct and differentiated, yet integrated in relationships'; to accept themselves with compassion and to accept the otherness of others, and for there to be a healthy balance between the two (Hobson, 1985, p. 279).

In discussing how psychotherapy fosters human relatedness Bromberg draws on Winnicott's thesis that the capacity to be alone develops through an internalisation of 'the relational bond' (2011, p. 107). It becomes possible because the inner world has become 'relationally nourishing' – a phrase which captures beautifully the contrast between internal working models based on safety, care and respect and models based on frightening, toxic, shaming relationships. With his keen sense of the importance of working through enactments, Bromberg stresses Winnicott's point that 'the internalisation of the relational bond is strengthened by having to deal with an absence of perfect harmony, provided the disharmony is reparable'. It is strengthened because a good-enough therapeutic relationship can provide what the past lacked, namely 'a self-reflective, involved and caring other who will not indefinitely protect his own truth by holding it to be self evident' (2011, p. 105). The more the client's own truths are not at risk, the more he or she can access and integrate truths that had to become 'not-me'. It is part of the growth of wholeness – 'a "myself" embracing a togetherness of my "selves" with those of another' (Hobson, 1985, p. 279) – of being a self with meaning and purpose, able to be more spontaneous and take new risks in relationships. We risk when we are open. We risk when we care. But if therapy can provide the client with 'safe surprises' it is possible for old self-with-other patterns to give way to alternative, flexible ways of relating (DeYoung, 2003, pp. 198, 206–8).

Margie comes to mind when I think of the internalisation of 'the relational bond' and of the development of a 'relationally nourishing' inner world. It was clear from all Margie said when she ended therapy that I and my room has become a secure base – a place that 'had something nourishing about it' which she could keep in mind and draw on as an ongoing resource. The woman in front of me in the final session was so different from the person who arrived in therapy. She had become three-dimensional (Wright, 2009b). She had developed a mind of her own, no longer identifying so adhesively with others, but able to assert her own views and follow her own dreams. The other major change was that Margie could now enjoy rich and meaningful relationships with others. When we first met she lost her voice and often her capacity to think when invited to social events, so fearful was she of others. But by the end she had become a 'myself' – finding pleasure and comfort in relationships and able to tolerate ambiguity and inner conflicts, and to withstand disagreements and 'disharmonies' when they arose.

I firmly believe that because of what psychotherapy and counselling offer experientially, and in particular the experience of a different form of relationship, something can change in all the dimensions of hope and that these changes are inherently integrative. Good-enough psychotherapy helps to integrate the shattered worlds of the deeply traumatised. As an active partner in the process of working through memories we help people to gain a more coherent sense of their history. When working with the body in mind we help them to integrate body, mind and emotions. Through our curiosity about and compassion for segregated, 'not-me' parts of self we support internal integration. Then, and this is true for all of us, with a greater sense of one's own subjectivity, of a self that is 'textured and multiple but integrated' (Mitchell, 1993, p. 261); a self with a past, present and future, and less need to sacrifice ourselves in order to be with others, we can develop a much richer engagement with life and other people.

Faith in something larger than the self

He who has a why to live can bear with almost any how.
(Nietzsche in Frankl, 2004, p. 109)

Throughout history, when there is literally no one else to turn to, a belief in something greater than the self has kept people going through unimaginable ordeals. Sometimes this 'bigger, wiser thing' is linked to a religious faith. For example, I once asked Bill if he could draw something to represent the 'ups and downs' which seemed to undermine moments of progress and hope. He drew a mountain path, full of twists, turns and unexpected hazards. When finished he said sadly, 'but I can't see the top. It's covered in mist.' This image powerfully captured the endlessness of his depression. Then he said calmly, 'but I'm not alone on the path. God is with me.' For Bill his faith gave him hope and courage to persevere. For other people – and this includes a number of clients who turned against religion because of their experiences – a connection to nature; to something that represents beauty or love or humanity; to a cause or to their community sustains them and gives them – a *'why'* to live. This, as Nietzsche clearly knew well, is fundamental to our existence.

And what about my own 'why to live'? What do I turn to when I fall into despair, whether this be because of something personal or in response to the work I do? Reflecting on this final dimension inevitably led to questions about my own relationship to something beyond the self and to a greater awareness of the need for all of us in the helping professions to have something in addition to our commitment to anchor us in the face of overwhelming suffering and despair. Even though I have never experienced quite the depths of despair that the people I have written about face regularly, there have been grey periods in my life when I felt I was hanging on, when I looked at death with a curiosity – but fortunately not a pull. What kept me going? Sometimes I have hung onto something very basic, like feeling my feet on the earth – just walking and knowing that the earth is still there. It's always there. Then I have imagined it stretching miles beyond me, its contours and textured surface like a vast body that I walk upon. This has kept me going – to know that the earth has been here a long time and weathered many storms and difficult times – and I believe that the earth, the sea and very old trees can teach us about surviving. The earth offers both a reassuring sameness in its repeated cycles and an important lesson in its capacity to adapt. Reminding myself that nothing stays the same helps me when I feel stuck in my own versions of despair. 'This too will pass!'

Change is inevitable and I have come to appreciate that the changes I have railed most against usually have something to teach me. Dom Helder Camara's words remind me of this:

Accept surprises that upset your plans,
Shatter your dreams,
Give a completely different turn
To your day and
Who knows? – To your life.
It is not chance
Leave the Father free himself to weave
The pattern of your days.

(1981, p. 92)

If we can cultivate what Orange calls 'an attitude of receptivity' – of embracing and welcoming unwanted surprises – they can indeed provide an unexpected and often beneficial turn to our lives (2011, p. 67).[9] My faith in something beyond myself and my suffering also encompasses appreciation. On the darkest days – my 'endless rain days' – small miracles have turned things around. I have kept going because of encountering something beautiful. This could be as small as raindrops glistening on a twig or a poem or piece of music or experiencing unexpected kindnesses from other people. There is something deeply important about experiences of shared humanity – moments of connecting, kindness, humour, being understood – that creates something bigger than me and whatever I am struggling with. To appreciate is a gift. I don't take it for granted and I know that when someone is caught in the web of despair it can be impossibly hard to see any beauty or feel part of a shared humanity. Nonetheless, I stay hopeful that in time my clients will regain a sense of connection to something that gives them joy and faith.

Having sources of faith and inspiration to sustain us when the going gets tough is crucial for us as therapists. We need hope to persevere with someone who is desperately stuck or keeps going down the 'snakes' as she faces one crisis after another; hope when we have exhausted our repertoire of techniques and potentially helpful strategies or when, even though we know something is changing, the client still complains about the things that brought him or her into therapy. There are times when I can feel an impostor. 'I've not met expectations or fulfilled the client's hopes. Should I really be doing this job?' *'Do you believe in what we are doing? That things will change? That one day I could ... ?'* These questions hang in the air between us. Sometimes only the bravest or most desperate client risks asking them. Sometimes it is a persistent call. *'Yes, I do'*, **and** I know that hoping is a risky business. As Mitchell warns, both love and hope are extremely risky because both mean 'imparting value in an inevitably uncertain future' (1993, p. 212). When working with desperate, traumatised individuals we *do* risk because, despite our committed care and ongoing hope for our clients, their future is uncertain. We can trust that what we offer will make a difference. We can hold a belief in the inherent potential of each individual. But we have to be willing to not know for sure, just to carry on in the certainty, as Havel said, 'that something makes sense regardless of how it turns out' (1990, p. 181).

Our 'faith' in something greater than the self is important here. Indeed, if we did not have access to something that represents each dimension, slipping into despair or into some of the countertransference reactions named in Chapter 8 would be inevitable as we listen to unspeakable horrors on a daily basis. Having said that – and I think this will have become clear by now – one of the tenets of my therapeutic 'faith' is that we **need** to be impacted by our desperate, troubled clients. We need to 'be upset to respond', to be disrupted out of the 'comfortable complacency' of our prejudices, theories, categories and concepts, all the things that keep people as objects rather than unique subjects (Orange, 2011, p. 63). And we need to let go the urge to understand, do something, succeed or be valued. 'The vulnerability of the other makes me vulnerable', wrote Donna Orange. 'It traumatizes me, takes me hostage, puts me in a state of suffering where the most I can do is offer my crust of bread, my hope from empty hands' (2011, p. 63).

In working with desperate and traumatised individuals we have to come to this place. But in surrendering to our mutual vulnerability and acknowledging the emptiness of what we have to offer, something new and healing does emerge. Indeed, it could be argued that this surrendering in order to truly be with another person and his suffering is an act of faith, even if not necessarily defined in a religious way. It is engaging with the transpersonal dimension of psychotherapy and the transcendent aspects of life – with the non-linear and complex. Paradoxically, although I have argued for the importance of being able to let go of magical hopes, I believe there is a place for mystery in our work. Sandra Bloom captured something of what I am trying to say when she wrote: 'Magic is the word I think of when a process outside of the bounds of linear thinking is at work.' 'When magic is present, transformative events occur. It does not matter whether the magic is on stage, in a movie, in a painting, a piece of music, a ballet, a poem, in school, a factory, a therapist's office, a day care centre, or in a room full of people talking. Magic is the emergent quality that is bigger than the sum of its parts' (1997, p. 257).

Concluding thoughts

Reflecting on how we can support each dimension of hope has made me appreciate how interlinked they are. Change might begin in one dimension but can then spread to others. For instance, experiences of mastery and a greater sense of control over body and emotions give us more confidence to try something new. Having the opportunity to make sense of our experiences helps to reframe our beliefs about our abilities or about how people will treat us, and, in time, this can strengthen relationships with others. With a greater sense of purpose our future expands and we can more truly 'live our own lives'. Finally, meaningful relationships or faith in something beyond the self can help us to endure periods of despair and encourage us on the first steps towards change. What strikes me again is the interconnectedness of hope and relationship. Something new and unexpected within a relationship may be the catalyst for hope. Even seeing hope in the eyes of others and hearing it in their voices could make a difference to the chronically hopeless.

Keeping the six dimensions in mind as we work can inform how we position ourselves. For instance, to support each dimension calls on different skills and sensibilities. We need what Jim Pye calls an 'integrative hospitality' – the capacity for an agile alteration between different ways of working and thinking about our work (personal communication, 2014). Such agility is guided by what we observe and feel in the moment, but also has an eye on the past – the reasons why our clients respond in the ways they do – and on the future – on what they are capable of. It can also be informed by our sense of where they are on the Hope Scale and the window of tolerance chart.

In Figure 11.1 I have drawn together some of the key elements of my approach to working with hopelessness with the dimensions of hope at the centre. At the bottom are the therapeutic tasks discussed in the last two chapters. Exploring alternative perspectives is a key factor in the process of finding meaning and helps open up a new sense of the future with meaningful relationships and things to do. Grieving and letting go of illusory hopes creates a bridge between past, present and future.

Above the dimensions are listed five basic therapeutic positions. When first playing with the diagram it was probably no accident that I put 'keeping hope alive' at the top. On noticing this I rather whimsically wanted to embed it in a star. Our hope for the client needs to be at the centre of all we do like a candle to inspire and guide the way. I love the Indian proverb: 'a candle is a

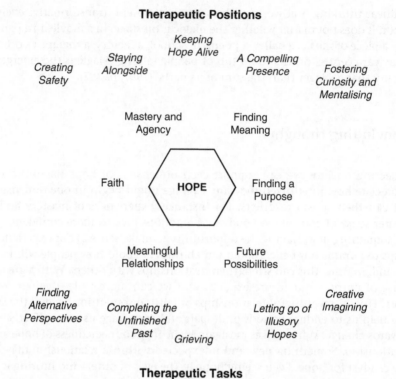

Figure 11.1 An Integrative Approach to Working with Hopelessness

protest at midnight. It begs to differ!' And in articulating our faith and belief in those we work with, we are repeatedly begging to differ and inviting them to see themselves and their future in a new way. When we value our clients as worthy partners in dialogue, rather than as problems to be fixed, we also beg to differ with the people who hurt, objectified and disconfirmed them.

Our emphasis on the other four positions will necessarily depend on timing and context. There are times when creating safety and trying to regulate arousal is crucial, and it would be counter productive to work on memories. Sometimes staying alongside and looking into the face of the other's suffering or gently supporting the flow of grief is the imperative. At other times we need to be more active in fostering curiosity and mentalising – for instance, when trying to find alternative perspectives or work on completing the unfinished past. There are also occasions when we have to become more compelling – to alert and reclaim someone who is stuck in hypoarousal and futility thinking; to expand their attention and encourage exploration and aspiration.

When we demonstrate a genuine interest in our clients' lives – and this can include talking about books, gardens, animals or sport – it helps bridge the gulf created by shame and self-doubt. When we respond to questions about our own interests we are allowing a genuine meeting with those we work with in order for them to discover more about themselves and about being with others. It taps into the quest to find and nurture what matters to them and to develop more meaningful relationships.[10] The compelling therapist is also someone who challenges stuck beliefs and illusory hopes in order to support more realistic, but still creative, forms of imagining. Ideally, our challenges should be when someone is in the window of tolerance and already beginning to entertain alternative perspectives, and they should come from a compassionate, non-shaming place. That is when inspiring curiosity – for instance about parts of self – helps. 'Is there a part of you who is still loyally waiting?' 'It sounds like that's a child's voice. Why do you think she's around right now?' 'How did believing that help you in the past?' Challenges land best when there is a mind to hear them, and of course sometimes, perhaps swayed by our personal hopes and fears, we get our timing wrong. Fostering our own curiosity and capacity to reflect after mistakes and ruptures is crucial. We have to keep questioning what is in our personal field and trust that something important will emerge from whatever went wrong.

Our hopes for those we work with will be coloured by our individual beliefs about faith, human nature, relationships and change. They also depend on our theoretical 'secure base' and our individual preferences for more active, solution-focussed ways of working, for creative or body-based approaches or for involving ourselves more fully in the process. But even within the reassuring safety of our 'mother model' I believe that we are repeatedly faced with choices about which way to turn and need to keep questioning whether we are colluding with illusory hopes or offering something genuinely reparative and growth building. There will be times, whatever our bias, when we get pulled into teleological mode or into discourses of shame and blame. When this occurs it is vital to draw on our personal resources in order to stay responsive, compassionate and curious. If we can 'dance with the resistance' – our own and that of our clients – and resist struggling to change them, the door opens onto something new.

Having said this, and as the quotation from Goethe heading the first dimension highlights, we don't have to passively accept someone as he or she is, nor the apparent hopelessness of a situation. We can be an advocate for future possibilities and challenge the withdrawal from social engagement as well as the dependency on illusory hopes and reliance on external solutions that so often goes with helplessness. Again this is about holding tensions and being ever mindful about how we position ourselves in order to avoid getting sucked into a client's 'system' and taking roles such as the 'longed for rescuer' or the 'useless, helpless other', and to flexibly shift between sitting with the client's despair and keeping the candle of hope alive.

We hold hope for our clients. Then one day we have to say goodbye. At this point what is the relationship of both therapist and client to hope, and how far do our respective hopes have to be relinquished in order to end? Do our clients go off into the 'happy ever after' or end up feeling disappointed or betrayed? Are we left feeling moved? proud? useless? sobered? Perhaps relieved that this particular dance between hope and despair is over? Writers from the psychodynamic tradition often stress that the hopes someone arrives with will, and need to, change during the course of a therapy, and the ending can be pivotal in this process.[11] Saying goodbye challenges people to finally let go of the wish – rooted in the magical hopes that kept them going long ago – that we will provide them 'what they need in order to change the story of their life and ease their pain' (DeYoung, 2003, p. 204). They have to come to terms with the fact that their 'fullest hopes, both the rational and the irrational, are never fully realized' and to reach the point when they can let go, not only of the past, but also 'of those longings that life cannot fulfil and try to seek satisfaction in more realistic ways' (Mitchell, 1993, p. 230; Molnos, 1995, pp. 79, 90). It is a process, as Mitchell pointed out, which can be painful and the occasion for real grief for both therapist and client. But, he adds, 'an analysis that has gone well is also the occasion for genuine hope on the part of the analysand and a renewed faith in the analytic method for the analyst' (1993, p. 230).

Jeremy Holmes emphasised the ambiguity of an ending when he wrote: 'poised between past and future, every ending encompasses both hope and regret, accomplishment and disappointment, loss and gain. The inherent ambivalence of endings tests our capacity as therapists to tolerate ambiguity, to encompass both optimism and sadness in the face of loss, and to hold onto a realist appraisal of our strengths and shortcomings' (1997, p. 159). Tolerating ambiguity can be much harder if both therapist and client have fallen into the trap of striving for the miracle cure or the perfect outcome – an addictive pursuit which brings with it anxiety about failing, and shame and hopelessness when the ideals cannot be met (Benton in Willock, 2014, pp. 25–32). With this in mind, how we can avoid seeing thwarted hopes or a less than perfect ending as a failure and both partners in the dance retain a sense of being good-enough?

I believe we can protect ourselves from slipping into the shame/blame paradigm by reminding ourselves that the dance between hope and despair is inevitable and plays out from our first meeting to the last. We should also remind ourselves that our hope as clinicians has to rest, not in being able to *do* something, but in offering a particular type of experience. Healing and insights will emerge in time from within the individual if we can provide an adequate relational safety net in which he feels safe enough to risk entering into a different relationship with himself and another person. When we try too hard or get caught in our own hopelessness and recriminations about not being good-enough we miss things. We stop listening out for the meaning behind our clients' urgent requests and our mutual pursuit of the perfect ending. We also miss hearing the child's voice underneath – perhaps the furious, entitled child whose needs were never met or the hurt child who really did need someone bigger, stronger, wise and kind to protect and care for her.

Of course, there are endings which really do challenge our ability to hold onto a realistic appraisal of our strengths and shortcomings such as a premature or tragic ending or one which left us bruised by an attack or complaint or still holding something unmetabolised for the client (perhaps because we did not provide the 'miracle' and are being punished). Such endings can trap us once more in 'if only' thinking. But in addition to not ignoring our feelings about what has happened, can we learn from them and grow? Can we stay resilient and not be beaten, in the same way that all through the therapy we can know and share our clients' despair but not be overcome by it? It we put such challenges to those we work with, we need to be able to do the same.

There will also be times when, after investing so much of ourselves in our work, we say goodbye without knowing how our clients' futures will evolve. We have to be able to let go without being able to read the final chapters and to tolerate not knowing whether a longstanding hope was eventually fulfilled or new dreams took its place. We don't know whether despair will catch them in its web again or if what they have learned in our relationship will be enough to help them through life's ups and downs. But we can stay hoping and trusting. Albert Schweitzer wisely summed this up when he wrote (1968):

No ray of sunlight is ever lost, but the green which it wakes into existence needs time to sprout, and it is not always granted the power to live to see the harvest. All work that is worth anything is done in faith.

Notes

1. Because some people have never experienced being somewhere consistently safe, I prefer to speak about a peaceful or comfortable place rather than use the term 'safe place'.
2. This activates the muscles involved in boundary setting and fighting.
3. I use a guided visualisation for this. If there are contexts in which our clients can spend time running for real and find this resourcing, even better.
4. The greatest damage was to the areas of the cortex which control the analysis, synthesis and organisation of complex associations into a coherent framework.
5. Although diagnoses risk objectifying people, there are other clients I can think of who began to let go of shame when they could understand themselves in the context of a medical condition.
6. This position is what Orange would call the 'hermeneutics of suspicion' (2011).
7. Sadly Zasetsky's story did not have the happy end he hoped for. Twenty-five years after the injury he still sat at his desk 'working on his story, trying to express himself better, to describe the hope and despair that are part of his continuing struggle' (Luria, 1987, p. 157). He tried and he kept hoping. What more can any of us do?
8. Interestingly, Erikson described this as a 'faith' or 'belief in the species', which fits my argument about our need for faith in something larger than the self. However, I disagree with his argument that productivity and creativity cannot replace what he means by generativity.
9. I am also inspired by Rumi's poem 'The Guest House', which ends with the words: 'Be grateful for whoever comes, because each has been sent as a guide from beyond.' (2004, p. 109).

10. Sometimes I have wondered, 'am I being a therapist?' after a session when we spent time talking about subjects of interest. The pull to 'do something' and show results is so endemic in our culture, and when one woman said, 'I never thought I might end up liking a therapist and enjoy talking about things with her', I wondered 'is that OK – for us both to enjoy our shared discussions?' But I know, because of observing what such conversations led to, that it was.

11. From an integrative perspective I question whether hopes always have to be relinquished and whether the psychodynamic view is overly pessimistic? Perhaps, because sometimes a hope is realised during the course of a therapy or it becomes 'not if, but when' – in other words, something our clients can hold on to as a growing possibility and a marker of a greater belief in themselves.

Bibliography

Aarts, P. and Op den Velde, W. (1996) 'Prior Traumatisation and the Process of Aging: Theory and Clinical Implications' in B. van der Kolk, A. McFarlane and L. Weisath (eds.) *Traumatic Stress: The Effects of Overwhelming Experience on Mind, Body and Society* (New York: Guilford Press).

Adams, M. (2014) *The Myth of the Untroubled Therapist* (London: Routledge).

Ainsworth, M., Blehar, M., Waters, E. and Wall, S. (1978) *Patterns of Attachment: A Study of the Strange Situation.* (Hillsdale, NJ: Lawrence Erlbaum).

Allen, J. (2001) *Traumatic Relationships and Serious Mental Disorders* (Chichester: John Wiley).

Allen, J. and Fonagy, P. (2006) *Handbook of Mentalization-Based Treatment* (Chichester: John Wiley).

Alvarez, A. (1991) 'Wildest Dreams: Aspiration, Identification and Symbol-formation in Depressed Children', *Psychoanalytic Psychotherapy,* 5, 177–89.

—— (1992) *Live Company: Psychoanalytic Psychotherapy with Autistic, Borderline, Deprived and Abused Children* (London: Routledge).

—— (2012) *The Thinking Heart: Three Levels of Psychoanalytic Therapy with Disturbed Children* (London: Routledge).

Anderson, R. and Dartington, A. (eds.) (1999) *Facing it Out: Clinical Perspectives on Adolescent Disturbance* (London: Duckworth).

Bateman, A. and Fonagy, P. (2004) *Psychotherapy for Borderline Personality Disorder: Mentalization-based Treatment* (Oxford: Oxford University Press).

BCPSG (2010) *Change in Psychotherapy: A Unifying Paradigm.* The Boston Change Process Study Group. (New York: W. W. Norton).

Beisser, A. (1970) 'The Paradoxical Theory of Change', *Gestalt Therapy Now.* www.gestalt.org/arnie.htm, accessed 2 April 2014.

Bentovim, A. (2002) 'Dissociative Identity Disorder: A Developmental Perspective' in V. Sinason (ed.) *Attachment, Trauma and Multiplicity: Working with Dissociative Identity Disorder* (Hove: Brunner-Routledge).

Bion, W. R. (1962) *Learning from Experience* (London: Maresfield Library).

Bloom, S. (1997) *Creating Sanctuary: Towards the Evolution of Sane Societies* (London: Routledge).

Boney-McCoy, S. and Finklehor, D. (1995) 'Prior Victimisation: A Risk Factor for Sexual Abuse and for PTSD-related Symptomatology among Sexually Abused Youth', *Child Abuse and Neglect,* 19 (21), 1401–21.

Boris, H. (1976) 'On Hope: Its Nature and Psychotherapy', *The International Review of Psychoanalysis,* 3, 139–50.

Bowlby, J. (1989) *The Making and Breaking of Affectional Bonds* (London: Tavistock/Routledge).

—— (1991) *Attachment and Loss: Volume 1. Attachment* (London: Penguin).

Briggs, S. (1999) 'How Does It Work Here? Do We Just Talk? Therapeutic Work with Young People Who Have Been Sexually Abused' in R. Anderson and A. Dartington (eds.) *Facing it Out: Clinical Perspectives on Adolescent Disturbance* (London: Duckworth).

Brown, J. (1997) 'Circular Questioning: An Introductory Guide', *Australia and New Zealand Journal of Family Therapy,* 18 (2), 109–14.

Bromberg, P. (2006) *Awakening the Dreamer* (Mahwah, NJ: Analytic Press).

———— (2011) *The Shadow of the Tsunami and the Growth of the Relational Mind* (New York: Routledge).

Buber, M. (1958) *I and Thou* (New York: Charles Scribner's Sons).

Buscaglia, L. (2006) *Living, Loving and Learning* (Thorofare, NJ: Slack Inc).

Camara, H. Dom (1981) *A Thousand Reasons for Living* (London: Darton, Longman and Todd).

Caroll, R. (2002) 'Panic, Seeking and Play in Psychotherapy' www.thinkbody.co.uk/papers, accessed 14 June 2014.

———— (2006) 'A New Era for Psychotherapy: Panksepp's Affect Model in the Context of Neuroscience and its Implications for Contemporary Psychotherapy Practice' in J. Corrigal, H. Payne and H. Wilkinson (eds.) *About a Body: Working with the Embodied Mind in Psychotherapy* (London: Routledge).

Chinen, A. (1994) *In the Ever After: Fairy Tales and the Second Half of Life* (Wilmette, IL: Chiron Publications).

Chodron, P. (1997) *When Things Fall Apart* (London: Harper Collins).

Corrigan, F., Fisher, J., and Nutt, D. (2011) 'Autonomic Dysregulation and the Window of Tolerance Model of the Effects of Complex Emotional Trauma', *Journal of Psychopharmacology*, 25 (1), 17–25.

Danielian, J. and Gianotti, P. (2012) *Listening with Purpose: Entry Points into Shame and Narcissistic Vulnerability* (New York: Jason Aronson).

Davies, J. and Frawley, M. (1994) *Treating the Adult Survivor of Childhood Sexual Abuse.* (New York: Basic Books).

Davis, M. and Wallbridge, R. (1981) *Boundary and Space: An Introduction to the Work of Donald Winnicott* (Middlesex: Penguin).

DeYoung, P. (2003) *Relational Psychotherapy: A Primer* (New York: Brunner-Routledge).

De Zulueta, F. (2000) *From Pain to Violence: The Traumatic Roots of Destructiveness* (London: Whurr Publishers).

Doidge, N. (2007) *The Brain that Changes Itself* (London: Penguin).

———— (2012) *Neuroplasticity: The Possibilities and Pitfalls*. Online seminar. National Institute for the Clinical Application of Behavioral Medicine.

Erikson, E. (1965) *Childhood and Society* (Harmondsworth: Penguin Books).

———— (1968) *Identity: Youth and Crisis* (New York: W. W. Norton).

Erskine, R., Moursand, J. and Trautmann, R. (1999) *Beyond Empathy: A Therapy of Contact in Relationship* (Philadelphia: Brunner/Mazel).

Feeney, J. and Noller, P. (1996) *Adult Attachment* (Thousand Oaks, CA: Sage).

Feldenkrais, M. (1984) *The Master Moves* (Soquel, CA: Meta Publications).

Fisher, J. (2011) *'Disorganised Attachment, Borderline Personality Disorder and the Traumatic Transference'* Online Webinar series.

———— (2012) *'Working with Trauma-Related Dissociation'* Online Webinar series.

Fisher, J. and Ogden, P. (2009) 'Sensorimotor Psychotherapy' in C. Courtois and J. Ford (eds.) *Treating Complex Traumatic Stress Disorders* (New York: Guilford Press).

Fonagy, P. (2001) *Attachment Theory and Psychoanalysis* (New York: Other Press).

Ford, J. (2009) 'Neurobiological and Developmental Research: Clinical Implications' in C. Courtois and J. Ford (eds.) *Treating Complex Traumatic Stress Disorders* (New York: Guilford Press).

Frank, J. (1974) *Persuasion and Healing* 2nd edn. (New York: Schocken Books).

Frankel, J. (2002) 'Exploring Ferenczi's Concept of Identification with the Aggressor: Its Role in Trauma, Everyday Life and the Therapeutic Relationship', *Psychoanalytic Dialogues*, 12, 101–39.

Frankl, V. (2004) *Man's Search for Meaning* (London: Rider).

Germer, C. (2009) *The Mindful Path to Self-Compassion* (New York: Guilford Press).

Gilbert, P. (2005) *Compassion: Conceptualisations, Research and Use in Psychotherapy* (London: Routledge).

―――― (2009) 'Introducing Compassion Focussed Therapy', *Advances in Psychiatric Treatment*, 15, 199–208.

Goethe, J. W. http://www.goodreads.com/author/quotes/285217.Johann_Wolfgang_von_Goethe, accessed 20 March 2013.

Gomez, L. (1997) *An Introduction to Object Relations* (London: Free Association Books).

Goodwin, J. and Attias, R. (1999) 'Traumatic Disruption of Bodily Experience and Memory', in J. Goodwin and R. Attias (eds.) *Splintered Reflections: Images of the Body in Trauma* (New York: Basic Books).

Hanson, R. (2009) *Buddha's Brain: The Practical Neuroscience of Happiness, Love and Wisdom* (Oakland, CA: Newharbinger Publications).

Havel, V. (1990) *Disturbing the Peace: A Conversation with Karel Hvizdala*, transl. P. Wilson (New York: Alfred Knopf).

―――― (1993) www.goodreads.com/author/quotes/71441.V_clav_Havel, accessed 21 June 2015.

Haynes, J. (2007) *Who Is It That Can Tell Me Who I Am? The Journal of a Psychotherapist* (London: Cromwell Press).

Herman, J. (1994) *Trauma and Recovery* (London: Pandora).

Hobson, R. (1985) *Forms of Feeling: The Heart of Psychotherapy* (London: Routledge).

Holmes, J. (1996) *Attachment, Intimacy, Autonomy: Using Attachment Theory in Adult Psychotherapy* (London: Jason Aronson).

―――― (1997) '"Too Early, Too Late?": Endings in Psychotherapy – an Attachment Perspective', *British Journal of Psychotherapy*, 14, 159–71.

―――― (2010) *Exploring in Security: Towards an Attachment-informed Psychoanalytic Psychotherapy* (London: Routledge).

Hosseini, K. (2013) *And the Mountains Echoed* (London: Bloomsbury).

Howell, E. (2005) *The Dissociative Mind* (New York: Routledge).

―――― (2011) *Understanding and Treating Dissociative Identity Disorder* (New York: Routledge).

Hoxter, S. (1983) 'Some Feelings Aroused in Working with Severely Deprived Children' in M. Boston and R. Szur (eds.) *Psychotherapy with Severely Deprived Children* (London: Routledge and Kegan Paul).

Hudson Allez, G. (2011) *Infant Losses; Adult Searches: A Neural and Developmental Perspective on Psychopathology and Sexual Offending* (London: Karnac Books).

Irvine, W. (2006) *On Desire: Why We Want What We Want* (Oxford: Oxford University Press).

Jackson, C. (2014) 'Should We Have the Right to Die?' *Therapy Today*, 25 (3), 17–23.

Jacobs, M. and Rowan, J. (2002) *The Therapist's Use of Self* (Buckingham: Open University Press).

Johnson, S. (2005) 'Broken Bonds: An Emotionally Focused Approach to Infidelity', *Journal of Couple and Relationship Therapy*, 4 (2/3), 17–29.

Joyce, P. and Sills, C. (2010) *Skills in Gestalt Counselling and Psychotherapy* (London: Sage).

Kabat-Zinn, J. (1991) *Full Catastrophe Living: How to Cope with Stress, Pain and Illness Using Mindfulness Meditation* (New York: Random House).

Kalsched, D. (1996) *The Inner World of Trauma: Archetypal Defences of the Personal Spirit* (New York: Routledge).

Karen, R. (1998) *Becoming Attached: First Relationships and How they Shape our Capacity to Love* (Oxford: Oxford University Press).

Karr-Morse, R and Wiley, M. (1997), *Ghosts from the Nursery: Tracing the Roots of Violence* (New York: Atlantic Monthly Press).

Kegerreis, S. (1995) 'Getting Better Makes it Worse: Obstacles to Improvement in Children with Emotional and Behavioural Difficulties' in J. Trowell and M. Bower (eds.) *The Emotional Needs of Young Children and their Families* (London: Routledge).

Klein, M. (1975) *Envy and Gratitude and other Works* (New York: Delacort).

Kluft, R. (2007) 'Applications of Innate Affect Theory to the Understanding and Treatment of Dissociative Identity Disorder' in E. Vermetten, M. Dorahy and D. Spiegel (eds.) *Traumatic Dissociation: Neurobiology and Treatment* (Arlington, VA: American Psychiatric Publishing).

Kurtz, R. (1990) *Body-Centred Psychotherapy: The Hakomi Method* (Mendocino, CA: LifeRythm).

Levine, P. (1997) *Waking the Tiger: Healing Trauma* (Berkeley, CA: North Atlantic Books).

Linehan, M. (1991) *Cognitive-Behavioural Treatment of Borderline Personality Disorder* (New York: Guilford Press).

Liotti, G. (2004) 'Trauma, Dissociation and Disorganised Attachment: Three Strands of a Single Braid', *Psychotherapy: Research, Practice, Training*, 41, 472–86.

Little, R. (2009) 'Understanding the Psychodynamics of Suicidal Clients: Exploring Suicidal and Presuicidal States', *Transactional Analysis Journal*, 39 (3), 219–28.

Luria, A. (1987) *The Man with the Shattered World: A History of a Brain Wound* (Cambridge, MA: Harvard University Press).

Lyons-Ruth, K. and Spielman, E. (2004) 'Disorganised Infant Attachment Strategies and Helpless-fearful Profiles of Parenting: Integrating Attachment Research with Clinical Intervention', *Infant Mental Health Journal*, 25 (4), 318–35.

Lyons-Ruth, K., Dutra, L., Schuder, M. and Bianchi, I. (2006) 'From Infant Attachment Disorganisation to Adult Dissociation: Relational Adaptations to Traumatic Experiences', *Psychiatric Clinics of North America*, 29, 63–86.

Malan, D. (2001) *Individual Psychotherapy and the Science of Psychodynamics, 2nd edn.* (London: Arnold).

Maroda, K. (1994) *The Power of Countertransference: Innovations in Analytic Technique* (Northvale, NJ: Aronson).

Marvin, R., Cooper, G., Hoffman, K. and Powell, R. (2002) 'The Circle of Security Project: Attachment-based Intervention with Caregiver-pre-school Child Dyads', *Attachment and Human Development*, 4 (1), 107–24.

Mearns, D. and Cooper, M. (2010) *Working at Relational Depth in Counselling and Psychotherapy* (London: Sage Publications).

Mearns, D. and Thorne, B. (2011) *Person-centred Therapy Today* (London: Sage Publications).

Meltzer, D. (1985), *The Kleinian Development: Part 11* (Reading: Clunie Press).

Middlebrook, D. and George, D. (eds.) (1991) *The Selected Poems of Anne Sexton* (London: Virago).

Mitchell, S. (1993) *Hope and Dread in Psychoanalysis* (New York: Basic Books).

—— (2000) *Relationality from Attachment to Intersubjectivity* (New Jersey: Analytic Press).

Molnos, A. (1995) *A Question of Time: Essentials of Brief Dynamic Psychotherapy* (London: Karnac)

Morgan, S. (2005) 'Depression: Turning towards Life' in C. Germer, R. Siegel and P. Fulton (eds.) *Mindfulness and Psychotherapy* (New York: Guilford Press).

Napier, N. (1993) *Getting Through the Day: Strategies for Adults Hurt as Children* (New York: W. W. Norton).

Nijenhuis, E., van der Hart, O. and Steele, C. (2004) 'Trauma-related Structural Dissociation of the Personality', www.trauma-pages.com/vdhart-93.htm, accessed 12 September 2005.

Obholzer, O. and Zagier Roberts, V. (eds.) (1994) *The Unconscious at Work: Individual and Organisational Stress in the Human Services* (London: Routledge).

Ogden, P. (2007) *'Beyond Words: A Clinical Map for Using Mindfulness of the Body and the Organisation of Experience in Trauma Treatment'*, Paper presented at Mindfulness and Psychotherapy Conference, UCLA/Lifespan Learning Institute.

—— (2009) 'Emotion, Mindfulness and Movement: Expanding the Regulatory Boundaries of the Window of Tolerance' in D. Fosha, D. Siegel and M. Solomon (eds.) *The Healing Power of Emotion: Perspectives from Affective Neuroscience and Clinical Practice* (New York: W. W. Norton).

Ogden, P. and Fisher, J. (2015) *Sensorimotor Psychotherapy: Interventions for Trauma and Attachment* (London: W. W. Norton).

Ogden, P., Minton, K. and Pain, C. (2006) *Trauma and the Body: A Sensorimotor Approach to Psychotherapy* (London: W. W. Norton).

O'Hara D. (2010) 'Hope – the Neglected Common Factor', *Therapy Today*, 21 (9), 17–23.

––––– (2013) *Hope in Counselling and Psychotherapy* (London: Sage).

Orange, D. (2011) *The Suffering Stranger: Hermeneutics for Everyday Clinical Practice* (New York: Routledge).

Panksepp, J. (1998) *Affective Neuroscience: The Foundations of Human and Animal Emotions* (Oxford: Oxford University Press).

––––– (2006) 'The Core Emotional Systems in the Mammalian Brain: the Fundamental Substrates of Human Emotion' in J. Corrigal, H. Payne and H. Wilkinson (eds.) *About a Body: Working with the Embodied Mind in Psychotherapy* (London: Routledge).

Partridge, K. and McCarry, N. (2009) Dissolving Blame: Systemic Therapy in Action' *Healthcare Counselling and Psychotherapy Journal*, 9 (3), 12–16.

Pearlman, L. and Saakvitne, K. (1995) *Trauma and the Therapist: Countertransference and Vicarious Traumatisation in Psychotherapy with Incest Survivors* (New York: W. W. Norton).

Porges, S. (2012) *Polyvagal Theory: Why this Changes Everything* Transcript of online seminar. National Institute for the Clinical Application of Behavioral Medicine.

Pynoos, R., Steinberg, A. and Goenjian, A. (1996) 'Traumatic Stress in Childhood and Adolescence: Recent Developments and Current Controversies' in B. van der Kolk, A. McFarlane and L. Weisath (eds.) *Traumatic Stress: The Effects of Overwhelming Experience on Mind, Body and Society* (New York: Guilford Press).

Racker, H. (1968) *Transference and Counter-Transference* (London: Hogarth Press).

Raphael-Leff, J. (2012) 'The Baby-makers' in P. Mariotti (ed.) *The Maternal Lineage: Identification, Desire and Transgenerational Issues* (London: Routledge).

Rogers, C. (2004) *On Becoming a Person* (London: Constable).

Rothschild, B. (2000) *The Body Remembers: The Psychophysiology of Trauma and Trauma Treatment* (New York: Norton).

Rumi, J. (2004) *Rumi Selected Poems* (London: Penguin).

Sachs, A. (1966) *The Jail Diary of Albie Sachs* (London: Paladin).

Scaer, R. (2007) *The Body Bears the Burden: Trauma, Dissociation and Disease* (New York: Routledge).

Schore, A. (2003a) *Affect Dysregulation and Disorders of the Self* (New York: W. W. Norton).

––––– (2003b) *Affect Regulation and the Repair of the Self* (New York: W. W. Norton).

Schweitzer, A. (1968) *The Wisdom of Albert Schweitzer: A Selection* (New York: Philosophical Library).

Scott King, C. (1985), *The Words of Martin Luther King* (London: Collins).

Sebag Montefiore, S. (ed.) (2005) *Speeches that Changed the World* (London: Quercus).

Segal, Z., Williams, M. and Teasdale, J. (2002) *Mindfulness-Based Cognitive Therapy for Depression* (New York: Guilford Press).

Shabad, P. (2001) *Despair and the Return of Hope: Echoes of Mourning in Psychotherapy* (Maryland: Jason Aronson).

Shapiro, F. (2001) *Eye Movement Desensitisation and Reprocessing* (New York: Guilford Press).

Shapiro, R. (2009) 'Introduction to Assessment and Treatment of Depression with EMDR' in R. Shapiro (ed.), *EMDR Solutions II* (New York: W. W. Norton).

Sharp, C. and Venta, A. (2012) 'Mentalizing Problems in Children and Adolescents' in N. Midgely and I. Vrouva (eds.) *Minding the Child: Mentalization-based Interventions with Children, Young People and their Families* (London: Routledge).

Shaw, D. (2013) *Traumatic Narcissism* (London: Routledge).

Shiff, J. (1975) *The Cathexis Reader: Transactional Analysis Treatment of Psychosis*, (New York: Harper and Row).

Siegel, D. (1999) *The Developing Mind* (New York: W. W. Norton).

———— (2010) *The Mindful Therapist* (New York: W. W. Norton).

Sinason, V. (1992) *Mental Handicap and the Human Condition. New Approaches from the Tavistock* (London: Free Association Books).

Solomon, J. and George, C. (2011) *Disorganised Attachment and Caregiving* (New York: Guilford Press).

Steele, K., van der Hart, O. and Nijenhuis, E. (2001) 'Dependency in the Treatment of Complex Posttraumatic Stress Disorder and Dissociative Disorders', *Journal of Trauma and Dissociation* 2 (4), 70–116.

Stern, D. B. (2010) *Partners in Thought: Working with Unformulated Experience, Dissociation and Enactment* (New York: Routledge).

Stern, D. N. (1985) *The Interpersonal World of the Infant* (New York: Basic Books).

Symington, N. (1992) 'Countertransference with Mentally Handicapped Clients' in A. Waitman and S. Conboy-Hill (eds.) *Psychotherapy and Mental Handicap* (London: Sage Publications).

Thich Nhat Hanh (1991) *Peace is Every Step: The Path to Mindfulness in Everyday Life* (London: Random House).

Turner, J. (2002) 'A Brief History of Illusion: Milner, Winnicott and Rycroft', *International Journal of Psychoanalysis*, 83, 1063–82.

Turp, M. (2010) 'Letter in response to O' Hara 2010', *Therapy Today*, 21(10), 36–7.

van der Hart, O., Nijenhuis, E., and Steele, K. (2006) *The Haunted Self: Structural Dissociation of the Personality* (New York: W. W. Norton).

van der Hart, O., Steele K., Boon, S. and Brown, P. (1993) 'The Treatment of Traumatic Memories: Synthesis, Realization and Integration', www.trauma-pages.com/vdhart-93.htm, accessed 12 September 2005.

van der Kolk, B. (1994) 'The Body Keeps the Score: Memory and the Evolving Psychobiology of Post Traumatic Stress', www.trauma-pages.com/vanderk4.htm, accessed 12 July 2005.

van der Kolk, B., McFarlane, A. and Weisath, L. (eds.) (1996) *Traumatic Stress: The Effects of Overwhelming Experience On Mind, Body and Society* (New York: Guilford Press).

Vygotsky, L. (1962) *Thought and Language* (Cambridge, MA: MIT Press).

Waddell, M. (1998) *Inside Lives: Psychoanalysis and the Growth of the Personality* (London: Duckworth).

Wallin, D. (2007) *Attachment in Psychotherapy* (New York: Guilford Press).

Wilkinson, M (2006) *Coming into Mind: The Mind-brain Relationship: A Jungian Clinical Perspective* (London: Routledge).

Williams, M., Teasdale, J., Zindel, S. and Kabat-Zinn, J. (2007) *The Mindful Way through Depression: Freeing Yourself from Chronic Unhappiness.* (New York: Guilford Press).

Willock, B., Coleman, R. and Bohm, L. (2014), *Understanding and Coping with Failure: Psychoanalytic Perspectives* (New York: Routledge).

Wilson, J. and Brwynn Thomas, R. (2004) *Empathy in the Treatment of Trauma and PTSD.* (New York: Brunner-Routledge).

Wilson, J. and Lindy, J. (eds.) (1994) *Countertransference in the Treatment of PTSD* (New York: Guilford Press).

Wilson, J. (2006) 'Trauma and the Epigenesis of Identity' in J. Wilson (ed.) *The Postraumatic Self: Restoring Meaning and Wholeness to Personality* (New York: Routledge).

Winnicott, D. W. (1958) *Through Paediatrics to Psycho-Analysis* (London: Hogarth Press).

———— (1965) *The Maturational Process and the Facilitating Environment* (New York: International Universities Press).

———— (1990) *Playing and Reality* (London: Routledge).

Wright, S. (2009a) 'Phase Conscious Approaches to Trauma Therapy: From Theory to Practice', *British Journal of Psychotherapy Integration,* 6 (1), 16–27.

—— (2009b) 'Becoming Three Dimensional: A Clinical Exploration of the Links between Dissociation, Disorganised Attachment and Mentalization', *Attachment: New Directions in Psychotherapy and Relational Psychoanalysis,* 3, 324–39.

—— (2013) 'As Long as You Have Hope: A Study of Hope and Despair in the Therapeutic Encounter', *British Journal of Psychotherapy Integration,* 10 (1), 19–42.

Index